Probation: Working for Justice

Probation

Working for Justice

edited by

David Ward and Malcolm Lacey

Whiting and Birch Ltd

MCMXCV

Published by Whiting and Birch Ltd, PO Box 872, London SE23 3HL, England. *USA:* Paul & Co, Publishers' Consortium Inc, PO Box 442, Concord, MA 01742.

British Library Cataloguing in Publication Data
A CIP catalogue record is available from the British Library

ISBN 1 871177 64 2 (cased)
ISBN 1 871177 65 0 (limp)

Printed in England by Antony Rowe, Chippenham

Contents

Dedication

This book of essays is dedicated to the memory of John Pendleton, who so sadly died when he was Chief Probation Officer for Warwickshire and still had so much to contribute to the Probation Service.

John will be remembered by many people for making us think about fundamental issues and for the way in which he brought his background as a Baptist minister and as Head of the Social Work Programme, later Special Professor of Probation Studies, at the University of Nottingham to bear on the policy and practice of the Probation Service.

As the essays in this book clearly demonstrate, much of his thinking was far-sighted in the way that he keyed into the matters that are now of central importance. In particular, he saw how the Probation Service could contribute to a more just society taking into account the needs of offenders while highlighting the way in which they should make reparation for the harm they had done to the victims of crime. He was closely associated with early schemes for mediation and reparation.

It is a particular delight that we have been able to reprint his essay 'More Justice, Less Law' as the first essay in this collection.

We wish to acknowledge the interest and encouragement of John's wife, Barbara, and his children, Andrew and Rachael, as this book has come together. However the responsibility for the content is solely that of the editors and contributors. We hope it is a fitting tribute.

Malcolm Lacey and David Ward

Section I

Justice in Focus

One
More justice, less law

John Pendleton

We hear much about 'law and order' these days. It is a key issue in the programmes of most political parties: politicians are acutely aware of rising crime rates, increasing urban decay and unemployment, to mention but some of the significant symptoms of the malaise of our civilization.

It is interesting that 'law and order' is the context in which such symptoms are seen – as though proscription and enforcement will somehow bring about order, will somehow keep the lid on! The 'rule of law' is a phrase constantly placed before us by our leaders as a reified entity before which all will somehow magically become obedient, coherent and thus ordered. In reality, the law of itself can do nothing.

The law actually provides two major components. One is a protection of people. The other is the provision of a negative framework for the regulation of human behaviour; the law mostly relates to the boundaries of human conduct by indicating what we may not do, or what in a civilized society is not permissible. This is not to deny the positive function of custom, law and regulation for as Fosdick has pointed out, 'they are as indispensable to personality as a trellis is to guide the growth of a living vine' (Fosdick, 1954). The problem occurs when the trellis becomes so over-elaborated that it begins to stifle the life of the vine!

J.S. Mill argued that the only purpose for which power can rightfully be exercised over any member of a civilized community against his or her will is the positive one of preventing harm to others. He therefore would only admit to one component of the law and that is the one of protection. However, as Robinson (1980) says:

> This may of course, involve prohibition or restriction. The raison d'être of the law is protection, not prohibition and

> where there is no need for protection it should not intervene. It is not there to express what Charles Davies has called 'the anger of morality' however abominable may be the object of its disapprobation. It is there as far as possible to enable people to be free, mature adult human beings. Of course, the law cannot make people adult human beings. It has a limited role in hindering the hindrances. It is limited because the free processes of influence, education, example and persuasion are so much more productive but as a last resort if a person refuses to respect the freedom of another, [or is dangerous to others or to himself], there must be provision to compel him to respect their freedom or to safeguard them from danger [author's addition in brackets].

What the law cannot do is create the conditions in which crime is less pervasive, for this involves not a reified concept but what actually happens between people both at the individual and personal and at the collective and political levels. This may be described as the creation of a quality of life that prevents and forestalls the wrongs that the law prohibits.

The contrast between the proscriptions, coercions and penalties of a legal system on the one hand and the creativity which produces quality of life on the other is, of course, arrestingly presented in New Testament terms by Paul. What he says is that when people trust legal regulation to do what only creative, spiritual life can do, they are riding for a fall: the code kills, the spirit gives life.

It should be noted that the law cannot entirely effect justice – if by justice, that is, one means a process which should lead to reconciliation at the centre of which is the notion of a change of heart and perception on the part of the wrongdoer and the wronged. The important issue about such a change is that it is in response to motivation towards making amends. This is an inward discipline; it is not in obedience to a discipline imposed from without.

Recently the concept of reparation has been very much a 'bandwagon' idea. Nevertheless, it is really, as I hope to show later, an integral part of the notion of justice. Lacey and others maintain that criminal justice is not simply a system for processing and punishing offenders; it is for 'righting wrongs' and basic to this is the concept of reconciliation between the offender, victim and society of which reparation is a part (Lacey et al., 1983).

The evidence for this view of the nature of criminal justice has been set out by many writers and broadly speaking can be traced to tribal communities. It did not, however, stop there. What is not sufficiently emphasised is that the distinctive idea of justice which formed the basis of western civilizations's judicial system up until the 17th century originated in the dynamic concept of justice proclaimed by the 8th century BC biblical prophets (Pendleton, 1974).

Let us consider briefly five characteristics of this prophetic view of justice (Pendleton, 1985):

1. The prophetic concept of justice was formed at a time of great inequality and social injustice. The prophets strongly argued that justice should be towards the poor and oppressed. They did not mean that the poor and oppressed should receive any different treatment from the rest of the community. Still less did they mean that wrong actions condemned in the rich were condoned in the poor. They held that there should be one law for all. In short, the 8th-century prophets saw justice as upholding the rights of the underdog. This was a key element in their notion of justice.

   In practice this notion of justice did not operate. The rich, the aristocrats and the businessmen sold out the poor, building up their own estates and fortune within the law as administered. The poor had no redress, for the influence of the wealthy held sway over the administration of the law. It was against this that the prophets spoke.
2. Justice for the prophets was about people and what happens to them and between them. The prophets were urgent and persistent in this view. The Hebrew language at this point in its development had very few abstract nouns; they mostly emerged later in the language's development. Words like righteousness, love and justice were not seen as ideas or as abstractions but as activities. In a sense there was no idea of justice as a concept but only as a just act. For example where wrongdoer and wronged have come together, or have in biblical terms 'atoned,' there to the Hebrew would be justice or righteousness. It was only in the syncretism which occurred later in the Judaeo-Christian tradition, largely through the influence of Greek thought, that more abstract and complicated notions arise. The prophets of course, related all this to God but even here their whole view was permeated by

what happens to people: even their view of God has not to do with whether God is or exists, but assumed that God does (Wheeler Robinson, 1949).

3. Prophetic justice has to do with the putting right of wrongs which existed in the community. This notion again was in no sense static, remote or legalistic – rather it was active, essentially based in the relationship within the community between those who committed and those who suffered wrong (Snaith, 1951).
4. There was a strong commitment involved in all this to the idea of contract. The word used was that of 'covenant', between the wrongdoer and the wronged, often assisted in its establishment by a mediator ('daysman'). The Hebrew notion of covenant was chiefly about God's covenant with Israel, but it was also about a contract between people and the loyalty (the approximate Hebrew translation means something like 'steadfastness') which should exist between the parties to it. The loyalty was expected from both sides, even if the parties were not equal.
5. Reparation was a key concept in the process of 'righting wrongs'. In early writers the word was used as a kind of shorthand for a way of bringing about reconciliation between people who are separated by wrongdoing on the part of one or both. In early biblical communities, reparation was often a sign in the form of an offering made by the guilty person to the victim (known as sin or guilt offerings). What is interesting is that this was usually done without recourse to litigation: ... the avoidance of litigation arose from the recognition that the community should take responsibility for its own problems and probably also because reconciliation is not a process which can be ordered or directed (Richardson, 1951).

Jesus followed in the tradition of the 8th-century prophets and went even further in his concept of justice and reconciliation. One example may assist in understanding its radical nature (Fosdick, 1954). In the case of personal injury at the time of Jesus, the victim could demand an eye from the aggressor if his own eye had been destroyed. The hard-line lawyers (Sadducees) of Jesus' day went along with its literal observance. The more liberal lawyers (Pharisees) went for financial compensation: though theoretically having to uphold and fulfil the law, they found their way around it by saying the victim could extract the aggressor's eye only if it were exactly like its own in size and colour and since this condition is never present, the principle of retaliation was retained without its fiendish expression. Now Jesus rejects this: 'He required undiscourageable goodwill even towards those who injure – the vindictiveness that desires an eye for an eye was conquered at its source in the heart of the injured man' (Fosdick, 1954). The whole point is that justice is essentially an inward matter developed by inward motivation. It is not something that can be compelled from without.

Perhaps the greatest emphasis of the Christian end of the Judaeo-Christian tradition in relation to justice is that it is essentially concerned with a change of heart and mind and thus of perception. This people-centred notion of justice arises out of the belief that people, and therefore structures, can change; it was not founded on any deterministic notion as, for example, in psychoanalytical approaches or in systems theory. Basic to this concept of justice is the idea that there can be no reconciliation, no putting right of wrongs, unless there is the motivation for it, that is unless that is the will on the part of both the wrongdoer and the victim. There can be no coming together without both parties having some desire to put things right. The idea of repentance is central here. The word, however, is often misrepresented and would be better understood in its literal sense of 'change of mind'.

Cupitt (1979) has shown that this point is one of some subtlety and complexity. This change of heart and mind happens in a disruptive way and is totally radical. What it does is to reverse ordinary human valuation so that, in the words of Jesus, there is a preference for the 'lost over the safe, the sick over the healthy and the sinners over the righteous', or as Cupitt puts it, 'sensible self-absorbed and busy people begin to look ridiculous and sick and needy people begin to look sensible'.

However, there is a second string to this because Jesus, as with the 8th-century prophets, saw justice not only in terms of changing the self, but also changing the structures, political and otherwise, of society in order to create equality. Both the prophets and Jesus looked towards a better society in which the oppressed, the poor and the ill could get justice. The Judaeo-Christian view of justice, therefore should be read both at the individual/personal, and political/structural levels. The values of change of heart, mind and perception occur when people become aware of the problems and the issues of others. This occurs, for example, when the wrongdoer becomes aware of what he has done to the victim, regrets it and begins to recognise something of the problems and needs of the victim. Similarly, the victim becomes more aware of the problems and needs of the wrongdoer and that the structure often fails to give equality to him or her.

There was some small evidence of this in a recent review of the Warwickshire Reparation Scheme in which some fifty of the attempts at reparation were examined. Although reparations were done indirectly, without victim-offender encounters, and were concerned with repairing properties by offenders for victims under the Community Service Scheme, the project seemed to be dealing with some of the components of change indicated earlier. For example, in almost all cases offenders became aware of the trauma which victims experience when their house is broken into. Victims also seemed to gain some understanding of factors which may be causal in offending behaviour. Victims often said that they had not realised that offenders were able to do such skilled work. Why was it that they were not given proper work to do by society? Why were their skills not being used? Though not earth-shattering, these comments are of great interest as they express some potential for change of attitude and value both individually and on a wider basis. If reparation is well effected, it seems to be one of the most significant ways in which the community can really learn about the causal factors of crime.

In recapitulation, justice according to the Judaeo-Christian tradition is about putting wrongs right within the community. It is about people being equal before justice. It is about what happens to and between people rather than about concepts. It is about what happens to people within a covenant or contract and as far as possible outside of litigation. Its implications are for a change of heart and mind, of policies and of structures. It is phenomenological, not deductive; dynamic not static, spiritual not legal. It is about the creation of a quality of life in which those who offend can face the consequences of their actions and take responsibility for their lives within the community. It is equally about victims and the community at large facing the issues of offending and its causes.

There are, of course, some problems inherent in the foregoing. The first and most obvious is that this idea of justice is not the one mainly in operation in the judicial system in this society. There are many reasons for this:

> To understand the social message of the prophets, we must banish from our minds a view that is deeply ingrained in western culture, namely that justice is behaviour that conforms to an ethical or legal norm (Anderson, 1979).

Justice is done, we say, when a judge decides impartially in terms of legal norms and precedents. People are righteous when they live up to standards accepted by their community, nation or religious tradition. But the 8th century prophets and subsequently the Christian tradition of justice also refer to the fulfilment of responsibilities that arise out of particular relationships within the community, an essentially communitarian approach. The question for the Judaeo-Christian tradition is, as Anderson says, whether 'one actually has the power to take part in the relationships of society with dignity and responsibility'. Essential to the whole notion of justice was that individuals 'live and move and have their being in a context of social relationships'.

Powerful influences over the centuries have changed our concept of justice. One of the most significant of these was that of the Greek ideas of justice which were static, uninvolved, 'objective' approaches as, for example, in the ideas propounded by the Epicureans (Snaith, 1952). Another major influence would be the rather more bureaucratic ideas of law developed by Rome and perhaps the other significant influence has been that of the Utilitarian approach developed from about the 17th century onwards. Out of this latter approach emerged a judicial system administered centrally. All of these influences contributed to a static and legalistic rather than a dynamic concept of justice.

The criminal justice system now seems largely geared to administering the law by way of processing offenders upwards through a tariff which is concerned with how much punishment deterrence or even treatment is necessary. The question often being posed is 'what is this offence worth and where does it rate?', rather than 'how can this wrong be put right?' This leaves out the victim and the community and the potential for facing issues about offending and its causes. It also divorces offenders from what they have done and from its implications. Even worse, the logic of the criminal justice system must be called greatly into question in that it continually seeks for alternatives to imprisonment, suggesting that the objective of the criminal justice system is the imposition of custodial sentences.

Another problem concerns size. What might have worked in small homogeneous communities is much more difficult to apply in complex, industrialised, stratified societies. When I contributed to a judicial seminar on this subject recently, several judges pointed out to me that though they were sympathetic to this idea of justice, they could not see it working in modern society. Yet, although it is clearly more difficult, I believe it would be right for us to make the attempt. The impressionistic evidence from attempts being made to use this approach around the country indicate that it offers a better chance of offenders facing the consequences of their actions and accepting responsibility for their lives, and of the community facing the consequences of its policies, than if the offender is in custody (Lacey et al., 1985).

Let us finally consider some implications if this dynamic and spiritual notion were to be adopted by our criminal justice system.

An area in which there are clearly difficult implications is that concerning equality before justice. This is not a matter which can be dealt with by the criminal justice system fundamentally: it has wider political, economic and psycho-social implications. If an 8th-century prophet visited this society now, he might not find oppression and injustice to the same degree as in his own era. However, he would find that most detected crime is committed by young, unemployed, often homeless or rootless people. He would find that the amplification by the press and media of the increase in serious violent offences masks the fact that much crime is not of a serious nature in the sense that it does not pose a great threat to others. These offences ought to be contained and dealt with in the community, but are often not. Though such offending must not be condoned, it would be evident that many young people between the ages of about sixteen to twenty five years are excluded from responsible participation in society. Because of this, they are placed at risk of offending against the law.

A prophet from the Judaeo-Christian tradition of justice would be quick to point out that such inequality has no place in a civilized society. Further, he would point out that it is quite immoral that many thousands of people in this unequal position should have to be sacrificed while we wait for this, that, or some other economic theory to work. The prophet would rapidly make clear that what matters is not systems and economic theories but people! A society like ours cannot wait; it must respond to the needs of those people who are oppressed now. Those who are oppressed need policies which will respond to the real range and depth of their needs which will create some real measure of equality.

> The health of a social organism depends upon the adequacy of its social structure as much as does the health of the body upon the bio-chemical processes. No degree of goodwill alone can cure a deficiency in glandular secretions; and no moral idealism can overcome a basic mechanical defect in the social structure (Neibuhr, 1949).

All of us in the criminal justice system, the National Association of Probation Officers, the Association of Chief Offices of Probation, the Law Society, the Central Council of Probation Committees, the Magistrates Associates and others, must keep pressing on those in political power that there will be no real justice while such basic defects in the social structure exist. Between us we have the evidence more than most other people that this is the case.

In the meantime, there are some rather more specific implications for the criminal justice system.

One is that, on the whole, it is better to keep as many people as possible outside the criminal justice system for what substantially needs to be done in putting wrongs right cannot in the end be done by sanctions. This would clearly only relate to early offenders and is very much in line with some of the crime prevention work which is being done in diversion schemes in juvenile bureaus such as those in Northamptonshire, Devon and in my own county. In these schemes, through cautioning [warning] and voluntary agreements with offenders and victims, good reparative and reconciliatory work is done. There is some evidence to suggest that people are beginning to learn to face the consequences of their actions and take responsibility for themselves.

A further implication which arises from this view of justice is that when offenders come to court, as clearly they must if offences are repeated and are of a more serious nature, they should come into a system which sees the community as the primary place for putting wrongs right and sees custody as the alternative only to be used when the issue of protecting the public and safeguarding them is paramount (Pendleton, 1982). If this were to be the case, one could get rid of tariff systems. The Probation Service and others would be able to develop opportunities within the community for putting wrongs right and creating the situation in which offenders could face the consequences of their action without having to concern themselves with 'high tariff interventions,' trying to guess what the court will buy, or finding alternatives to imprisonment.

I think that a prophet imbued with the Judaeo-Christian view of justice would be arguing for more justice and less law. The development of what are called reparation schemes, is in fact, a way of invoking the old Judaeo-Christian notion of justice and would not require greater sanctions such as reparation orders by statute; use could be made of what already exists. The probation order could be used a lot more but in doing so it should be recognised that reparation and reconciliation rely on the motivation of the parties involved. It should be possible more and more to offer to the court an agreement between the victim and the offender which has been freely negotiated, particularly in which the victim has freely consented. This is paramount in any such arrangement. Victim support schemes have a very important role here: it is necessary for the victim support scheme visitor to assist the victim and to ensure that the victim agrees freely and not under any kind of pressure to help the offender. It would need to be demonstrated, of course, that such agreements actually work. In Warwickshire (and I believe in some other areas) the probation service has adopted a policy of agreements with offenders which are offered to courts without recourse to special conditions in probation orders. So far the impression is that these work well, although detailed evidence is yet required.

The old biblical communities often used a mediator or daysman enabling reparation and reconciliation to take place in order to help work out an agreement. When one considers the potential for change it may be necessary often to have someone who is skilled enough to organise and assist this process. There have been many suggestions about how this should be done: some have opted for systems of well trained volunteers, for example in some schemes in the United States. If the Probation Service were to be involved, then this could be done using officers already involved in conciliation methods in civil work, from which the Service has learned a great deal. It has been argued elsewhere that the Service could well transfer some of these methods to its work with offenders for this is all about the skills of helping to resolve conflict (Lacey et al., 1983). If the Service were to develop a conciliation and mediation service, it would have the advantage of being able to transfer those skills increasingly into the criminal justice element of its work. It would also mean that officers involved in mediation would not be those who worked directly with offenders and would therefore be able to be seen, particularly by victims, as impartial.

Finally, the notion of 'putting things right' or of reconciliation within the community is often seen as esoteric or idealistic. What is not recognised is that it is extremely practical. This fact is already being demonstrated by victim/offender mediation schemes of a voluntary nature and also via probation services in both the United States and Great Britain.

One of the problems with such schemes is that they tend to be peripheral. They are seen to exist only on the margins of mainstream criminal justice and because of this eventually may die. Indeed, one of the vested interests of institutional justice is to keep such schemes on the edges of the system, for to regard them as fundamental in any way would in itself be disruptive.

The way forward is for those of us who work in and around the criminal justice system to persist in creating imaginative approaches and schemes which cannot be ignored. It is also to be like the 8th century prophets: persistent and urgent in representing that the only significant way to restore the hurt caused by offending must focus on the community. It is only here that those who offend may be prepared to take the consequences of their actions and take responsibility for their lives. Only here can those offended against accept responsibilities for the policies which help to create the climate in which offending occurs. In these factors, after all, lie the prerequisites of reconciliation.

Note

'More Justice Less Law' was first published as a monograph in an Occasional Paper series, *New Perspectives on Crime and Justice.* It is reproduced here with permission from the Mennonite Central Committee Canada, Victim Offender Ministries Program and the Mennonite Central Committee US Office of Criminal Justice

Two
Working for justice - I
Fairness

Malcolm R. Lacey

> In justice as fairness men agree to share one another's fate (John Rawls).

Over the last twenty five years and especially during the last decade the Probation Service has been subject to fierce political and managerial demands, outlined by David Faulkner in his essay, which have tested the resilience of the Service to the limit. Those demands are not going to slacken because they are not simply ideologically driven though that has often been the dominant experience.

The root causes lie deeper. The British economy has failed to compete effectively in the new world market. Too many people have been left without the skills necessary for paid work in companies which now require advanced technological and administrative skills. British society has become pluralistic with many different cultures and moral frameworks in a way that has been experienced as fragmenting and competing rather than enriching and rewarding. The virtues of neighbourliness, stability, and cohesion have become harder to maintain when the language of the market and the virtues of competition have become pervasive.

Public sector organisations have not been immune. In fact, they have been singled out for the introduction of managerial techniques which, though often necessary and potentially creative in their own right, have often taken precedent over professional values and insights for the Probation Service. This has been accompanied by the expectation of delivering punishment in the community rather than simply a social work service to the courts and for offenders. The result has been a weakening of its sense of identity and a loss of shared purpose, with management often perceived as imposing new methods and expectations against the instincts and beliefs of front line staff.

This essay is offered as an exploration of the concept of justice and its significance for the Probation Service, recognising the importance of both procedural and social justice. It is more inclusive than the traditional probation debate about care and control, placing the Probation Service much more firmly in its social context rather than almost exclusively delivering individualised casework to offenders; and, I believe, with greater resonance for the concerns of other agencies in the criminal justice system and for all our fellow citizens. It owes its genesis to John Pendleton's interest in these ideas and the work that he, Gordon Read and I did together in the short article 'Supervision in the community: the righting of wrongs'. The tone may now be more sombre but I hope that he would recognise that the conviction is still as strong and the possibilities still as fruitful.

A quarter of a century has elapsed since the then Home Secretary, Roy Jenkins, said that the Probation Service was moving towards the centre of the criminal justice system – words repeated almost verbatim in the Decision Document *Organising Supervision and Punishment in the Community* (Home Office, 1990). It is difficult to test the truth of such statements. Are they patronising, a way of encouraging people of low status within the system to believe they are indispensable? Are they political, part of a move to shift assumptions about sentencing? Whatever lies behind them, they have been used by the Service to bolster its position, claim a right to influence policy and improve the standing of probation officers. And, during the decade that led up the Criminal Justice Act 1991, it certainly felt as though the success of the strategy to force a shift towards more community sentences depended on the Services being prepared to shoulder that responsibility and to live with the compromises it demanded. Difficult though it was for some members of the Service, no-one can deny that it responded positively and committed itself to making a success of the Act.

That hold on influence always seemed tenuous enough. The architecture of the court did not change. The adversarial system still provided clear, defined spaces for Judge or Bench, the defendant, witnesses, prosecution and defence; but seating for the probation officer is always marginal to that central process of the establishment of guilt or innocence and the pronouncement of sentence. The Pre-Sentence Report may be of key significance but it is squeezed into a short moment in the total drama. Probation officers still complain of their low status when it comes to the listing of cases. Barristers and solicitors always seem to take precedence while probation officers kick their heels during yet another case even though their breach action or report could have been dealt with in a quarter of an hour. They do not feel as important in the system as in fact they are and sometimes, perhaps, fail to assert themselves as positively as they might. The National Association of Probation Officers certainly felt that their generally co-operative approach to the Criminal Justice Act 1991 had not been rewarded in the following pay negotiations when they had made a specific claim for extra pay to recognise the new responsibility laid on them.

The amendments to the Criminal Justice Act 1991 in the Criminal Justice Act 1993 underlined the fragility of the gains that had been made. As a *Guardian* leader on the 18 December 1993 put it, the reason lay in:

> ...(the) policy's shallow roots. Too little was done to convince the public of its benefits. Both ministers and officials were nervous of the tabloids. Had they been more open, they might have built a consensus that could have protected the sane approach.

Perhaps the Service had, unwisely as it turned out, identified itself too closely with the Act, because it did offer the possibility of dealing much more constructively with a wider range of offenders. Even so, the amendments came as a morale-shattering blow at all levels. This was followed by Mr Howard's '27 Points' announced at the Conservative Party Conference in October 1993 which reinstated the primacy of prison and claimed an efficacy for it which seems based, at best, on rather insubstantial evidence. Moving centre stage no longer seemed an apt description of the future of the Service.

THE CENTRALITY OF THE SERVICE

But that is to take far too pessimistic a view. There are at least four strong reasons on which to base a claim for being at the heart of the criminal justice process.

The first is that probation officers deal with defendants or offenders at almost every stage following arrest. Occasionally, and fairly frequently in Youth Justice teams, they may act as the 'responsible adult' when children or young people are questioned by the police. They are involved in cautioning panels; in Public Interest Case Assessment schemes, where they exist, in providing information for the Crown Prosecution Service to decide whether or not to prosecute; and in bail information and bail support schemes and bail hostels. Once a case comes to court, they prepare pre-sentence reports on all the most serious offenders. They are responsible for all community sentences. With the advent of sentence planning, in addition to the welfare and therapeutic activities they have carried out for many years, they now play a significant role in decision-making about how a prisoner should use his time and how his release should be planned; and they resume authority for the oversight of the licence for all prisoners who have served more than 12 months.

This range of work, wider than any other players in the system, produces a network of contacts, not just within the criminal justice process itself, but with other voluntary and statutory services as well as many in the private sector especially in connection with accommodation and employment. The Government has recognised this in its drive to promote partnership by forcing the Service to spend part of its budget (currently 5%) on grants to and contracts with other agencies which can further Service objectives as set out in the *Probation Service Three Year Plan 1995-98* (Home Office, 1994d).

Unless Probation Services grasp this opportunity to become enabling authorities then they will certainly become more vulnerable to externalisation and privatisation. Used sensitively, genuine partnerships can be fostered by this new ability to fund positive community initiatives especially if ways are found to consult the community, through the membership of voluntary agencies and through public consultative meetings, on how the money should be spent and on defining the kinds of scheme that local people feel are useful in preventing crime or rehabilitating offenders. Such initiatives would capitalise on the pivotal position that the Service occupies in mobilising resources and public support for the methods it uses in rehabilitating offenders.

Part of this network are the victims of crime. Probation officers were active in starting and supporting Victim Support schemes. The rationale for community service is reparation if usually in an indirect way to society as a whole rather than the actual individuals who have been harmed. There have been experimental mediation and reparation schemes which have included meetings of offenders and victims. The Service now has a duty to consider the potential effect of release on licence of prisoners on their victims, a duty that is not easy to carry out and to which I will return later.

The second reason is the nature of the workload that the Service now carries. Concentrated within the caseload of probation officers are some of the most difficult and demanding cases in any public service. Professor David Smith (1993), reporting on the research carried out at Lancaster University, has said:

> ...it is clear that the life experience of people who are known to criminal justice agencies differs in important ways from that of the population as a whole. They are more likely to be poor, unemployed, educationally unqualified, homeless or in insecure housing, unmarried, to have spent some time in local authority care, to be in debt, to suffer from chronic illness or disability, to be dependent on alcohol or other drugs, and to have disruptive or abusive family relationships.

These factors are borne out in the research of Pritchard et al. (1992) in whose sample 33% of those under supervision have been in care, 45% have been in prison, 75% are unemployed and 28% have chronic housing problems. In addition, 46% have problems with alcohol, 35% with drugs, 14% have mental health problems, 10% have attempted suicide and 15% are vulnerable to HIV infection. As Smith puts it:

> ...not only are they relatively poorer and more deprived, they are also absolutely more committed criminals, much less likely to be first offenders...and much more likely to have been in prison.

It is clear that probation officers are often working with people who have little to lose and, as a result, feel little obligation to the normal ties of society and little recognition of the harm they do. The harm is considerable. It goes beyond the direct effect of their crimes. A few of their victims suffer direct physical hurt; many more have to receive treatment for the depression and stress which result from it. The mix of drug-taking, especially by needle, prison and promiscuity produces a really high risk of HIV vulnerability and the potentiality to pass it on to sexual partners. There is also a connection with much theft, credit card fraud and burglary. This group is not only disadvantaged, it at the least can cause inconvenience, at worst it can pose dangers to others as well.

Any supervision must start from the assessment of risk and the protection of the public. This requires a re-ordering of priorities for the modern probation officer. Traditionally, the focus has been mainly on the offender and his or her needs. What is being argued here is not any lessening of that concern, but placing it within a wider context. It means raising with the offender that he or she must shoulder responsibility not just for what has been done but also to change so that it will not happen again.

It is not unusual for an area Service to have 10% or more of its cases on high risk registers – people who have caused or are at risk of causing death or serious personal injury. These cases include sex offenders for whom Probation Services now have to provide specialised intervention and management programmes during periods of extended supervision or licence. The Service so far has avoided the kind of hostile media attention that Social Services Departments have had to suffer but clearly the risk of public criticism when one of these offenders commits a further offence – as is bound to be the case – is rising fast.

Arising from the range of the Service's responsibilities and the nature of the caseload is the third reason for the Service's growing importance. Such work cannot be done without a high level of professional responsibility and discretion. Professionalism implies the trust of the public to apply a high level of knowledge and skill to difficult issues without prejudice and with respect for all concerned, victims and offenders alike. This is clearly essential in an area where there are so many conflicting interests, where there is much public concern, where the risks are high, and where emotions are strong. It is therefore difficult to overemphasise the high level of responsibility which probation officers carry in the preparation of Pre-Sentence Reports, in the supervision of those under orders of the courts and for the oversight and possible recall to prison of those who have been released on licence.

Pre-Sentence reports are called for in all cases, (subject to the amendments in the Criminal Justice and Public Order Act 1994) which are defined by the Criminal Justice Act 1991 as being 'serious enough' to attract a community sentence or 'so serious' that a prison sentence may be the only appropriate sentence. They are not prepared on people who have committed offences which courts can deal with by means of fines or discharges. This excludes defendants about whom the court may have concerns on welfare grounds, which is a matter of regret to many magistrates, and does call for the Service to develop ways of offering help on a voluntary basis, once the court proceedings have been completed, probably through volunteers or arranging for help by a voluntary agency. The main point, though, is that the Pre-Sentence Report has a unique function in helping the court to pass a just sentence. Because of the history of the Probation Service, entering the courts to offer more compassionate ways of dealing with offenders, it is often misconstrued as a mitigating document. On the contrary, its strength lies in the fact that, at its best, it is an even-handed document which paints a full portrait of the defendant and so offers the possibility of understanding why *this* particular person committed *this* offence at *this* time and what was the nature of the predicament he or she was responding to or trying to solve. It is not about estimating the seriousness of the offence – that is for the court to decide – though it must take account of where that estimate is likely to fall; but this full picture can contribute to indicating the level of risk that the offender presents and the kind of response that he or she might make to a community sentence, or the likely outcome, in personal or family terms, of a prison sentence. This task belongs to no-one else and much depends on the quality of this assessment. It is the core skill which underpins all probation work and should be undertaken by the most skilled and experienced practitioners who have already had substantial experience of supervising people on probation orders. It is quite strange how the Service allows this task to be undertaken by students even if the reports are counter-signed by a practice teacher.

How does this impartiality square with the motivation of probation officers who, after all, enter the Service keen to help and rehabilitate offenders? The first answer is obviously that impartiality is a key element in any just decision-making process and therefore the role demands it. The second, and more interesting one, has been given by Alvin Gouldner (1975) in his fine essay *The Sociologist as Partisan*. He is responding to Howard Becker who argues that it is virtually impossible to escape from writing from the position of superiors, of those who are in power. So it is essential to adopt a kind of underdog identification. But that brings in its train a loss of objectivity and that in turn entails a loss of credibility. Gouldner turns the argument on its head. Retaining as much objectivity as we can, but focusing on the underdog, the sociologist:

> ...gives us new information concerning social worlds about which many members of our society, including ourselves, know little or nothing ...(and) it may give us new perspectives on worlds we had thought familiar and presumed we already knew (p.35).

He goes on:

> ...these dominant conceptions of reality,...to grasp...the reality of the suffering of those beneath them. ...a sociology truly concerned with representing the standpoint of the underdog would most especially seek to communicate the character of his suffering, its peculiar sources and special intensity, the ways and degrees in which it is avoidable, the forces that contribute to it, and his struggle against it...a sociology of the underdog is justified because, and to the extent that, his suffering is less likely to be known and because – by the very reason of his being underdog – the extent and character of his suffering are likely to contain much that is avoidable (pp.36-37).

The parallels with Pre Sentence Reports are vivid and striking. Each report turns a spotlight onto areas of life that most of their readers will know little about. Reading a sample of reports one cannot but notice the frequency with which the subjects have had to contend with family breakdown, illness and bereavement (often at an early age). While the 'peculiar sources and special intensity' of these experiences may have been unavoidable, it is also true to say that Pre-Sentence Report writers can also often identify ways of coping or offering new opportunities that may make 'the extent and character of his sufferings' avoidable in future. It echoes David Smith's point, quoted earlier, 'The life experience of people who are known to criminal justice agencies differs in important ways from that of the population as a whole'. *'In justice as fairness men agree to share one another's fate'.*

This understanding is not just for the sake of the offender; it must be for society as a whole. Its particular contribution is to remind everyone that what has happened is a breakdown of human relationships and that sentencing has to take full account of the person. But the person of the victim is left shadowy. The criminal justice system is beginning to respond to the needs of victims, though everyone is still struggling with the legacy of centuries of tradition, when the personal nature of the affront to the victim has been almost incidental to the legal process that has been dominated by the requirement of the State to ensure 'the Queen's Peace'. So it is hardly surprising that probation officers have not yet taken on, as a matter of course, writing to the victim, offering to see him or her, or to receive their comments. It may be that such an offer would go beyond the proper role of the probation officer and, certainly, such a new departure would need a lot of discussion and some pilot schemes, but it may be this kind of re-focusing of attention is a pre-condition of a re-positioning of the Service in the public's perception. It seems to say something about justice as fairness. It depends to a large extent on whether the victim's point of view is adequately expressed directly or by other people in the system. By and large, victims do not seem to think so. Probation officers see themselves as holding the middle ground, as mediating between the offender and the demands of the law:

> The major skill of court work, however, was undoubtedly seen, as one officer put it, as 'the ability to be a wo/man for all seasons'. This amounted to 'the skill of steering the middle course – knowing the expectations and concerns of judges and magistrates, communicating that you understand that they have to have regard for society's interests, but retaining your independence, not getting sucked in, not colluding, whilst being prepared to stick your neck out for the client, but being open and honest about the risks'.. It was the skill of mediation, balance, being the bridge (Boswell et al., 1993, p.161).

Nevertheless, we seem to shrink from a full acceptance of the logic of this position which certainly should include the interests of the victim, an identified person, not just those of a generalised 'society'. It would be emotionally demanding. It would need care to avoid giving the impression to the victim that he or she was having the final say. It might be difficult to retain the trust of the offender in later working with him or her. But these are essentially problems of practice not of principle.

This kind of assessment can influence sentencing in a distinct and valuable way. The same exercise of this core skill is fundamental to good supervision of community sentences, sentence planning and oversight of licences. The responsibility is direct not just advisory as it is in court. Continuous assessment has to be harnessed to a commitment to helping which offenders can probably gain from no other source. It is notable that in two surveys carried out on homeless people, one in Surrey (Stockley et al., 1993) and one in Dorset (Pritchard and Clooney, 1994), both came up independently with the finding that homeless people, many of whom have been in trouble, said that probation officers were the most helpful people they had contact with. And in an anonymous survey of people under supervision in Dorset (Pritchard et al., forthcoming) some 95% of respondents reported positively on their relationship with their probation officer; many added extra comments on how well they had been dealt with and the assistance they had been given. One interesting finding was that probation officers were regarded more favourably than Probation Service Officers. This seems to be a consequence of the training that they have received which promotes respect for people, in continuing to be reliable and concerned, no matter what their situation or their ability to be responsive. These findings replicate Roy Bailey's research in Northern Ireland (Bailey and Ward, 1992).

This can be illustrated through some work carried out by an employment 'mentor' with an offender. She devoted a lot of time to him, gave excellent advice, made practical arrangements – and then was dismayed that the offender did not follow it through. It was all the more puzzling, because the offender was capable of university level training. That counted for nothing in face of his over-powering self-destructive impulses for which he needed counselling, perhaps therapy – skills and understanding which someone without social work training did not and could not have been expected to have. Another way of illustrating this is through a comment made by someone working with people in prison who have AIDS: 'If people feel dis-enfranchised they won't value themselves, so will not feel themselves worth protecting' – and, one can add, so can become a danger to others. This kind of dynamic extends far beyond those suffering from AIDS and applies to many, if not most, of the people whom probation officers work with. This kind of understanding has to become ingrained – a word I use because some people seem to have an innate gift for it while for others it has to be realised and maintained through training. It is not a 'common-sense' understanding, it needs constant renewal and – something we are not good at – communication of value to the external world.

In her novel *Beloved*, Toni Morrison (1987) has two striking sentences: '...she returned their disapproval with the potent pride of the mis-treated' (p.97) and 'Freeing yourself was one thing; claiming ownership of that freed self was another' (p.95). In order to be effective, probation officers need to understand that so many offenders have to simulate self-esteem through aggression rather than assertion, that their harmful and destructive behaviour has its roots in a search for meaning and significance. And also, once they have been helped to free themselves from that kind of impotence, great skill is called for in helping them to own their freed selves. In the new enthusiasm for cognitive approaches, which do genuinely offer real advances in intervention techniques, it will be important not to lose these dynamic insights which are based on values, attitudes and knowledge and are the only basis on which programme delivery and re-education can be effective. In particular, the Service needs to retain a purchase on other approaches which seek the same humanistic ends but by other means. User-centred, empowerment and social action approaches have relevance and the Service must not shrink from uncomfortable and risky questions about the effects of the economic and social policies of, and the goals set for the Probation Service by, the government of the day.

In this essay, I am attending to the criminal side of the Service's work, but the same kind of case can be made for the skills of Family Court Welfare Officers when they engage divorcing couples in negotiating agreed arrangements for the care of their children or undertaking investigations about the welfare of the children when the parties cannot agree.

The fourth element giving the Probation Service a unique role can best be illustrated by an anecdote. A group of long sentence prisoners were meeting with a parliamentary spokesman on penal affairs. Asked about the contribution of probation officers, there were a number of ribald comments to the effect that it was almost impossible to get to see them, and that when you did it made little difference. But the mood changed quickly and an agreement emerged that it was unreasonable to place all the responsibility for getting anything done on to the probation officer. The Service seems to represent, not only for prisoners but for sentencers and others too, the hope that change or improvement can happen in a system that all too often experiences repeated failures. This is not to claim that judges, police or prison officers have no belief in people at all; most are helpful and compassionate and take a real interest; but the focus of their role is different – to investigate crime and catch the criminal, to weigh the seriousness of the offence, to ensure that prisoners do not escape. Only the Probation Service has a primary role to 'advise, assist and befriend' or, as the *Statement of Purpose* puts it, 'Working at all times to bring out the best in people' and 'Reconciling offenders and communities, recognising the obligations of both'. The commitment to hope for change and improvement is explicit.

In all these ways, then, the Probation Service has a distinctive and indispensable purpose. It is questionable, though, whether its existing rationale (or, indeed, the length and thoroughness of its training) reflects this purpose and whether its staff's own understanding really matches up to and supports them in sustaining the duties and expectations laid on them; and, most importantly, whether it is convincing enough to explain to the public why the Service's role has taken on such importance since it was founded nearly a century ago.

WORKING FOR JUSTICE

Probation was born when there was an urgent need for penal reform. It offered the same mix, back in 1907, of economic and social advantage that the invention of community service did some 60 years later. It widened the scope of sentencing which till then had been limited to prison and, to a small extent, fines and discharges. It struck a humane chord for dealing with the host of minor offenders who were then imprisoned – we should not forget the example of Winston Churchill, when he was Home Secretary, visiting prisons and ordering the immediate release of some prisoners, convinced that their punishment was excessive. It was clear that many of those prisoners could be released without much risk and some with a real chance of rehabilitation. It was natural that the Probation Service should commit itself to that concept, one which the early Police Court Missionaries had helped to invent; and should concentrate on younger offenders who seemed in need of 're-education' as in the title of Elizabeth Glover's (1956) famous book *Probation and Re-education*. No doubts then about net-widening.

But the key problem we face now is not penal reform – though Judge Tumim's reports keep us alive to the extraordinarily various destructive possibilities that prison offers, and the ministerial team in the Home Office alerts us to how easily punishment for its own sake can be re-introduced – but crime and our response to it. The number of reported crimes rises inexorably and the fear of crime is endemic whatever the objective likelihood may be. It is forcing the police to ask themselves, and the wider public, what they are in business for. Law and order have risen to the top of the political agenda and with it has come a coarsening of language. During the 1980s the Home Office deliberately avoided the language of warfare; now it is returning. Even more significant it is using a hyena as the logo of the campaign against car crime and words like vermin and scum and monsters are used by official spokesmen. The disgust that these words express carry also the impression that criminals are sub-human, not part of civil society, their very nature preventing them from being integrated. This is the rhetoric of retribution and exclusion, the very antithesis of the values on which probation is founded. But it serves a purpose beyond scape-goating. It diverts attention from the Home Office's own research which shows that one man in three has a conviction for an indictable offence by the age of 35, even though only one crime in fifty reaches court (if we take the estimate of the *British Crime Survey* which suggests that only one third of crime is even reported). But an even more difficult issue is that as property crime is rising so must also be the outlets for selling the expanding proceeds. Again, this has been highlighted by a Home Office researcher (Sutton, 1993). How do politicians raise these issues with the electorate – an electorate which consists of a high proportion of convicted people (mainly men) and many more who prefer not to ask questions about the bargains they pick up through second-hand shops, car boot sales and pubs?

The rhetoric of exclusion does, however, have a core of plausibility. Again, it is Home Office research which shows that 5% of convicted offenders are responsible for around two-thirds of reported crime. The same seems to be true of juvenile offending where it is said that the new secure units are needed to control the activities of 'some hundreds' of persistent young offenders. This seems to justify the assertion that it is worth imprisoning this core of persistent offenders to give the rest of us a break. Anecdotally, it is supported by magistrates and police officers who notice a respite from a spate of burglaries when a gang of thieves has been arrested and sent down. However, it is a complicated issue. Recent research by Hagel and Newburn (1994) indicates that persistent young offenders are responsible for only a small amount of crime. And an analysis of cautioning indicates that about 85% of those cautioned in 1985 and 1988 were not convicted of a 'standard list' offence within two years of their caution and 72% of the 1985 sample had not been convicted within five years (Home Office, 1994b).

It is within this context that the Probation Service has to describe and define itself. Can it re-position itself without losing its core commitment to respecting persons as ends in themselves despite their offending, of holding on to the importance of condemning evil acts while believing in the potential of most offenders to change for the better? We must recognise how difficult this is because probation officers are now supervising some people whom they find it almost impossible to stay in the same room with, so dreadful have been their offences, and whom we do not have the knowledge or skill to change.

> Some whose eyes I don't meet,
> hands I don't shake, one that cut
> NF in a man's back and left him
> choke on his testicles, the knife
> still in him and ran with the video.

Ken Smith (1988), whose poem 'Wormwood' highlights the range of emotions engendered by the work vividly expresses the impact of working with people who have committed such crimes. It was written when he was writer-in-residence at Wormwood Scrubs prison. John Hopkins, who wrote some fifty episodes of 'Z Cars', was filmed on BBC 2:

> The stories I tell took me down dark roads into areas that have not been good for me. I'm not well , I have Parkinson's but, more important than that, the work I have done over the last 30 years has taken such a toll on my ability to deal with this and that I've written about and thought about and tried to understand. But it's an incurable obsession that will wreak its havoc on me. In the end the only thing you want to do is to understand why one person wants to hurt another. Even while you know, that the explanation is only in you (quoted by Nancy Banks-Smith, *The Guardian*, 1 June 1993).

The work stains you even, if you also realise that such potentialities lie within each of us.

There are profound personal and organisational issues raised here for people, working in a service whose rationale has been an anti-custodial stance believing that most offenders can be helped to live within and contribute to society. As will become clear later, this value system is of tremendous social importance at the present time and it remains true that we can live safely in the community with most of the people on probation officers' caseloads. This can be convincing only if sufficient emphasis is laid on assessing those who may need to be in custodial conditions. The Service must also help its staff to cope with the feelings surrounding these cases, including secretarial staff who are working in reception areas and typing reports.

So the question is: can the Probation Service use the central position it has achieved to contribute an understanding – in both senses of the word – of the offender without losing sight of the harm that has been done or the risk that might be run in the future? Such an understanding must be a contribution to justice informed by a sense of fair dealing to all those involved. It will mean paying much more attention to the impact of the offences, and sometimes of the actual proximity of the offender, on the victim. It is a radical shift, both in practice and in the projection of a different image of the Service to the public at large, which at present seems to view the Service as marginal and on the side of the offender.

It is here that the work of John Rawls in his book *A Theory of Justice* (1973) can help with a theoretical underpinning of probation as a contribution to justice. We have done little to explore the concept of justice, perhaps because it seems a self-evident good, a common-sense conviction. Rawls argues that the basis of justice is fairness. His reason for starting from this point is that there are many visions of the Good and what a good life should be but, in the end, there is no way of deciding between them. No democratic society can commit itself to the pursuit of a single ideal since there can be no consensus about the nature of that ideal. In fact, it is a characteristic of totalitarian regimes that they do have such a commitment and justify any coercion in its pursuit. So justice cannot be based on a notion of an ultimate Good; what it can represent is a society that is rule-governed, where each individual is equally free to pursue his or her own ideal so long as it does not impede or violate any other citizen's right to their belief. Justice is a way of regulating competing claims. It is a practical matter:

> ...a society in which all can achieve their complete good, or in which there are no conflicting demands and the wants of all fit together without coercion into a harmonious plan of activity is a society in a certain sense beyond justice (p.28).

A rule applies to everyone; it 'requires equality in the assignment of basic rights and duties' (p.14). It is the first of his principles: 'Each person is to have an equal right to the most extensive basic liberty compatible with a similar liberty for others'. His second, and rather more unusual, principle is:

> Social and economic inequalities are to be arranged so that they are both (a) reasonably expected to be to everyone's advantage, and (b) attached to positions and offices open to all (p.60).

The thrust of this second principle is that any inequality can only be justified if the advantages it brings to everyone outweigh the losses that others are likely to incur.

The two principles are explicitly designed to address both liberty, that is freedom from oppression, the right of conscience and to freedom of expression; and social justice, namely, the distribution of wealth and income and the hierarchies of authority. The second principle

> ...represents...an agreement to regard the distribution of natural talents as a common asset and to share in the benefits of this distribution whatever it turns out to be. Those who have been favoured by nature, whoever they are, may gain from their good fortune only on terms that improve the situation of those who have lost out. ...The natural distribution is neither just nor unjust...What is just and unjust is the way that institutions deal with these facts...The social system is not an unchangeable order beyond human control but a pattern of human action. *In justice as fairness, men agree to share one another's fate* (pp. 101-2).

The courts are primarily concerned with the first principle, liberty, which Rawls acknowledges is always primary and no retreat from it can be justified on social or economic grounds:

> The suspicion that others are not honouring their duties and obligations is increased by the fact that, in the absence of the authoritative interpretation and enforcement of the rules, it is particularly easy to find excuses for breaking them...the existence of effective penal machinery serves as men's security to one another (p.240).

He takes this a step further:

> We see that the principle of responsibility is not founded on the idea that punishment is primarily retributive or denunciatory. Instead it is acknowledged for the sake of liberty itself (p.241).

One strand in the public debate leading to the Criminal Justice Act 1991 was that social considerations, that is to say the individualised needs of the offender, had been so emphasised that public understanding and confidence in our system of justice had been eroded. It was therefore necessary to assert a principle of 'just deserts', focusing on the seriousness of the crime rather than the characteristics of the offender. Perhaps its expression was too subtle for at the same time there was a re-ordering, a kind of codification, of the definition of seriousness, leading to more lenient punishment for lesser property offenders and increased severity for violent and sexual ones. Public opinion did not seem ready for this. Even the principle of unit fines designed to make the impact of the penalty more equal on people in differing material and financial circumstances has been abandoned when what was needed was an adjustment of the administrative calculations. The present ministerial team at the Home Office seem to feel that severe punishment needs to be emphasised. They believe that too many people are finding excuses for anti social behaviour because the courts are failing to take seriously the ordinary citizen's view of the legal system as a procedural one which focuses on the gravity of the offence and ignores, or at least minimises, mitigating factors of causation and motivation.

If the importance of the Service within the system is as great as I have suggested, then we may have to acknowledge the strength and indispensability of Rawls' first principle, noting that it stresses responsibility, not deterrence, retribution or denunciation. It is an affirmation of the offender's dignity, responsible for his or her own actions. It is in line with good social work principles. For example, the first requirement in work with sex offenders is to confront them with the fact that they have abused their position in coercing someone weaker than themselves, and cannot pass responsibility off onto their victim for enticing them. Again, with burglars, their familiar argument that the insurance will pay has to be shown to be the rationalisation that it is before much effective work can be done on changing behaviour. Practice has changed, as probation officers have dealt with more committed offenders, from the days when a probation textbook could suggest that, as the relationship developed, its originating offence would tend to be forgotten (Monger, 1967). Rooting this change more deeply into a framework of justice will give it greater force and coherence, both for practitioners and for a public to whom we must increasingly explain and justify what we do. Such work starts from the rights of the victim, a theme which some practice incorporates but one which needs to gain a much higher prominence. The presence of the victim brings responsibility home.

Rawls' second principle, social justice, while it can never override the requirements of liberty, is necessary to gain a general acceptance of a system of justice. This depends on the substantive matters of fair access to the basic goods of opportunity, income, wealth and the bases of self esteem. They are more difficult to establish because they encounter the existing structures of power and advantage. He argues that there are conditions:

> ...that encourage hostile outbreaks of envy. The first of these is a psychological condition...persons lack a sure confidence in their own value and in their ability to do anything worthwhile. Second...many occasions arise when this psychological condition is experienced as painful and humiliating. The discrepancy between oneself and others is made visible by the social structure and style of life of one's society. The less fortunate are therefore often forcibly reminded of their situation, sometimes leading them to an even lower estimation of themselves and their mode of living. And third, they see their social position as allowing no constructive alternative to opposing the favoured circumstances of the more advantaged. To alleviate their feelings of anguish and inferiority, they believe they have no choice but to impose a loss on those better placed even at some cost to them selves, unless of course they are to relapse into resignation and apathy (pp. 535-36).

If we take these frames of mind in turn, we can see how graphically they describe many of the people that probation officers are now supervising.

The first operates at a psychological level. Nevertheless, it demonstrates for Rawls that 'the primary goal of self-respect...turns out to have a central position in the moral psychology underlying justice as fairness' (p.433):

> ...(for) it includes a person's sense of his own value, his secure conviction that his conception of his good, his plan of life, is worth carrying out. And second, self-respect implies a confidence in one's ability, so far as it is within one's power, to fulfil one's intentions. When we feel that our plans are of little value, we cannot pursue them with pleasure or take delight in their execution. Without it nothing may seem worth doing, and we sink into apathy and cynicism (p.440).

The second aspect, that is 'the discrepancy between oneself and others...made visible by the social structure' has been addressed by Sir Ralph, now Lord, Dahrendorf, in a lecture in 1987 which describes the process by which structural unemployment has produced in the United States a group of people who have 'no stake in the world in which they are living. (They) cannot be expected to comply with its norms and they do not.' Dahrendorf notes that many are young, as are the majority of perpetrators of crime against property and crimes of violence.

In Britain, according to Dahrendorf (1987), developments are moving in the same direction. There are inequalities, although as yet they do not extend to the point where people doubt 'the underlying assumptions of society'. But the majority do lock out the less fortunate. Dahrendorf concludes: '...there is a moral case for not dropping any human being and it is strong.' But there is a social and practical case as well.

> ...citizenship has become an exclusive rather than an inclusive status. Some are full citizens, some are not. This in turn means that doubt in the validity of prevailing values is built into the structure of society itself..., extending full citizenship rights to all is therefore the main task of social policy.

The reality of this has been vividly described in Beatrix

Campbell's (1993) account of the 1991 riots in Cardiff, Oxford and Tyneside. She tells the story of seventeen-year old Dale Robson who was killed in a gruesome crash while being chased in a stolen car by the police.

> In an attempt to dignify his life, his grieving father, Mick Robson, made a public statement shortly after his death, reported in the *Newcastle Journal* on 9 September, in which he insisted that his son was not a joyrider, he was a professional car thief. ...His efforts were regarded by respectable society as a mockery of making a living, and by Meadowell citizens as ruining their community's reputation. Nonetheless, he had made a poignant effort to give his son the status of a skill. This gave the dead boy, who had been an exile in his own society, much more than talent, though his father was paying tribute to that, too: it redeemed him as a social person by imagining a career and therefore a context, history, relevance and relationships... It was a quest to clothe a life in moral virtue when it had ended in disgrace (p.55).

Campbell makes the point strongly that this social disintegration has a particularly pernicious effect on young men. She seems to me to make an irrefutable case but what I want to draw attention to here is the way in which our culture becomes internalised for good or ill. Self-esteem is not an individual's achievement, it is a product of the relationship between the individual and the society which is not only important but inescapable to him or her:

> For a lad whose culture celebrated a man's authority and power, and lethal weapons as the solution to social problems, the discovery of his own illiteracy or incompetence could, of course, carry the dread that 'being inside society' meant 'being defeated'. That was the scenario some of these lads repeated in the riots, where *power* meant only *brute force*. 'They have no idea how society works', says one of their lawyers (p.96).

It is striking that Rawls contrasts his theory of justice as fairness with what he clearly feels is the predominant conception, the utilitarian view. That asserts as a first principle the right of each individual to maximise his or her own satisfaction so that the greatest amount of happiness within society as a whole may be achieved:

> ...there is no reason in principle why the greater gains of some should not compensate for the lesser losses of others; or more importantly, why the violation of the liberty of a few might not be made right by the greater good shared by many (p.26).

The utilitarian drive behind current politics becomes only too evident in the light of remarks by senior Conservative politicians. 'The rise in unemployment is a sacrifice well worth making' and 'There is no such thing as society, only individuals and families'. Like the priest in Adam Thorpe's novel *Ulverton* we might well say: 'For a zealous wind doth blow amongst us, withering the vine. And the armies of the flashing mind devour the poor secretly. Then beware, my children' (1993, p.25).

Utilitarianism is intimately connected with the theory of the market, historically and intellectually. Its hold now is so strong that even in the public services, not only is there the drive to create internal markets and to subject as much as possible to competition, but it is becoming increasingly difficult to avoid the use of the language of commerce – marketing, consumers, customers – even when such language distorts the true purpose of the relationship or the social transaction that is taking place. The inevitable consequence, as with any utilitarian position since it can never give primacy to a moral ought, is an increasing reliance on 'back to basics' or 'Victorian values' at the softer end of persuasion, or open reliance on coercion. As the Home Secretary put it when addressing the Conservative Party Conference on 6th October 1993:

> I am announcing the most comprehensive programme of action against crime that has ever been announced by any Home Secretary [applause]. Action to prevent crime – action to help the police catch criminals – action to make it easier to convict the guilty – and action to punish them when they are found guilty. And this is just the first instalment.

It has to be a first instalment because, if justice is not seen to be fair in a social as well as a legal sense, it contains the seeds of its own destruction – it leads to Rawls' third category of people who feel 'they have no choice but to impose a loss on those better placed'.

I am one, my liege,
Whom the vile blows and buffets of the world
have so incens'd, that I am reckless what
I do to spite the world (Macbeth III.I.108).

Or, to put it in the modern context that Campbell gives:

> ...he has lived his life in an era which disinvested in the social skills he might otherwise have acquired – literacy, work and co-operation. He was capable of deadly dangerousness (1993, p.194).

The element of consent has been retained for community orders despite their becoming a sentence rather than a 'proving' period instead of a sentence. The original Probation of Offenders Act in 1907 had this profound insight into both its pragmatic and political necessity. Unless offenders are prepared to go along with the Order, then any change will only be skin-deep. Campbell describes many young men, like the one just described who withhold their consent, withhold it largely because our era has disinvested in social skills such as co-operation. For them, the court's orders have no legitimacy and leave probation officers struggling to establish some meaning and rapport at a personal level which has never been offered within their wider experience. Consent can only really operate within a wider context of legitimacy.

Probation is a great social invention but like all inventions it needs maintenance and sometimes a major refit. We cannot ignore the changed times we now work in or the magnitude of the difficulties we now face. This essay acknowledges that the Service is under the most sustained ideological attack it has ever had to face; it takes account of the impact of the Victim Support movement which has by no means run its course in influencing thinking and attitudes within the criminal justice system; it recognises the difficult task that probation officers now have in working with committed and dangerous offenders, with some sense of wonder at the way they persevere and prove themselves the one reliable and concerned person in the world of so many of them; and it offers a framework for holding together all these conflicting pressures in the belief that probation officers are still as inventive, imaginative and morally concerned as ever they were, and that their blend of pragmatism and compassion is too valuable for society to lose.

Three
Working for justice - II
Punishment

Malcolm R. Lacey

You punish because you punish (Nils Christie).

As public anxiety has grown about the increase in crime and the vulnerability to it that more and more people feel, so there has been a greater emphasis on the importance of punishment. This has made a great impact on the Probation Service because it has changed its founding purpose from the supervising of offenders 'instead of a sentence' to supervision ' as a sentence'.

It is impossible not to give some attention to this issue in any consideration of justice, not least because there is all too often a belief that bringing someone to justice is more than bringing him or her to trial, it is an expectation of punishment.

John Patten, in his speech at the ACOP Conference in 1988, highlighted punishment as one of the 'essential issues' (p.5) in the Green Paper *Punishment, Custody and the Community* (Home Office 1988) and dealt with it in a man-of-the-world, common-sense kind of way: 'Offenders must be punished for what they have done. It is strange to someone like me from outside probation how difficult some in the service find this' (p. 5.). Later, he deals with this at more length:

> My reason for this is that it deals with *some basic truths* about the way the criminal justice system operates and how the public perceives it (p.12. my italics). *The fact is that all probation based disposals are already in varying degrees forms of punishment. For example, the offender who has to report to a probation officer, or work specified hours on C.S. or spend 60 days at a day centre, is clearly being punished. It is bizarre to scratch around to find polite euphemisms for what is going on* (p.12., his italics).

That speech was made in the process of working out what were to become the measures to be contained in the Criminal Justice Act 1991. Since then that Act has been significantly amended and the philosophy of punishment has been given its definitive, contemporary expression. Mr Michael Howard in his speech to the Conservative Party Conference on 6 October 1993, which I have already quoted in the previous essay, ended:

> When Jim Carpenter spoke in our debate of the need for punishment he wasn't speaking for himself; he wasn't speaking for this Conference; he was voicing the concern felt by millions of people in this country'. And he added...'At the same time I shall be toughening up community sentences. I want them to be proper punishment'.

That speech, with its 27 Points, has been bitterly criticised:

> Suddenly the law and order problem has again become very simple. Complexity vanished in the gale of conference demands that more police, more courts, more punishments and more prisons are the only answer. Those solutions were offered from the floor with the usual certainty that any alternative, or any scepticism whatever, was a gutless treason on the British people. It is the task of the platform, not always shirked, to disabuse the floor of such crude simplicities. Howard's debut revealed a man, instead, whose capacity to muse about deep social forces doesn't deter him from playing to every atavistic impulse the party conference exhibits...By the end, he was almost screaming (Hugo Young, *The Guardian,* 7 October 1993).

But maybe the leader in *The Times* (7 October 1993) struck a note that is more representative:

> Michael Howard's exhilarating speech...addressed the anxiety of ordinary people about law and order and the rising fear that the Criminal Justice system is weighted in favour of the offender.

In all the press stories about a 'teenage tearaway...given a home of his own after an adventure holiday failed to straighten him out' (*Daily Mail,* 12 August 1994) and 'Teenage Joyrider

Cheats Jail' (*Daily Express,* 18 August 1994), there is a serious debate trying to get expressed. Sometimes it does, as in a thoughtful leader in *The Daily Telegraph* (12 August 1994):

> The dispatch of a 14 year-old for a holiday at Center Parcs seems to reflect serious misjudgement by Essex County Council. Whatever the merits of intensive therapeutic treatment for young offenders, this policy cannot be sustained without public confidence. Such follies as the Essex case widen the credibility gap, for they appear to promote a policy of rewarding anti-social behaviour. *The punishment of mischief and reward of good conduct are fundamental tenets of all morality...*A nation-wide debate is urgently needed about the kind of environment that is desirable in these new custodial centres. At the root of much juvenile delinquency is a failure of parenting. There is room for therapies that seek to heal deep wounds by the intensive application of professional skill (my italics).

We can neither ignore nor side-step these arguments nor just refuse to become involved in punishment. We must recognise that the way in which Mr Patten and Mr Howard use the word does resonate with many, perhaps most, people. We have to engage with it and formulate a response which aims at changing that popular perception and unearthing other, more valuable, insights which are in danger of being permanently buried. The purpose of this paper is to sketch out a background for arguing such a viewpoint which has been well expressed by Terence Morris (1988):

> By its very title *Punishment, Custody and the Community,* it presumes that non-custodial forms of disposal *ought* to be punitive, whereas it has been received wisdom for more than a generation that the objectives of such sentences as probation, and more recently of community service, should be identified as rehabilitative; the very need for the offender's assent would seem to suggest that these are not punishments, per se, but rather contractual forms of social expiation.

TRADITIONAL JUSTIFICATIONS

It is important to start with the usual justifications of punishment. Walker (1972) for example, states: ' I do not believe retribution is a proper aim for a secular penal system' (p.6.) and goes on to argue:

> The reduction of prohibited conduct must be the main aim of any penal system, but must be tempered by both economic considerations and humanity if the system is to be practicable and tolerable (p.38).

A similarly utilitarian argument is put forward by Benn and Peters (1959):

> Our main contention has been that punishment is a technique for preventing breaches of rules; like any technique, it must be judged by its results...As a technique employing deliberate suffering, it must be counted, in moral terms, as costly (p.195).

Or, as the old utilitarian master, Jeremy Bentham (1823), himself put it: 'All punishment is mischief; all punishment is in itself evil' (p.281). That stricture is worth bearing in mind. All punishment is a failure not a self-evident good as the more raucous tabloids sometimes come near to suggesting. In this context, it is of interest to note that *Cruden's Concordance* lists over 50 references to punishment in the Old Testament, and only 9 in the New Testament.

Against this utilitarian rejection of retribution, Ashworth (1983) in an authoritative book, says:

> The general justifying aim of sentencing is probably a modified version of what might be termed *modern retributivism*...The fact of his having broken the law may justify singling out a person for punishment, but the justification for inflicting punishment upon him seems to some extent instrumental. Punishment is not only permissible but desirable; it is not merely inherent in the idea of law but also socially necessary in order to maintain laws (pp.16 & 18).

The characteristic of a retributive theory of punishment is that it looks backward to the crime whereas a utilitarian one looks forward to what the punishment may achieve. It will be obvious that this is a parallel debate to that between desert and rehabilitation.

I am not suggesting that we can ignore these insights into the nature of punishment and their justifications. Indeed, we need to pay attention to an article by two leading theorists, Wasik and von Hirsch (1988), when we try to justify a greater use of non-custodial penalties. They argue that:

> ...non-custodial sentences have developed in a largely unprincipled way...minimal Court of Appeal guidance exists...The view that community service should be tied into the tariff has now attracted judicial approval, and some scale of commensurability between community service and custody has emerged, albeit in rudimentary form. With the decline of the rehabilitative ideal, efforts have been made by some writers to redefine probation in something approaching a desert model, with greater emphasis upon the type of condition which may be written into such an order, and their enforcement, instead of the traditional emphasis upon the probation officer's duty to 'advise, assist and befriend' the offender (p.556).

This was a very important paper which was influential in the calculus of seriousness which became the key principle in the Criminal Justice Act 1991. The Act did address the anarchic state of sentencing principles especially in the area of community orders. It also adopted their argument about the place of the probation order in such a scheme:

> Traditionally, *probation* has been regarded as...a period 'on trust' which, if successfully completed by the offender, will result in no penalty being given for the offence...For our purposes, however, it seems preferable to regard the various conditions of a probation order as constituting the offender's penalty...It seems clear to us...that it is unrealistic now to regard probation as anything other than a non-custodial penalty...Whilst probation supervision has historically purported to emphasise treatment, it could instead stress *surveillance*...(making) it more difficult for the offender to offend, or intimidate him from doing so (pp.568-69).

Both the rhetoric of public debate and the pragmatic of new legislation are therefore forcing members of the Probation Service to see whether it is possible to define a position in relation to punishment, seriousness and desert which is compatible with our rehabilitative motivation and yet can satisfy this legitimate concern.

A DIFFERENT APPROACH

If we are to do so, then I think we have to start from our own experience, and that of friends and colleagues, when we have been the victims of crimes, sometimes quite minor in themselves. Almost invariably, we react with hurt and anger – 'just let me get my hands on him'. Simply put, the only place to start is with the hurt of the victim. It is significant that both retributionist and utilitarian theories concentrate on the offender; the retributionist wishes to inflict some disadvantage on the offender to restore the balance that has been upset (a peculiarly negative approach when one comes to think about it) while the utilitarian looks to ways in which sanctions might be used to prevent future breaches of the rules that are necessary for civilised society.

This is no mere debating point. A constant complaint from victims is that they are not kept informed about what they regard as *their* case. This comes out strongly in the research of Shapland et al. (1985):

> Victims felt aggrieved if they were not told and could not easily find out...Even victims who were police officers found difficulty in following what was happening to the offender...
>
> Truly reparative measures have, on the whole, been neglected for reasons that are not altogether clear. In civil law the concept of damages is of ancient establishment, but in the context of the criminal law the position of the victim has been limited for the most part to that of being a witness. A criminal offence in common law is 'against the peace' – that is the Sovereign's Peace – which though it may have some legal convenience as an abstraction has minimised the fact that the victims of many crimes are real people who suffer actual loss or injury...When the Criminal Injuries Compensation Board was established to make provision for the victims of crimes of violence there was some feeling in legal circles that this novelty might set a dangerous precedent for the compensation of the victims of property crime in that the State would be

> admitting to failing to protect them, too, from the depredations of offenders (pp 139-40).

It is essential to start from this intuitive sense of outrage. To clarify it, it is easiest to start with heinous crimes, where the point is well made by Peter Berger, in his book *A Rumour of Angels* (1971), where he discusses the Eichmann case:

> A somewhat different sort of reasoning is involved in what I will call the *argument from damnation.* This refers to experiences in which our sense of what is humanly permissible is so fundamentally outraged that the only adequate response to the offence as well as to the offender seems to be a curse of supernatural dimensions. For here is a case in which condemnation can be posited as an absolute and compelling necessity, irrespective of how the case is explained or of what practical consequences one may wish to draw from it. Indeed, a refusal to condemn in absolute terms would appear to offer prima facie evidence not only of a profound failure in the understanding of justice, but more profoundly of a fatal impairment of *humanitas*. There are certain deeds that cry out to heaven. These deeds are not only an outrage to our moral sense, they seem to violate a fundamental awareness of the constitution of our humanity (pp.84-85).

One of the most painful aspects of the Moors Murders case is the continuing blight in the lives of the parents and the way their lives have been eaten away by their continuing corrosive bitterness. It seems possible that this may be as a result of the fascination exerted by the perpetrators and the comparative neglect of the families, perhaps because their pain is too great for us to bear. In some of the televised discussions in which they have taken part, one almost feels they are being put in the wrong for not accepting that Brady is mad and Hindley may have become religious. It is, however, a logical conclusion of our theory of punishment because the State has put huge resources into understanding the offender and only derisory ones into understanding and helping the victim, even those who have been subjected to monstrous evil.

Most crime is not of the order of Eichmann and Brady and Hindley. I have concentrated on it only to highlight the importance of the feelings of anger, hurt and outrage which crime brings out in us, because I think the same feelings, though less intense, are aroused with lesser crimes, and *are equally justifiable*, constituting a part of our humanity.

This is clearly exemplified in an article by Graham Hutton, 'A family betrayed by the system' (*The Guardian* 14.9.94):

> Until my niece, Roxy Geransar, was killed in May last year by a drunken driver, I had never had any personal involvement with our criminal justice procedures. But in fact 'The System' which was supposed to punish the man who had killed Roxy instead treated him with the most ridiculous leniency.
>
> I believe it was that leniency that ultimately caused my niece's mother – my sister – to commit suicide...Because it was her terrible distress over the court case and the sentence the drunk driver received which tipped the balance of her mind...She had suffered the unspeakable tragedy of losing her beloved daughter, and now the judicial system appeared to be spitting on Roxy's memory...she felt totally betrayed by the people she had always assumed were her natural allies in life – people who believed in decency and law and society...if so-called justice in this country continues in this manner it won't be long before ordinary people feel so disillusioned that they decide there is no alternative but to take the law into their own hands.

Nils Christie in *Limits to Pain* (1982) is the person whom we shall find most helpful in formulating a position from which punishment can be recognised as necessary while at the same time combating those vengeful desires for inflicting pain and restrictions, almost for their own sake, which are at the root of our worries about embracing punishment.

Christie suggests an analogy with sorrow. First, it is a *personal* matter. How difficult we find that. Meetings between perpetrators and victims are so unusual that they are filled with apprehension, not just because feelings may run high, but because they run counter to our expected ways of dealing with crime, which are distanced, professionalised and impersonal. Second, it is an *emotional* matter. Just as it is reasonable to grieve, though not for ever, so it is reasonable to be angry, though not to excess. Third, *mourning is an act without purpose*, by which he means that it is not carried out in order to get over the loss, it just is, it is part of what being human intrinsically means. Christie argues strongly for an absolute theory of punishment: 'Absolute because no reasons are given. You punish because you punish'. He maintains that this would have a limiting effect because people would have to concentrate on the morality of inflicting pain rather than on some hoped for utilitarian result which might justify it. He does not deny that the effects of deterrence have to be evaluated as well, only that the absolute view of punishment encourages us to get what was behind it into the open:

> All I suggest, is that there is more behind some part of the claims for punishment than stated in the simplistic, utilitarian version. And it is important to get that 'more' out into the open, make it explicit, and start a debate on it. Our situation is one where incentives for 'an absolute type of punishment' are transformed into a system suited for handling utilitarian punishments. This leads to a perpetual dissatisfaction with law and order in society. Within penal law, this leads to an everlasting demand for more punishments carried out by representatives who rightly in the impossible situation in which they are placed – perceive themselves as a buffer between a savage population filled with a lust for vengeance, and some misfits in need of protection against receiving too much pain (p.103).

I want to strengthen this point by quoting a lengthy passage from William Morris in *News from Nowhere* (1931, Chap. 12) in which the narrator talks to the old man, Hammond, who lives in a Utopian vision of a future England, a dream where 'instead of the unsatisfied aspirations rebelling against the poverty of the present, the fulfilled aspirations reveal the poverty of the past:

> ...'Yes,' I said, 'but consider, must not the safety of society be safeguarded by some punishment ?'.
>
> 'There, neighbour' said the old man, with some exultation. 'You have hit the mark. That *punishment* of which men used to talk so wisely and act so foolishly, what was it but the expression of their fear? And they had need to fear, since they – i.e., the rulers of society – were dwelling like an armed band in a hostile country. But we who live amongst our friends need neither fear nor punish.

Surely if we, in dread of an occasional rare homicide, an occasional rough blow, were solemnly and legally to commit homicide and violence, we could only be a society of ferocious cowards. Don't you think so, neighbour?'

'Yes, I do, when I come to think of it from that side', said I.

'Yet you must understand', said the old man, 'that when any violence is committed, we expect the transgressor to make any atonement possible to him, and he himself expects it. But again, think if the destruction or serious injury of a man momentarily overcome by wrath or folly can be any atonement to the commonwealth? Surely it can only be an additional injury to it'.

Said I, 'But suppose the man has a habit of violence, – kills a man a year, for instance?'

'Such a thing is unknown', said he. 'In a society where there is no punishment to evade, no law to triumph over, remorse will certainly follow transgression'.

'And lesser outbreaks of violence,' said I, 'how do you deal with them? for hitherto we have been talking of great tragedies, I suppose?'

Said Hammond: 'If the ill-doer is not sick or mad (in which case he must be restrained till his sickness or madness is cured) it is clear that grief and humiliation must follow the ill-deed; and society in general will make that pretty clear to the ill-doer if he should chance to be dull to it; and again, some kind of atonement will follow, – at the least, an open acknowledgement of the grief and humiliation. Is it so hard to say, 'I ask your pardon, neighbour?' – Well, sometimes it is hard – and let it be.

'You think that enough?' said I.

'Yes,' said he, 'and moreover it is all that we *can* do. If in addition we torture the man, we turn his grief into anger, and the humiliation he would otherwise feel for *his* wrongdoing is swallowed up by a hope of revenge for *our* wrongdoing to him. He has paid the legal penalty, and can 'go and sin again' with comfort. Shall we commit such a folly, then? Remember Jesus had got the legal penalty remitted before he said 'Go and sin no more'. Let alone that in a society of equals you will not find any one to play the part of torturer or jailer, though many to act as nurse or doctor' (pp.191-92).

IMPLICATIONS FOR PRACTICE

What practical conclusions can we draw from the insights in these quotations?

First, we must not just recoil from the emphasis on punishment but use the intensity of public concern as an opportunity to get the issues 'into the open' and offer an alternative set of meanings which can be contained within the word, while recognising that it is a difficult time to bat on this wicket.

Second, in this we are talking not just about probation, but about the criminal justice system as a whole. In particular, there is an argument that the fine should be abolished and compensation orders made instead. In cases where there was no direct victim, or a claim was not made, or the victim provoked the offence, then the money would be paid into a compensation fund. Victims would then be compensated directly by the Court. The ability to pay would be separated from the principle that compensation ought to be made. This would have a tremendous symbolic public effect. It could be heightened by retaining the fine for motoring offences, offences of strict liability under Public Health and Factory Acts, and victimless offences such as possession of cannabis – 'acts...which...are not criminal in any real sense but...acts which in the public interest are prohibited under a penalty' (Sherras v. De Rutzen (1895) 1 QB 918, quoted in Morris, 1988, p. 56).

Third, we should recognise that offenders should rightly suffer pain but that as far as possible it should be the pain arising from 'humiliation and grief'. Probation officers may be instrumental in bringing offenders to experience such pain as part of the process of expiation. This may involve quite strict discipline, as in community service, where offenders are often not willing to discharge, or are by themselves incapable of discharging, their obligations. It is not accidental that the founders of the Pennsylvania System called their prisons *penitentiaries*; it was an attempt to get offenders to recognise their own responsibility, not just 'to pay their dues'. Any system run by the Probation Service ought to have similar *personalising* aims though we should recognise that we may often fail in this, and that there is no shame in getting someone just to pay his or her dues in a non-degrading, recognisably useful way. In general, we could argue the case for 'Making Amends' so well thought out by Martin Wright (1982) where he devotes a whole chapter to setting out such a scheme.

Fourth, the Probation Service should recognise that we have

not responded as positively as we ought to have done to the Combination Order. We have been so concerned that the extra demands such orders may put on offenders will cause them to put themselves at risk of further punishment by breaching the conditions that we have overlooked the powerful arguments for combining the reparative element of community service with the helping element of probation. So long as it were not administered in a conventional and routine way, it would be a signal to the offender and to the public that the harm done had to be acknowledged and actively made amends for.

Fifth, it is significant that the element of consent has been retained in the making of a probation order, even though it has now become a sentence in its own right. This may seem rather odd so it is important to be clear that the Court, by gaining consent, is not asking the permission of the offender, but is beginning to engage him or her in the 'dialogue' which Christie argues, and I agree with him, is the key to any personal acceptance of responsibility, not 'punishment but a contractual form of social expiation'. Ironically *consent* which has been so often derided as a charade becomes the key to re-formulating the purpose of punishment within the criminal justice system.

Sixth, we should recognise that some offences are so serious that they require the infliction of a penalty over and above what might seem adequate for reparation – for example, attacking an old lady in her home in the course of a burglary might 'cry out' for the infliction of a penalty over and above the actual value of the property stolen or the injury caused. This seems to be the kind of dividing line between probation-based measures and others such as punitive fines and imprisonment. As mentioned in the first essay, this has been recognised in the Criminal Justice Act 1991.

Similarly, we can wholeheartedly support the penal system when it is used for 'protection' though we may feel that this argument is sometimes used too glibly and inappropriately. However, the 'denunciatory' aspect of sentencing becomes much less sustainable in the kind of system I have outlined which is predicated on satisfying the outrage suffered by the victim.

Seventh, we need to change the vocabulary we use to describe the work we do. There is now a general acceptance that we should avoid the word 'client' and describe people as defendants, ex-offenders, parolees, residents, or simply people. This is quite a small change but we need to go much further and place much greater emphasis on the accurate description of what probation officers now do – assessment of risk, with a priority on public protection, the analysis of offending behaviour, the management of programmes for offenders often in partnerships with other agencies both voluntary and statutory. And with regard to supervision, we need to stress the work done on awareness of the victim's hurt, the making of amends, learning how to take responsibility, and the emphasis on the learning of skills to enable offenders to begin to contribute positively to the society in which they live.

This new changed vocabulary only reflects many of the changes that modern practice already incorporates. However, we have done relatively little work in a theoretical way to help students, staff and the general public to understand and legitimise the process that is involved. We need to *re-frame* the concept of supervision.

I use the word re-framing as a modern, secular version of repentance. It means a sense of deep regret and guilt for some misdeed. What is interesting is that it is a translation of two words – from the Greek *metanoia*, which means transcending or going beyond the present state of mind in order to amend what is wrong; and from the Latin *penitentia* which relates to sorrow for sin or confession especially as expressed in the payment of a penalty. In secular language, we can express this as a re-framing of the situation from one of paying a penalty (deprivation of liberty as it is expressed in the Criminal Justice Act and associated rules) to one of making amends. In practical terms, it is a usefully different way of engaging motivation.

A PARADIGM FOR PRACTICE

So I am suggesting that an 'ideal model' of practice would have four stages:

1. **Protection.** The offender to be made aware that he or she has forfeited certain rights and that the safety of others will assume precedence. This may make it easier to approach the expectations in National Standards that the interests of victims will be considered when releasing prisoners, especially those who have committed serious offences. For some offenders, it may be reassuring to know that their badness is being contained. For others, whose self-esteem is negligible, it

may be meaningless or even damaging if not handled well, though this is not a reason for avoiding it. For many, whose own experiences have been such that they construe the world as a place where 'dog eats dog' and any empathy with the effect that these self-regarding survival actions have on other people is non-existent, the primary demand to consider the victim may be a necessary part of any effective rehabilitation.

It is worth noting that the defining characteristics of effective therapists (as researched by Truax and Carkhuff, 1967) are non-possessive warmth, *genuineness* and *empathy*. It is no coincidence that the *skills* taught under 'Reasoning and Rehabilitation' (Ross et al., 1988) programmes fall into two types – those that teach offenders skills of self-assertion and competence and those that teach empathy or understanding the world of other people.

2. **Re-framing**. This is the act of taking responsibility. It will usually be accompanied by depression because it entails feelings of guilt for harm done. It is a pre-requisite for emotional and social growth. Nevertheless, for most of the people whom we supervise, it is a difficult time which they will try to avoid. It is therefore very important to use this time to offer opportunities for enjoyment (sport and music) and skills, especially those which can lead to some productive outcome – if not work, then at least an NVQ. The point is that the offender is doing some work on him- or herself to enable re-entry – or entry for the first time – into the world of citizenship.

   The evidence of Mediation UK to the Royal Commission on Criminal Justice (1991) contains the following:

   > Reparation is the act of making amends by the offender; it may comprise compensation to the victim, an apology, payment to a charity, work for the victim (especially a corporate victim such as a business or club) or work for the community (e.g. a charity). *The offender can also make reparation by co-operating with any training or rehabilitation that he or she needs – an outcome that victims are often glad to accept.*

3. **Reparation**. This is implicit, as the quotation shows, in re-framing. I suggest that all orders ought to contain some element of direct or indirect reparative work.

4. **Reconciliation.** This is an end-point which may or may not be reached. The practical implications are that offenders should be introduced to club or activities where they can participate as non-stigmatised equals and make *friends*. It is worth noting that the root of the word is 'to make friendly' and this connects directly with the dominant purpose of probation's aim in its founding period 'to advise, assist and *befriend*'.

None of this diminishes our responsibility for emphasising that very many offenders belong to an 'underclass', under-educated and under-trained, increasingly unemployable, on the fringes of the housing market, themselves often the victims of childhood abuse and neglect. It is essential not to over-simplify nor to use slogans. Neither Christie nor Morris does, but they are also very clear that our present penal system is a product of the way our society is organised: 'Societies of calculating individuals, deeply embedded in the exchange of commodities to maximise individual benefit...Nothing could be more in harmony with a market model of exchange than neo-classical thinking around just deserts' (Christie, 1982, p.101). And Terence Morris (1988):

> If the aim of those who operate the apparatus of social control is the establishment of order then penal reformers must not avoid the question 'whose order'? Yet even the most sensitive and humane of reformers seem sometimes unaware that there is such a question for they so seldom doubt the legitimacy of what passes for the status quo. Nor is there much to suggest that in seeking to moderate the blunter excesses of the penal system with humanitarian zeal they recognise that control is about power, and that power in the last analysis turns upon the axes of economic and political interest (p.141).

Probation is not just an organisation, it is also a movement. It is not by chance that William Morris, Terence Morris and Nils Christie are used by me here because they are all looking towards a future state. We should not forget that the three great penal successes of this century are probation and community service and the impact of the Social Enquiry Report (now the Pre-Sentence Report) on sentencing. They are enormous achievements. They are the practical expression of the inclusive philosophy of rehabilitation which has dominated penal legislation and practice during the twentieth century.

It would be foolish to deny that there is a sea-change happening in the terms of public debate. The widespread repetition of the belief that too much has been done, and is still being done, for the offender and too little for the victims marks this change. It is a shift from an inclusive to an exclusive philosophy, to methods that *remove* offenders from society through a greater use of imprisonment and secure detention centres for juveniles and the wish to identify and stigmatise offenders undertaking community service.

It often seems surprising how much attention the Home Office pays to the role of the Probation Service as a small, cheap and reasonably efficient part of the whole criminal justice system. It is less surprising once one realises that it is the fulcrum on which the argument about inclusion or exclusion turns, not in theory, but as its political and institutional expression. One of the most important things we might learn from Christie is that a new emphasis on punishment in an absolute, personalised way might begin to relieve probation officers of the burden of acting 'as a buffer between a savage population filled with a lust for vengeance, and some misfits in need of protection against receiving too much pain'.

This is an issue which is absolutely central not just for the future of probation but for the purpose and acceptability of the whole criminal justice system. It is strange that the Probation Service has never really engaged with the idea of justice, despite the profound and complex questions it poses for its very existence. It is time to move on from discussions of care and control, help or surveillance into articulating a framework of meanings and justifications that are significant for the system as a whole. If we can rise to the challenge, then we can build on the very considerable achievements of the Service so far and formulate a theoretical basis for becoming a genuinely community-based service.

Four
The Criminal Justice Act 1991: Policy, legislation and practice

David Faulkner

THE ORIGIN AND PURPOSE OF THE ACT

This chapter considers:

- the origin and purpose of the sentencing provisions of the Criminal Justice Act 1991;
- the parallel and closely related developments in the management and professional orientation of the probation service;
- the present situation and future prospects as they appear in the summer of 1994.

The Purpose of the Act

The Criminal Justice Act 1991 was the central part, but only one part, of a set of policies whose purpose was to prevent and reduce crime, and to provide a more rational and coherent system for dealing with it. The objectives were:

- more logical and consistent sentencing and the removal of anomalies, including anomalies in the relationship between sentencing and parole;
- consolidation of community sentences as sentences in their own right and no longer as (by implication second best) 'alternatives to custody';
- moderate use of imprisonment, on remand and under sentence, and a more stable prison population for which provision could more reliably be planned in advance;
- demanding but also progressive regimes for those under supervision in the community or in custody, with an emphasis on the reduction of re-offending;

- a serious programme to prevent and reduce crime in the community, using both 'physical' measures to improve security and the likelihood of detection, and 'social' means to influence the attitude and motivation of potential offenders;
- more consideration, support and respect for victims;
- effective communication and co-operation between all parts of the criminal justice system, including central government and the judiciary.

The Assumptions

Underlying assumptions were that prison sentences could not be justified for any supposed deterrent or rehabilitative effect on the individual offender; that attempts to influence offenders' future conduct were more likely to be successful in the community than in custody; and that any serious programme for reducing crime, or for dealing with it more effectively when it occurred, required a collective effort on the part of all the organisations involved in the criminal justice process and the co-operation of the wider community. Tackling crime could never be seen simply as a matter of law enforcement, detection, conviction and punishment.

These policies had a coherent, if politically precarious, foundation in research, professional and academic thought, and developing professional practice. This foundation was not easily expressed in legislation (that is not the tradition of British legislative drafting) or in Ministerial speeches (which had to appeal to a range of opinions within the Conservative Party). It was however expressed more clearly in the Green and White Papers (published in 1988 and 1990) which preceded the 1991 Act; and – very importantly – in the Woolf Report on the disturbances which took place in Strangeways and other prisons in April 1990. Similar influences were at work in the police - the development of community policing, following the disturbances in Brixton in 1981 and the Scarman Report in 1982; the Police and Criminal Evidence Act 1984; the increasing recognition of issues of race and gender; and the Quality of Service initiative launched in 1989.

The Wider Context

The context included:

- financial stringency, and the Government's Financial Management Initiative;
- the application throughout the public service of what has

come to be called the 'new public management', with its emphasis on output measures and performance indicators, individual and collective targets and objectives, the creation of internal markets, the development of contracts and quasi-contractual relationships, and performance-related pay;

- political distrust of professional, as distinct from managerial or commercial, judgements and of professional (or 'provider') influences on the setting of priorities and the use of resources;
- professional emphasis on issues of culture, race and gender and a developing awareness of their significance for more general issues of professional integrity;
- increasing recognition of the need for accountability in the provision of public services and the performance of public duties, starting with an emphasis on inspection and audit but extending (for example in the Woolf Report) to wider concepts of natural justice and legitimacy;
- the Government's Next Steps initiative in 1988 and the Citizen's Charter in 1991.

These features had different origins in different parts of the country's social and political framework; some of them were potentially in conflict with one another; but all were influential.

Sentencing

It has always been difficult in this country to establish any clearly defined or generally accepted principles of sentencing, or any generally understood purposes which sentences are supposed to serve. Sentencing is at the meeting point between three separate and very different institutions of state – Parliament, which makes statute law and sets the legal framework; the judiciary, who interpret and apply the law, but also make it through the development of jurisprudence and the common law; and the executive which gives effect to the sentences imposed. All three have different and potentially conflicting aims and interests, and all three operate in an environment which makes not just agreement but even discussion hard to achieve. As a result, there is no generally recognised responsibility, or even machinery, for establishing common aims or principles, or for reconciling different points of view, still less for developing a 'sentencing policy'. This might not matter in a community which has confidence in itself and in its institutions, services and professions; with a single culture; with rising prosperity; and with a stable penal system which can readily accommodate all those to whom the courts might give custodial sentences. This was broadly the situation in this country until the 1960s. But few of these conditions apply today, nor can they easily be restored.

Questions about the purposes and principles of sentencing have during the last ten or twelve years emerged from the obscurity of academic debate to become issues of national importance. In a complex modern society it is not acceptable to have wide variations between sentences resulting from idiosyncratic views of the seriousness of particular offences or types of offences, or from the different emphasis which the sentencer may place on considerations such as rehabilitation, deterrence, retribution or protecting the public. It is still less acceptable for sentencing to depend on local custom, or how the sentence is likely to be reported in the press. Some common understanding of purposes and principles is needed, and some framework of accountability to make sure that they are observed.

This is especially so at a time when, rightly or wrongly, rehabilitation and deterrence are by many people dismissed as unrealistic aims of sentencing, at any rate so far as they can be achieved in our existing society or through the existing criminal justice system. Nor will it do, at a time of increasing economic difficulty, for sentences to be passed without any regard for the means and cost of putting them into effect. Most western countries would now recognise that although the sentence to be imposed in any particular case must be a matter for the judiciary alone, to be decided without interference from government, sentencing principles and sentencing policy are matters of general public importance and need to be publicly determined. A resolution to this effect was passed by the Eighth United Nations Congress on the Prevention of Crime and the Treatment of Offenders in 1990, and subsequently endorsed by the General Assembly.

The situation in England and Wales has been complicated by the existence of a number of statutory provisions which allowed for executive interference (as it was seen) with the operation of the sentence as imposed by the court. These provisions could in theory and sometimes in practice conflict with the judge's intentions when the sentence was passed, and they have always been deeply resented by the judiciary. The most obvious was the parole system, especially as it operated before the Criminal Justice Act 1991; others were the procedures for release from sentences of life imprisonment (still a matter of friction between the judiciary and the government) and, until 1982, the indeterminate sentence of borstal training. Overshadowing all discussion of sentencing during the past 30 years has been the problem of chronic overcrowding in the prisons, together with the cost of maintaining and expanding the prison estate. There has also been the constant prospect of serious prison disturbances, potentially – as at Strangeways in April 1990 – on a scale which could undermine the operation of the whole criminal justice system. Any government comment on sentencing was usually seen by the judiciary as influenced by considerations not of principle but of prison management and finance.

Earlier Legislation

From 1961 to 1988 there was a series of legislative and administrative adjustments to the framework in which sentencing took place and effect was given to the sentences imposed. An early example, much disliked by the judiciary, was the provision in the Criminal Justice Act 1961 which made borstal training the standard medium-term custodial sentence available for young offenders under the age of 21, and the withdrawal for most cases of the parallel (and in the judges' view more flexible) sentence of imprisonment for terms of between six months and three years. Later examples were the introduction of parole and of suspended sentences in 1967, with the compulsory suspension of short sentences which was brought to an end in 1972. The rate of change accelerated rapidly in the 1980s. The Criminal Justice Act 1982 abolished the indeterminate sentence of borstal training and substituted the determinate sentence of youth custody. It also introduced statutory restrictions on the use of custodial sentences for young offenders (the forerunner of the restrictions on custodial sentences generally which later appeared in the Criminal Justice Act 1991). There followed the introduction of the 'restricted policy' which severely curtailed the grant of parole to life and long sentence prisoners; and the reduction in the minimum qualifying period, which resulted in prisoners serving any sentences of 12 months to two years spending what were seen as equivalent periods in custody. The former, as applied to prisoners serving life sentences, came under pressure in the European Court of Human Rights and in proceedings for judicial review in the domestic courts. The latter provoked an angry response from the higher judiciary who saw it as an encroachment on their sentencing discretion. It led to Lord Carlisle's fundamental review of the parole system (published in 1988) and to amending legislation in the 1991 Act.

Other changes were the introduction of partly suspended sentences of imprisonment (a provision in the Criminal Law Act 1977) in 1982; an increase in remission on sentences of 12 months or less from one-third to one-half in August 1986; and the introduction in the Criminal Justice Act 1988 of the Attorney General's power to refer an apparently over-lenient sentence to the Court of Appeal (for a discussion of its effects, see Shute, 1994).

Some of these changes were designed as progressive reforms to make sentencing and the penal system more fair and flexible; some were in response to judicial or to political and public opinion; some were intended to control the prison population. Several were a mixture of all three. A common feature was an attempt to increase the range of sentencing options available to the courts, to place constraints on their use of imprisonment, and – significantly – to require them to give reasons for their sentencing and other decisions.

The Judiciary

While these legislative changes were taking place, the judiciary were making their own moves to respond to their changing environment and to criticisms of inconsistency in sentencing. An important early development, initiated by Lord Lane as Lord Chief Justice, was the Court of Appeal's practice of issuing 'guideline' sentencing judgements intended to introduce greater consistency into sentencing practice, and in some instances to encourage more or less severe sentences for particular types of offence. These were published in sentencing reports and periodically collected and made available to judges in Dr. Thomas's (1979) sentencing handbook. Some early judgements acknowledged the shortage of prison accommodation as a relevant consideration. The Magistrates' Association subsequently issued, and from time to time updated, a more comprehensive set of guidelines covering the main types of offence likely to be dealt with in magistrates' courts. The Judicial Studies Board, originally appointed in 1979, was re-organised and its scope extended.

The 1980s were therefore a difficult and unsettled period so far as sentencing was concerned. There was continuous criticism of inconsistency and of undue severity or, more often, excessive leniency. Concern also began to be expressed about the possibility of racial discrimination in sentencing practice (Hood, 1992). The Prison Service suffered a series of crises due to overcrowding, disturbances or industrial action by prison officers, with prisoners being held in police cells or in camps because no normal prison accommodation was available. Judges responded to political pressure by increasing their use of imprisonment between 1984 and 1988, and subsequently by reducing it between 1988 and 1990. The Court of Appeal's guideline judgements were welcome for the offences to which they applied, but they did not apply to the middle range of robberies, assaults, burglaries and thefts which provide most of the Crown Court's business and account for a large part of the prison population. The Court of Appeal's ordinary sentencing judgements, which have the same formal authority as its special guidelines, were sometimes thought to have an inflationary effect on sentencing generally. The reason was the Court's reluctance to interfere with a sentence unless it was wrong in principle or manifestly excessive, and its difficulty in substituting a community sentence for a custodial sentence when part of the custodial sentence had already been served. The new sentences imposed might therefore be higher than they would have if the Court had been sitting as a court of first instance. Some of the Court's judgements were also inconsistent in the way in which they dealt with, for example, previous convictions or related offences.

The Need to Act

By the end of the 1980s, the government had decided that this politically and operationally precarious situation could not be allowed to continue. Some framework was needed to ensure reasonable consistency in sentencing and reasonable stability in the prison population. Neither the government nor the judiciary had developed any generally applicable sentencing principles in the legislation they had promoted and the judgements they had given during this period, and the first requirement was seen to be a set of recognised and coherent principles against which particular sentences could be decided, explained to defendants and victims in court, and publicly justified.

The problem was how this was to be done. The government had no authority to determine sentencing principles or seek to impose them on the judiciary, and the judiciary would have rejected them as unconstitutional and an infringement on their independence if they had. The judiciary themselves had no appetite for the task, preferring to deal with individual cases as they arose, and their institutions were not structured for the purpose – the Court of Appeal because it could only deal with individual cases as they came before it, and the Judicial Studies Board because it had no authority independently of the Court of Appeal. The judiciary had dismissed the suggestion of a Sentencing Council as a threat to their independence. The Sentencing Commissions in Canada and the United States were not models which anyone wanted to copy: no action had been taken on the report of the Canadian Commission (published in 1986), and the work of the Commissions in the United States had mostly been associated with steep increases in the prison population (Towry, 1987; Ashworth, 1992; Von Hirsch and Ashworth, 1992).

Principles of the 1991 Act

The government therefore turned to Parliament, as the only institution which had the authority to establish principles which the judiciary and the government would both respect, by enacting them in statute.

The government's proposals adopted broadly the principle of 'just deserts', or of proportionate justice – although not by any means in its most austere or academic form – for which there was some degree of consensus in this country and in most other common law jurisdictions. It avoided the problems which had been found with the ineffectiveness of rehabilitation and deterrence, and it was thought to represent a 'common sense' view of punishment (although appeals to common sense have subsequently been used to justify a quite different approach). The main consideration in deciding on the type and length of a sentence was to be the seriousness of the offence for which the offender had been convicted, with provision for longer sentences to be imposed in cases of serious violent or sexual offences if they were needed for the protection of the public. There was intended to be a deliberately high threshold for an offence to be 'so serious' as to justify custody, but the courts' sentencing powers in relation to violent or sexual offences were considerably strengthened. Non-custodial sentences were to be treated as sentences or punishments in their own right and not as alternatives to custody. Unit fines would enable fines to be calculated more consistently and more equitably, with more systematic regard for the means of the offender. The suspended sentence was to be retained, although strictly speaking inconsistent with the 'just deserts' approach, in order to give courts flexibility, but the partly suspended sentence was to be abolished. 'Seriousness' was not to be defined in statute but left to the interpretation of the courts, again to provide flexibility. Previous convictions would only be relevant to a decision on sentence if they were relevant to a judgement of the seriousness of the current offence. An important and significant provision was a requirement for the court to explain to the offender in open court and in ordinary language the reasons for any custodial sentence it might impose. In many respects, including the treatment of previous convictions, the Act was intended to follow previous judgements of the Court of Appeal.

The sentencing provisions of the Criminal Justice Act 1991 were part of a more comprehensive approach to crime and criminal justice, some of which was set out in other parts of the Act and some of which were pursued by other means. Another important part of the Act was the reconstruction of non-custodial sentences, now to be called community sentences, designed to establish their authority and credibility in their own right and to displace imprisonment as the only 'real' or 'serious' penalty which the courts could impose. The probation order became a sentence in its own right and no longer an alternative to a sentence. A new combination order was introduced enabling courts in effect to combine the element of punishment implicit in a community service order with the supervision and support available under a probation order. Provision was made for curfews and their enforcement by electronic monitoring. Section 95 dealt with the publication and use of financial information and with the avoidance of discrimination on improper grounds such as race and gender: very little information has so far been published in accordance with it, but it was an important new element in making the system more publicly accountable. Other policies were concerned with the prevention and reduction of crime (for example Safer Cities and the formation of Crime Concern), and with recognition and support for victims – both recognising implicitly that these are not matters which can be dealt with effectively through the operation of the ordinary criminal justice process on its own.

Professional and Managerial Change

The sentencing provisions of the 1991 Act were closely linked to, and depended upon, changes in the probation service's professional orientation and its management systems and practice. Some of the changes were driven by the service's own need to re-assert its credibility with the courts and the public, to demonstrate more confidently its capacity to deliver programmes which protect the public and prevent re-offending, and to respond more readily to – and contribute to shaping – its working environment. Others were driven centrally by the Government's programme for increasing efficiency and effectiveness throughout the public sector. To a considerable extent, the different interests co-incided. Even so, there was some friction, suspicion and hostility, both within the probation service and between the probation service and central government, as the various changes took place. The service had to re-balance the relationship between the care and control of offenders, and to come to terms with the political and judicial language of punishment. It had to respond to and accommodate more points of view and to work with and respect different professional cultures. It had to reconcile its duties to offenders with duties to the courts and the public which were becoming progressively more insistent and demanding. The changes were however completed, for the most part successfully, by means which included a major programme of training before the Act came into force, and the service which set about implementing the Act on 1 October 1992 was undoubtedly more professional, more competent and more highly regarded than it had been ten years previously.

The service at the beginning of the 1980s was still in many respects a welfare organisation providing social casework for the benefit of the defendants and offenders – universally referred to as 'clients' – who were entrusted to its care. It functioned largely as a collection of individual operators, working with their own caseload or projects, loosely co-ordinated by a permissive management. The service for the future needed to be an integrated service, operating reliably and consistently throughout the country and doing so as part of a fully co-ordinated criminal justice system alongside, and on equal terms with, the police, the Crown Prosecution Service, the court services and the Prison Service.

The changes took place over several years, and went through several stages. They included the following:

- The development of a collective sense of direction and purpose, a sense that the service as a whole had certain tasks to perform and results to achieve from them. This was stimulated by, among other things, the *Statement of National Objectives and Priorities* (Home Office, 1984), and backed up in many areas by local statements applying to local situations. The main priorities were to prevent re-offending, to re-integrate offenders with the community, and to divert offenders from custody.
- Efforts to increase the courts' and public confidence and to demonstrate the effectiveness of community based penalties, with local action plans and intensive probation programmes targeted on young adult offenders, followed by the progressive introduction of national standards for various aspects of probation work.
- Progressive adoption of performance targets and indicators to show what progress was being made and what results were being achieved, with a stronger lead from management in allocating resources, setting objectives and monitoring the outcome.
- Closer and more productive working with other services and organisations, and greater authority with those organisations based on the service's breadth of experience and expertise, resulting from its understanding of a wide range of social issues and its involvement in all stages of the criminal justice process.
- A shift from the direct provision of a limited range of services to the design, management and delivery of more comprehensive schemes of supervision, often involving a wide range of other agencies – statutory, voluntary or commercial – with different attitudes, cultures and areas of expertise.
- The development of new or existing skills and techniques, both in assessing and reporting on an offender's situation and prospects, and in helping – or requiring – offenders to control their behaviour.

There was a relatively short period during which Ministers questioned the capacity and the will of the probation service to deliver the kind of service which their policies required, and to achieve the transformation to enable itself to do so. Social work was no longer held in the esteem which it had once enjoyed, and some of the service's attitudes – to offenders, to the courts, to the police, to the protection of the public and to notions of punishment and social control more generally – were represented by its critics as 'soft' or even subversive. A break- up of the service was briefly considered, perhaps into separate purchasing authorities and providing organisations which would compete for contracts.

This idea did not make progress, for various reasons. One was the service's success in bringing about the professional and managerial changes already described. Another was the scale of the effort which would have been required. A third was the absence of any obvious source of similar expertise, and a fourth was the limited benefits which could have been produced. But competition and contractual relationships are still very much part of the Government's approach to the management of public services of all kinds, and similar proposals could be revived at any time.

What the Government Was Trying to Achieve

The objectives of these policies, taken together, could be summarised as being to:

- prevent and reduce crime;
- establish a more coherent and principled basis for sentencing and parole;
- avoid the unnecessary use of imprisonment and stabilise the prison population;
- develop schemes of supervision in the community which would effectively reduce re-offending;
- give greater consideration to victims;
- make the system more efficient, effective and accountable.

These objectives were made clear enough in Mr. Douglas Hurd's speech to the Conservative Party Conference in 1989 (for which he received the customary standing ovation), but other presentations were more ambiguous, emphasising the 'tough' aspects of the proposals and playing down others. The impression gained by many of those involved in giving effect to the Act was that it was simply intended to prevent the courts from sending so many people to prison in order that the Government could reduce expenditure on the prison building programme. The principles on which the Act's sentencing provisions were based were never set out in the Act itself, perhaps because to do so would have been contrary to the traditions of English legislative drafting; and when the Act came into force in October 1992 the Home Secretary – by then Kenneth Clarke – took no part in celebrating or promoting it. The signal was clear – Ministers were no longer committed to important parts of the Act and the way was open for the judiciary, the press and other critics to attack and undermine it (for a general discussion, see Lacey, 1994).

THE ACT AS AMENDED: PRESSURES AND PROSPECTS

The Political Context

It is not the purpose of this chapter to speculate about the reasons for the change in political mood, affecting all political parties, which took place after the 1992 General Election. The politics of that situation, including the influence of the media on the Government (and vice versa); the significance of the debate about crime in the context of other political issues and events such as the Maastricht Treaty; and the way in which that debate was conducted, including the systematic intimidation of all critical opinion, would provide interesting material for a political historian. For the present purpose it can simply be said that the Government moved from the approach described earlier in this chapter to one which relied on law enforcement, and especially the disabling effect of imprisonment and the supposed deterrent effect of conviction and punishment more generally, as the principal means of tackling crime. This approach paid little attention to prevention, to the social and economic circumstances in which crime becomes prevalent, or to the influences which affect a person's behaviour or pattern of life. It relied more on its popular appeal than on any process of consultation or evidence of its likely success. It was an approach which was deeply possimistic in its view of society and of human nature; it was dangerous in the encouragement it gave to oppressive forms of policing and to the arbitrary administration of justice; it was divisive in risking the creation of an excluded and criminalised underclass; and it was operationally precarious in the strain it placed, especially on the Prison Service, but also on other parts of the criminal justice system.

Liberal opinion cannot however afford to criticise or to be complacent. Crime had been increasing throughout the 1980s, and although it was absurd to attribute the increase to the criminal justice policies pursued during that period, without reference to the social and economic influences which were at work, the emphasis on diverting young offenders from the criminal justice process may, for example, have resulted in the neglect of the relatively small number of very disturbed and persistent juvenile offenders. More generally, a high level of crime has itself a corrupting effect on the fabric of society, as well as a sometimes devastating effect on individuals. Whether or not it is exploited for political or media purposes, it can generate not only feelings of fear and anger, but also a defensive or 'fortress' mentality, where people become increasingly obsessed with security, with erecting stronger and stronger physical defences and with more elaborate personal protection. Ordinary social life becomes restricted, and ordinary social contact can become hesitant and suspicious. There are inevitably, and properly, demands for 'something to be done', which the media will exploit and to which both government and criminal justice services, including the probation service, have to respond. It takes political courage to avoid the easy response of calling for more certainty of conviction and greater severity of punishment, but if a defensive mentality is to be prevented, and repressive criminal justice policies are to be avoided or moderated, other means have to be found which genuinely affect people's experience and perception of crime. Some of these must be sought outside the criminal justice system altogether and are outside the scope of this chapter. Within the criminal justice system the emphasis must be on prevention as well as enforcement, and for the probation service it must be on preventing re-offending by those once convicted and placed under its supervision. The service, and the values which it represents, will lose all credibility if supervision is seen, however unfairly, as allowing a pattern of offending to continue unchecked, or as providing benefits which are not available to other people.

Wider Criminal Justice Issues

Other, more fundamental, questions are now beginning to present themselves. They include:

- the nature of criminal responsibility and its implications, especially for children or those who are mentally disturbed;
- the position of the victim in the criminal justice process, the extent, if any, to which victims should be entitled to influence decisions taken by the courts or the criminal justice services,

and the nature of the recognition and support which they should receive from society more generally;

- the continued validity of traditional principles such as the burden of proof and the presumption of innocence (taken for granted by the Royal Commission on Criminal Justice in its report published in 1993 but now being increasingly questioned and implicitly challenged by some of the provisions in the Criminal Justice and Public Order Act);
- the proper scope of the criminal law and the criminal justice process, and the extent to which dangerous or troublesome behaviour can be dealt with acceptably and more effectively by other means; and even
- the purpose of the criminal justice process itself and whether justice is an objective in itself, or simply a means of achieving a different objective such as social stability or the protection of the public (or of its 'law abiding' or deserving members).

These are serious questions, some of which have a long history of earlier discussion, and some of which are relatively new. The answers are not necessarily those which would come most easily to traditional liberal opinion. All of them need to be re-examined in the context of the modern political, social and judicial climate; a forum – perhaps the Criminal Justice Consultative Council, on which the probation service is represented – is needed in which that re-examination can take place; and the probation service is one of those who have a contribution to make, whose voice should be heard, and who will be deeply affected by the answers that are given.

The Prospects

There are several positive features in the probation service's situation as it looks forward to the twenty-first century. Despite the difficult political climate, the degree of public concern and anger about the general state of crime and the surrounding uncertainty, the probation service has a large fund of good will among those with whom it works; it enjoys increasing authority and confidence with the courts and other criminal justice services; it has so far been reasonably well funded; and it has not yet been subjected to the distraction of fundamental changes in its organisation or structure. A new debate is developing about communities and citizenship: these are familiar concepts to the probation service and they can give a valuable new focus to its work. Although important changes have been made to those parts of the Criminal Justice Act 1991 which dealt with unit fines and with previous and related offences and the offender's response to previous sentences, the structure of the Act remains and has been endorsed by both the Home Secretary and the Lord Chief Justice as providing a fundamentally sound basis for sentencing. Even where the Act has been amended, the courts still have discretion, and are to some extent required, to apply the principles which the Act in its original form was tended to reflect: for example that fines should be related to the offender's means, and that previous convictions should not automatically lead to a more severe sentence than would otherwise be appropriate, but should only be taken into account where they are relevant (i.e. to a judgement about the seriousness of the current offence). The former is a statutory requirement of the Act as amended; the latter is incorporated in the Magistrates' Association's guidelines for magistrates' courts, and it appears to have been accepted by the Lord Chief Justice although there has not so far been definitive guidance from the Court of Appeal.

Many probation officers will regret the need for some of the provisions in the Criminal Justice and Public Order Act, especially those introducing secure training centres and secure training orders for children aged 12-14, the increase in the maximum custodial sentences available for young people aged 15-17, the restrictions on the grant of bail, and the creation of new criminal offences relating to demonstrators, squatters, travellers and 'raves'. The problems addressed by these provisions should whenever possible be dealt with by measures which do not rely on the criminal law but which typically involve greater co-operation between the services – often including the probation service. Probation officers will particularly regret the decision to abolish in most instances the requirement for courts to obtain a pre-sentence report before imposing a custodial or community sentence. All these provisions will however operate at the discretion of the courts or the operational services: it is to be hoped that they will need to be used rarely in practice and that more suitable means will continue to be found for dealing with the situations to which they apply. Especially in relation to bail and Pre-SentenceReports, it will be the task of the probation service to develop working arrangements with the courts and with other services which will ensure that reliable and up-to-date information is always made available to the courts when and in the form that it is needed, and that best practice continues to develop within the discretion provided by statute.

The greatest challenge to the probation service will undoubtedly be to its ability to devise and sustain schemes of supervision which succeed in preventing re-offending; to maintain and develop the skills of assessment which are required to match those schemes to the needs and circumstances of individuals; and to communicate effectively with the courts, other relevant agencies and organisations, the wider public and central government so that the service's work, and the principles and values on which it is based, continue to command confidence and respect.

Characteristics of successful schemes of supervision are likely to include a clear description of what is involved, and a complete understanding on the part of offenders and others concerned; a firm structure of requirements and checks that they are observed; and reliable procedures to ensure that what is supposed to happen does in fact happen in practice. The scheme should be accepted and 'owned' by the offender as fair and relevant, and should not be felt as arbitrarily or pointlessly imposed. It should be based on mutual understanding and respect, with a sense of mutual obligation and perhaps regarded as a form of 'contract'. It should acknowledge and if possible address the offender's whole situation as well as specific aspects of his or her behaviour (McGuire, 1995). Intensive and sometimes intrusive programmes will have a place, and may well involve a degree of compulsion (perhaps greater than has been contemplated in the past), but they must preserve the offender's dignity and autonomy and avoid humiliation, manipulation or exploitation.

Accountability and Legitimacy

A service which exercises coercive powers, and which influences the exercise of coercive powers by others, must operate according to the highest standards not only of accountability but also of legitimacy. Most recent discussion of accountability in the public service has focused on its responsibility for obtaining value for money and for acting in accordance with government policy – on the basis that central government provides through taxation all or most of the funds by which the service is financed. The Citizen's Charter provides a wider view of public accountability with its emphasis on published information and on responsiveness to the customer, consumer or user, but it has important limitations. It enables the customer to complain if the service is not provided to the advertised standard, but not to demand higher standards or a different kind of service, and its principles are not easily applied to criminal justice functions. Experience throughout the public sector is demonstrating the difficulty of relying on the techniques of accountancy and on responsibility through Ministers to Parliament as providing an adequate framework of accountability for public services (for example in health or education as well as criminal justice) in whose operation not only the user but also society as a whole has an acute and proper interest. The issue is especially important in relation to services which exercise coercive powers, which need to be not only accountable but also legitimate in the sense that they must function with the consent and support of society as a whole, including those against whom coercive powers may have to be exercised. The authority of those who exercise such powers, and the use they make of them, have to be respected in their own right and not simply imposed on those made subject to them. The point was acknowledged, but not developed, in the White Paper *Supervision and Punishment in the Community*, published in 1990; it was discussed more fully in Lord Woolf's report on prisons published in the following year, where it became a major theme (Bottoms, 1994).

A proper foundation of accountability and legitimacy requires openness and accessibility throughout the process, and in particular:

- clearly stated objectives, standards and expectations;
- monitoring of performance to establish how far they are being met;
- independent inspection and audit;
- reasons for decisions, especially where they are likely to be unwelcome to those affected by them;
- opportunities and a recognised structure for question, challenge and complaint;
- effective means for correcting mistakes, abuses or errors of judgement, and for identifying those responsible and holding them to account;
- recognition and sensitivity to issues of race, gender and culture;
- informative, well-presented, published reports;
- a statutory framework which, in the last resort, enables the above requirements to be enforced through the courts.

Many of these features are already in place for the probation service; some are in place but need to be developed or formalised; and some – including the service's future statutory base – still need to be established. These are all matters to which the service should itself pay urgent attention, and not wait to respond to an initiative from central government.

Management Structure and Style

As well as a suitable framework of accountability, the probation service needs a management structure and a management style which match its professional functions and values. Changes of structure and style have to a large extent been influenced by the government's own programme for improving the service's efficiency and effectiveness, as described earlier in this chapter. Most of those developed during the 1980s were necessary and inevitable; in many instances the service contributed to their development and their application to its own particular functions and circumstances; and the service has for the most part welcomed or accepted them. There are however several aspects of the new public management which the service should approach with caution. In particular, an excessive preoccupation with output measures and performance indicators, especially if they are rigidly quantified and closely defined, can narrow vision, drive out initiative and imagination, distort priorities and have a flattening effect on quality or true levels of performance. They can lead to a 'filofax' mentality in which time and resources are efficiently managed but the purpose of the enterprise is lost from sight. They can produce an institutional conformism, a practice of self-censorship, a reluctance to question the institution's received opinions and customs, and ultimately to secrecy and defensiveness.

An emphasis on cost-effectiveness can also distract attention from equally important considerations of equity or natural justice. A process of setting targets from the 'top down', of monitoring performance according to narrow and rigid criteria, and of rewarding it accordingly (whether by performance related pay or by selection for senior posts or the renewal of contracts), reflects a management style based on low trust, low levels of discretion and a view of personal and professional motivation which conflicts with the values and identity of the probation service and of other public services which have traditionally been based on a sense of public duty and devotion to the public interest.

From a wider perspective, a managerial approach to justice can lead to an instrumental view of its purpose (a criticism which has been made of the terms of reference and the report of the Royal Commission), to a coarsening of standards and perhaps – even if unintentionally – to a more repressive, and more pessimistic, approach because measures such as arrests, convictions, sentences, prison escapes and disturbances, and 'failures' generally are easier to quantify than offences which might otherwise have been committed or patterns of offending or re-offending which might otherwise have developed and become more serious. A narrow managerial approach can also distract attention from issues which may be regarded as marginal and not specifically reflected in the performance measures of the organisation, but which may nevertheless be of public importance. Examples include the interests of those who are mentally disturbed or of young people at risk, issues of race or gender, problems of drug abuse or alcohol misuse, preventive work of all kinds.

Partnership and Contracts

Schemes of supervision will increasingly, and rightly, include partnerships with other organisations in both the statutory and the independent sector. These organisations will have their own skills and expertise which will be relevant to the tasks to be performed and they will be chosen on that account. The probation service should not seek to contain all the relevant skills within its own organisation, or directly to provide all the facilities or activities that may be required. Part of the skill of the modern probation service is to identify and commission the facilities and activities that are needed, and to establish suitable purchasing and contractual arrangements where it is appropriate to do so. Although the radical changes discussed in *Punishment, Custody and the Community* (Cmd 424, 1988) were not pursued at the time, the issue of partnerships has been revived in a more limited way by the Home Office Circular 17/1993 issued on 6 December 1993. Purchasing and other partnership arrangements should however be decided by reference to the needs and the situations they are intended to meet, and not by any dogmatic or politically determined view of the mechanism or of the source from which services should be provided. Whatever arrangements are made, they should observe the principles of accountability and legitimacy already indicated in this chapter, and purchasing and providing organisations should share the same professional values.

Recruitment, Training and Careers

The probation service must inevitably ask itself whether the present patterns of recruitment, training and career development are still appropriate in the present situation of rapid change and professional re-orientation. The service's development and present standing undoubtedly owes a great deal to its social work base, as well as to other influences on its identity and character. But there are now many specialist posts in the service for which a social work qualification is unnecessary or even irrelevant; and relatively few, especially above the basic level, for which no other experience or expertise is necessary or desirable. Nor is it easy to demonstrate the specific contribution which social work training can make to the task of preventing re-offending or of achieving social stability or social justice more generally. On the assumption that generic social work training will continue indefinitely in more or less its present form, it must always be the hope that many social workers will continue to seek a career in the probation service, and that the service will continue to value the training they will bring with them. But the service is unlikely to benefit in the longer term from a continued division between its 'professional' members trained in social work and its other members who may be of equal value to the service and who may have equally demanding qualifications in other disciplines.

The task for the future will be to identify a range of professional skills – in assessment, social casework, communication, negotiation, the interpretation and use of information, the management of contracts – and to develop a pattern of recruitment, initial training and subsequent progress through postings, secondments and in-service training. Aptitudes and existing skills would be identified on first appointment and members of the service would then be encouraged and enabled to obtain additional skills as their careers progressed. Where possible, training should be arranged on an inter-agency basis with members of other services or voluntary organisations. The likelihood is that in the probation service, as elsewhere, an appointment will in future be seen less as the start of a lifetime career and more as one of a number of moves which the individual will make on his or her own account, as he or she assembles a portfolio of portable skills and qualifications and takes them to the service or position which appears most professionally and personally rewarding for the next stage of their career. This need not be a matter of regret provided that all members of the service share its fundamental values and commit themselves to its objectives; and provided that they have enough security and confidence to retain those values and their own professional integrity.

Five
Victims: Towards a reorientation of justice

Helen Reeves and Martin Wright

For a number of people biblical teaching on criminal justice seems to be summed up by 'an eye for an eye'. The importance of neighbourly concern for the victim of crime, brought out by the story of The Good Samaritan, is less often remarked. Another valuable biblical concept is *shalom*, the community peace and harmony which crime breaks and which should be restored.

The past two decades have seen the gradual growth of new thought and practices aimed at dealing with the problem of crime in society. Many, but not all, of these initiatives have paid increased attention to the position of 'victims': the people at the receiving end of crime. Victims of crime do now have a place on the political agenda; the question is, whether they will be offered humanitarian support independently of the criminal justice process; or will they be accorded a place in the existing process, on the basis of assumptions about their needs and views; or will the process itself be modified to take greater account of their needs and their rights?

'Criminal justice' tends to be a somewhat narrow concept, though of course a necessary one. Its focus on the accused's apprehension, trial and punishment necessitates emphasis on safeguards and due process for the defendant. Until recently there has been little awareness that victims and other witnesses should have anything more than walk-on parts in the courtroom drama, in which the stage directions – the rules of criminal procedure – often subordinate their rights to those of the defendant.

When victim support was introduced in Bristol, England, in 1974, the expectation was that victims' problems would be primarily related to the crimes they had suffered. But it became clear that many of them also suffer other forms of social injustice, such as poverty and poor housing (Gay et al., 1975).

Later it emerged that they are often victimised by the system itself, through some of the procedures of courts, coroners and the police (Shapland et al., 1985; NAVSS, 1988; Victim Support, 1990; Raine and Smith, 1991).

If an organisation created to support victims remains on the margin, the established criminal justice system will continue to follow its own devices; but if it becomes involved with the system it risks legitimising the traditional practices, although it may succeed in securing some improvements. As Victim Support said in its evidence to the Royal Commission on Criminal Justice in 1991:

> The criminal justice process is not just a process by which the State brings wrongdoers to justice on behalf of the community. It is also, or should be, a recognition that a citizen has been the victim of a crime, and a process which helps the victim's recovery, or at least does not hinder it. .... This is, moreover, in the interests of the criminal justice process, which depends on victims reporting crimes and giving evidence.

Ideally, in our view, the concept of 'criminal justice' should be extended to become a 'response to crime', in which victims would be accorded just and humane treatment in their own right, not merely for the sake of the system. The response would also accord proper safeguards to the defendant, and would monitor cases to address the wider questions about how crime happens and possible ways of reducing it.

We begin by suggesting that it is wrong to assume that there is a 'victims' movement' with a shared philosophy. We shall trace the development of victim support and awareness of the needs and rights of victims in Britain. Then we shall show how this independent voluntary work has become concerned about the way victims are treated in the traditional, adversarial criminal justice process. Finally, we shall ask whether it is right to concentrate on making this process less painful for victims, or whether it is time to take a new look at the process itself.

IS THERE A VICTIMS' MOVEMENT?

There is a natural human tendency to try to impose a pattern on phenomena, and this may be the reason why the idea of a 'victims' movement' with a shared philosophy has gained momentum. We believe this idea, however, to be erroneous – not surprisingly, given the different origins of interest in victims.

For academics, for example, victims offered the prospect of a new '-ology' (the coining of the word 'victimology' is credited, if that is the right word, to Mendelsohn, 1947, followed by von Hentig, 1948), whose original focus was to establish the extent to which crime was 'precipitated' by victims' behaviour. Then a penal reformer, Margery Fry, promoted the idea of compensation for victims of crimes of violence as an additional means of demonstrating society's denigration of such crimes. She was supported by the law reform organisation Justice (Fry, 1951, 1959; Justice, 1962), and the concept was realised in New Zealand in 1963 and the United Kingdom in 1964.

The idea of emotional and practical support for victims arose from a study group including police, prison and probation officers, lawyers and magistrates, a lecturer in public policy, and two ex-offenders; the prototype scheme was implemented by the South West Council of the National Association for the Care and Resettlement of Offenders (NACRO). They were aware that penal reforming groups were often criticised for not being concerned about the victim, and felt that 'the newly-developing field of victimology was notably lacking in information about victims as *people with needs*' (Holtom and Raynor, 1988, p.18, italics in original).

The study group started by interviewing a number of victims. Among its findings were the major emotional impact of crimes, including burglaries; the fact that relatives, friends and neighbours were less supportive than might have been expected; that the 'official' system almost ignored the victim, except as a source of evidence, and appeared actively to prevent any spontaneous reparative gesture by the offenders. They also observed that no statutory or voluntary body took responsibility for helping victims of crime in general, although there was the Criminal Injuries Compensation Board for the small proportion who had suffered physical injury, and a limited use of compensation orders by the courts (Holtom and Raynor, 1988). There was, however, provision for specific groups: by the mid-

1970s children were the responsibility of social services; housing departments and voluntary agencies were providing basic accommodation for the homeless; and Women's Aid was establishing refuges for battered women. These categories, however, were not thought of under the same label of 'victims of crime'.

In North America, concern for victims took a different course. For independent groups, many with a strong feminist orientation, women and children were almost the only categories regarded as victims, for whom they established safe houses and rape crisis centres. The criminal justice system focused originally on assistance to victim-witnesses: that is, their concern was at least as much with encouraging the victim to assist in keeping the wheels of justice turning as with meeting his or her needs. Many such services were accordingly based on police or public prosecutors' departments, or the courts. A list of North American victim services in the mid-1980s included compensation by the State and the offender, victim-witness programmes, social service referrals, crisis intervention for 'the emergency needs of selected victims', victim advocacy, mediation, and crime reduction – but nothing comparable to the British model (Elias, 1986, pp.297-99).

Concern was disproportionately with violence, even by American standards; examples given by the President's Task Force on Victims of Crime (1982, pp.2-3) included only one non-violent crime among the murders, violent robberies, shootings and rapes. The debate in the United States and Canada has concentrated more on victims' legal rights and legislation than in Britain, where the effort has gone primarily towards service provision.

Victim Support in the United Kingdom has also resisted the notion, common in America, that victims should be given an active role in determining the outcome for the offender, on the grounds that it would at least place a heavy burden of responsibility on victims (and there is no evidence that many of them want it), and at worst would place them at risk of intimidation. The task belongs in the courts, whose sentencing is already inconsistent enough; what is important is that the courts should have all the relevant facts about the victim on which to base decisions about bail, compensation by the offender and sentencing. Accordingly, the *United Nations Declaration of Basic Principles of Practice for*

Victims of Crime and Abuse of Power, in 1985, adopted a more general wording: judicial processes should:

> ...(allow) the views and concerns of victims to be presented and considered at appropriate stages of the proceedings where their personal interests are affected, without prejudice to the accused...

In some of the United States, where judges and prosecutors are elected, it is easier for candidates to use the rhetoric which claims that victims are helped by tough measures against offenders than to educate the electorate in the complexities of criminal justice and victims' real needs. In Germany, the largest organisation for victims, the 'White Ring' (der 'Weiße Ring'), was the offshoot of a popular 'Did You Witness the Crime?' television programme, 'XY Unbekannt', similar to the British 'Crimewatch', and in its early years adopted a similar stance. In France, victim services often operate in tandem with victim/offender mediation. With such a range of approaches, it is clearly misleading to suggest that there is a 'victims' movement' with a common philosophy.

THE DEVELOPMENT OF VICTIM SUPPORT IN THE UNITED KINGDOM

When the Bristol Victim Support scheme was established, a number of principles were decided, and these have, in the main, stood the test of time.

A primary concern of Victim Support has always been with people's emotional reactions to crime – the need to be listened to, and if necessary reassured. They may want to express anger or fear, or to feel that the seriousness of the offence has been properly recognised – and they may, as many do, feel deeply reassured by the offer of help without needing to accept any specific services. It was soon found that all victims could benefit from the recognition offered by Victim Support, and that those people who needed specific support were not necessarily those who might be expected to be vulnerable: they may be young or old, male or female, affluent or on low incomes. It was often those most needing help who did not find it. Victim Support has therefore adopted a policy of outreach, asking for individual victims of all types of crime to be referred automatically by the police, with a few exceptions:

- victims of rape, and families of murder victims, are not referred without their consent;

- Victim Support schemes do not follow up thefts of or from motor vehicles, unless exceptional problems have been identified;
- child abuse is the responsibility of statutory social services and the National Society for the Prevention of Cruelty to Children (NSPCC);
- domestic violence was originally regarded as the province of Women's Aid, but Victim Support is now working with them and other agencies towards providing an integrated service.

Victim Support has avoided the common misconception of regarding victims as objects of pity to be treated as a separate group. Victims of crime are ordinary members of society experiencing what will, it is hoped, be a temporary crisis after which they can regain their autonomy through the provision of relevant information, advice and community support. It does not use publicity materials calculated to provoke fear or anger.

The original intention was that victims who had been deeply traumatised by some of the more serious crimes would be put in touch with specialist resources such as counsellors, but it soon became clear there were few specialists with any experience of victims' problems and many Victim Support workers themselves knew as much as anyone, having learnt at first-hand. Nowhere was this more clearly demonstrated than in the action research project on services to families of murder victims, in which families themselves were asked about the types of help which they would find most beneficial. Victim Support has, as a result, developed additional training programmes to enable volunteers to provide longer term support to victims of the more serious crimes (Victim Support, 1990).

An essential part of the service provided by Victim Support is the provision of information on such matters as home security, insurance and compensation. Local expertise is recruited to assist with training on these issues and referral for expert advice is usually available. Support in dealing with the various aspects of the criminal justice process has become a special area of expertise.

To confirm the importance of the involvement of the local community, each local scheme has its own management committee which must include representatives of the police; probation or social services; a voluntary organisation (or church); and of the scheme's own team of volunteers. The independence of the scheme is thus assured. The link with the police is especially close, however, since they are the source of the great majority of referrals. This has meant that schemes have not been dependent on publicity to find clients; but efforts are being made to encourage self-referrals, for example among victims of racial harassment and those attending accident and emergency departments of hospitals, who for various reasons do not always report the crime to the police.

The experience of a supportive community is further confirmed by the employment of trained volunteers as the primary providers of service. Equality and normality implied in the relationship with a 'good neighbour' and the dangers of stigmatisation or over-dependency which may be inherent in psychotherapeutic services are avoided. There has not been, as in Germany, a big debate about volunteers versus professionals (Weißer Ring, 1992: Thema I; Wright, 1994, p.8). Volunteers do, however, need to be backed up by good training, supervision and support, and by the ability to call upon professional advice when required. The role of the local co-ordinator is therefore crucial and increasingly these posts are filled by paid professional staff.

An important part of Victim Support's policy is what it does *not* do: from the earliest days, a conscious decision was made to avoid comment on offender related issues, other than those which directly affected victims or the development of services for them. There were many attempts to hijack the newly discovered victims and use them to bolster up both sides of the debate on the punishment or rehabilitation of offenders, each side claiming that victims would benefit from the solutions they espoused. Victim Support had to work hard to establish that victims were important in their own right and there was a new need to promote community responsibility for the effects of crime. A by-product of this policy was that it enabled the Association to benefit from politicians' discovery of 'the political advantages of a tangible concern for victims', and from the police interest in emphasising the more outward-looking and caring side of their work (Holtom and Raynor, 1988, pp.22-24).

REFORMS IN THE CRIMINAL JUSTICE PROCESS

The National Association of Victims Support Schemes (now known as Victim Support), formed in 1979, began to receive reports that the criminal justice process was not only ignoring victims but causing them considerable inconvenience and even distress: leaving them in the dark, not even being told that 'their' offender has been caught until they read in the paper that he had been convicted and sentenced; not being allowed to bury a murdered relative in case the defence wanted a further post-mortem; being summoned to give evidence in cases that were repeatedly adjourned, without explanation; being ignored by the barrister prosecuting in what they regarded as 'their' case; being asked to speak up as they described painful events in a courtroom with much distracting coming and going and without an amplification system; being unable to reply to hurtful allegations made by the defence in mitigation and often published in the local press.

These reports were supported by independent research, including the findings of Victim Support operational research projects. Shapland and colleagues (1985) found that initial satisfaction with the police declined as victims were left without information. In Victim Support's project on racial harassment, there were also mixed reactions to the police, and one young Asian man was even arrested after reporting that he had been attacked by a white neighbour, because of unsubstantiated cross-allegations from the perpetrator (Kimber and Cooper, 1991, pp.46-47). In a survey of witnesses, one in three would have liked more information on court procedures; 58% felt there had been insufficient consultation over the date of the hearing; in 37% of cases the hearing did not take place on the scheduled day (of whom 7 out of ten were unaware of the change until they arrived at court). Most were given too little information; nearly half were kept waiting more than four hours (Raine and Smith, 1991, p.61).

Victims complained that they were not allowed to tell their story in their own words, and objected to procedural devices such as a plea of guilty to a lesser charge, which failed to recognise the extent of the harm suffered by the victim. Some of the problems arise from the retributive basis of the system, which necessitates extensive safeguards for defendants, and gave rise to the dictum that it is better to acquit ninety-nine guilty men than to convict one innocent – but the victim is conscious that both types of miscarriage of justice leave the real perpetrator at large.

Awareness of the victim's perspective began to spread through the criminal justice agencies as a result of their own involvement with Victim Support, particularly on management committees. The police saw a broader range of needs than those apparent when they interview victims in the immediate aftermath of a crime. Probation officers learnt about the effects of crime on victims, and some of them resolved to make offenders aware of it. Initially, the Magistrates' Association would not allow magistrates to participate, for fear of an appearance of conflict of interest, but Victim Support argued successfully that there is no conflict involved in an expression of concern for victims, and the Lord Chancellor agreed that they could without impropriety serve on management committees or, outside their own court areas, as volunteers. Clear contacts are now developing through court user groups, with court officials and with the Crown Prosecution Service (CPS), in the Crown Court Witness Service (of which more below).

A number of proposals for reform have been put forward by Victim Support in evidence to government committees, in working party reports, and through the twice-yearly Victims Steering Group which brings together senior representatives of the relevant agencies and government departments. Victims and witnesses are (to an increasing extent) receiving information leaflets, victims or relatives are beginning to be contacted before the release of life-sentence prisoners, and the Royal Commission on Criminal Justice has included several recommendations relating to victims, eleven of which the Home Secretary has undertaken to implement (*Victim Support Magazine*, 1993a, 1993b).

An initiative bringing Victim Support into closer than ever contact with the criminal justice system is the Crown Court Witness Service, in which Victim Support volunteers are available to support witnesses. Funding to extend the service to all Crown court centres by the end of 1995 has been announced. The service has been carefully planned and piloted, and the volunteers trained to follow a special code of practice. It has helped to promote awareness of the victim/witness's point of view in the CPS, which in 1993 responded by issuing a statement on the treatment of victims and witnesses.

However, no man is a hero to his valet, and any voluntary organisation working so closely with statutory agencies is bound to become aware of individual shortcomings and defects in the system itself. It has to tread a careful path between acquiescing (explaining to the victim why certain practices are necessary), complaining (for example, about individual cases of insensitive treatment of victims), and campaigning for change (for example, that prosecuting barristers should introduce themselves to their witnesses before the trial or that coroners should be brought within the ambit of the Courts Charter). If the voluntary organisation protests too forcefully, it could forfeit co-operation so that its clients would suffer. But if it remains silent, it is merely helping to perpetuate a system in which inconvenience and distress for victims are still inevitable. The manner in which victims and other witnesses are required to give their evidence, and indeed the style of cross-examination which follows, are issues which are only now beginning to receive the attention they deserve with the recent introduction of special protection for children.

JUSTICE FOR VICTIMS

When, despite preventative efforts, crimes occur, what should be society's response? If there are individual victims the first concern, we suggest, should be to care for them, and as far as possible restore them to their former condition (or to improve it, if they were in need). This should be an integrated response, not from Victim Support alone but from other voluntary and statutory agencies such as Citizens' Advice Bureaux, law centres, Age Concern, the Women's Royal Voluntary Service, local government departments, the National Health Service, and others as appropriate. It should include compensation, involving comprehensive and complementary provisions by both a State compensation fund and the Department of Social Security.

With regard to offenders, the usual concerns are with questions such as deterrence or rehabilitation, and a procedure that is fair to the defendant. We should like to suggest, in addition, that victims should be consulted about any compensation they would like, and that offenders should be enabled, or even required, to make reparation. The procedure must not, however, aggravate the victim's inconvenience or distress. Courts, for example, should pay compensation orders and recover them from the offender later to avoid the current problems experienced by victims when payments are extended over many months.

People who were fortunate enough to have worked with John Pendleton will know of his passionate concern for a new approach to justice. His work with the Probation Service is well known, but it may not be known to everyone that he was deeply involved in the development of Victim Support in the 1980s. During his employment at the University of Nottingham, he became a founder member of the Nottinghamshire Victim Support scheme, and on his return to the Probation Service he became closely involved in the work of Victim Support in Warwickshire. He was also an active and enthusiastic member of the National Council of Victim Support and its Policy Advisory Committee. His deep concern for the rights and well-being of both victims and offenders led him to a vision of justice which would embrace the two and restore humanity to the processes of criminal law. The ideas which he helped to formulate have more recently come to be known as reparative or restorative justice and in recognition of John Pendleton's significant contribution a brief description of the main points is given here.

Reparation is a broader concept than compensation. It may include an apology, the payment of money, or, if the victim does not wish to receive anything from the offender, service to the community or co-operation with rehabilitative measures. This gives the offender an incentive to make amends constructively, but without burdening the victim with responsibility for sentencing.

Victim/offender mediation, which may be offered with reparation or separately, involves communication between victims and offenders in the presence of trained mediators, or indirectly, with the mediators as intermediaries. The *British Crime Survey* found that half the victims who had reported an offence 'would have accepted the chance of meeting the offender in order to agree a way in which the offender could make a repayment for what s/he had done', and a further 20% would like such an agreement without meeting. The main reasons for wanting to meet were: to arrange for the offender to pay money in compensation; to see what s/he was like; to ask why s/he did it; so that s/he could see the effect of the crime on the victim; or 'to give him a good piece of my mind' (Maguire and Corbett, 1987, pp.227-31). This is a promising initiative, but the interests of victims should be to the fore: reparation and mediation services should not aim mainly to influence offenders or to divert them from the criminal justice process; they should, like Victim Support, be under independent management and observe agreed practice standards such as those of Mediation UK (of which, incidentally, John Pendleton was a founder member).

Home Office research has shown that meeting the offender was felt to be valuable by 82% of victims. The primary reason which victims gave for agreeing to meet their offender was to help reform them and help stop them re-offending. Almost all offenders considered that their victims had been reasonable; the very 'niceness' of the victim could add to the embarrassment (Marshall and Merry, 1990, pp.165, 168, 157). For some offences, particularly those that originated in personal disputes, satisfactory reparation or a mediated agreement will mean that prosecution is no longer in the public interest and can be discontinued.

In cases which go to court, some victims welcome the opportunity of communication with the offender, whether to express their feelings, ask questions, demand reparation, or simply to try to influence the offender's future behaviour and attitudes. At present, some cases are diverted out of the system, often with a caution for the offender, and the decision is commonly made with reference to its effect on him or her. But the first consideration should be given to the interests of the victim, and one way of doing so is to offer the opportunity for reparation, mediation, or both.

A CRIMINAL JUSTICE PROCESS THAT RESPECTS VICTIMS

The increased awareness of victims and of the harm which has been caused to public confidence by their neglect has provided a new perspective from which all of these issues can be seen in a new light. Some fundamental questions may have to be asked about society's response to crime; for example:

- To what extent should crime be seen as against the individual victim or against society as a whole?
- Should the response be based on the actual effects of the crime rather than, as at present, the intent?
- On whose behalf does the State intervene?
- Should crimes be regarded as significant individual events, or as the tangible indicators of wider social phenomena? – a question which is particularly relevant in domestic violence or racially motivated crime.
- Should more resources be deployed for prevention; for healing the harm caused to the victim and the community; or for learning to live with the problem?

When cases have to go to court the State should have a responsibility to ensure that victims are not further traumatised, and that:

- relevant information about the background of the offence and future risks and fears is sought and valued;
- victims are given full information and explanation of the progress and outcome of their case;
- the victim is treated with sensitivity and respect by all members of the criminal justice system;
- victims are given any assistance possible to achieve a speedy recovery from the effects of crime through comprehensive and accessible services for support, with any special professional or long-term facilities they may require, and through compensation or reparation if they wish it.

Enormous advances have been made in recognising the true position of victims in relation to the crime. Comprehensive services are now in place throughout the country and they continue to be improved as our knowledge increases. There is more awareness of victims and the treatment which they have a right to expect from criminal justice. Concern for victims is mentioned in most new policy initiatives involved with crime.

There is still a long way to go, but we should never again accept a system of justice that does not also show justice to victims.

Section II

Justice in Practice

Six
Troubles come not singly but in battalions: The pursuit of social justice and probation practice

Malcolm Cox and Colin Pritchard

John Pendleton's contribution to British Probation was motivated by a concept of a continuing pursuit of 'Social Justice' which he saw as a dynamic mission, and crucially interpreted the philosophical meaning of 'Justice', into practical action. We see Probation as essentially a Social Work Service within the forensic field. It represents a key element within democratic societies, that even when the individual appears to be in conflict with society, the State continues to seek equity and fairness in its search for justice for its erring citizen.

Democratic states, unlike totalitarian regimes, accept the classic theme within Magna Carta (1215), 'that no person is condemned without due process of law, and, is assumed innocent until proven guilty'.

Thus the defendant remains first a citizen and only at the point of conviction and sentence is his/her full citizen's right temporarily suspended or removed. What does this 'citizen-offender' concept mean for social work in the Probation Service?

Parallels can be seen in a range of legislation such as, the Mental Health Act 1983; the National Health Service and Community Care Act 1991; the Children Act 1989, and the various Criminal Justice Acts, that the social work profession is part of the State's effort to reach out to various troubled, vulnerable, disturbed and disturbing citizens. The purpose is to treat them, care, rehabilitate and/or reintegrate them as citizens, yet at the same time to control the individual, be they 'patient' or 'offender'. Such an approach implies a degree of consensus within a pluralistic society. Pritchard and Taylor (1978) argued that it was possible to identify, within democratic societies, welfare systems which linked different 'political' value bases, relevant to social work and probation practice. They took as self-evident that totalitarian regimes, either from the left or right, are incompatible with a value system which sees the citizen, the individual, as central to the concerns of that society.

Few would quarrel with this position, apart perhaps from stressing that in terms of 'protection', society and the 'innocent' should be Probation's primary concern. There has been, however, a considerable disagreement and questioning of the implied social work 'rehabilitative' and 'welfare' role for Probation (Bottoms and McWilliams, 1979) and recent legislation has created a new emphasis upon Probation being a form of community punishment. But Harris and Webb (1987), and others have put up a spirited defence for the importance of the welfare role (Raynor, 1993b; Webb and McBeath, 1989).

We base our appeal for social justice, and the practice of a democratic and civilised Probation Service, upon a document which unites all democratic ideologies. This is found in the *United Nations' Universal Declaration of Human Rights* (1948), in which Britain can take a pride as one of the founding signatories. In the preamble we see an assertion which joins Conservatives, Liberals and Democratic Socialists together:

> ...the recognition of inherent dignity and of the equal inalienable rights of all members of the human family is a foundation of freedom, justice and peace in the world.

and

> ...disregard and contempt for human rights have resulted in barbarous acts which have outraged the conscience of human kind and the advent of the world in which human beings should enjoy freedom of speech and freedom from fear and this has been proclaimed as the highest aspiration of the common people.

and

> ...the peoples of the United Nations have reaffirmed their faith in fundamental human rights, in the dignity and worth of the human person and in the equal rights of men

> and women and are determined to promote social progress and better standards of life in larger freedom – pledge themselves to achieve in co-operation the notion of universal respect for an observance of human rights and fundamental rights.

Who could quarrel with any of this? We subscribe and embrace totally all the 29 articles, and explore particular clauses which form the basis for a full, mature and autonomous citizenship, which is viewed as the ultimate goal of all societies. As will be seen, the Declaration includes not only 'active' rights but 'active' responsibilities as well. When we have perused these international standards and aspirations, we will contrast them with the life experiences of probationers in Britain in the mid-1990s. We draw attention to the articles of particular relevance to Probation practice. Interestingly the argument about whether or not Kantian ethics should apply to social work, in any setting including Probation (Webb and McBeath, 1989) can we believe, be firmly affirmed *providing that* the contextual disadvantages are acknowledged and *compensated* for. We will ultimately show that the inherent right and dignity of the citizen to accept the moral justness of punishment for infringing other citizens' rights in crime can be just but only if the totality of the personal and social history of the person is understood. Based upon current empirical work and the UN Declaration, we propose an ethical framework for practice and the further development of the empowerment of the person whose citizenship has been impaired.

In the Declaration, everyone is entitled to full equality and to a full public hearing by an independent and impartial tribunal in the determination of their rights and obligations and of any criminal charge against them:

> i) Everyone charged with a penal offence has a right to be presumed innocent until proven guilty according to law and in a public trial he/she has all the guarantees necessary for his/her defence.
> ii) No-one should be held guilty of any penal offence on account of any act or admission which did not constitute a penal offence, under national or international law at the time when it was committed. Nor shall a heavier penalty be imposed other than the one that was applicable at the time the penal offence was committed.

> iii) The family as the natural fundamental group unit of society is entitled to protection by society and the state, in accordance with the organisation and resources of each state, of the economic, social and cultural rights indispensable to his/her dignity and free development of his/her personality.
>
> 23i) Everyone has a right to work, to free choice of employment, to just and favourable conditions of work and to protection against unemployment.
>
> 25i) Everyone has the right to a standard of living adequate for the health and well-being of himself/herself and his/her family, including housing and medical care and necessary social services, and the right to security in the event of unemployment, sickness, or other lack of livelihood in circumstances beyond his/her control.
> 25 ii) Motherhood and childhood are entitled to special care and assistance. All children, whether born in or out of wedlock, shall enjoy the same protection.

Finally, uniting active rights with positive responsibilities:

> 29i) Everyone has duties to the community in which alone the free and full development of his/her personality is possible.
> 29ii) In the exercise of his/her rights and freedoms everyone should only be subjected to his/her limitations that are determined by law solely for the purpose of securing due recognition of respect for the rights and freedom of others and of meeting the just requirements of morality, public order and the general welfare in a democratic society.

It is argued that despite the Declaration being more than forty years old, this is still a comprehensive review of a full citizenship, though it may make uncomfortable reading for some.

Crucially, it focuses upon active, not just passive rights, which, of course, is the essence of full citizenship. No individual should be left passive or non-contributory to their society, and each should contribute according to their abilities. We will argue that a range of disadvantaged circumstances results in a series of prejudices, not just the obvious ones of ethnicity, or gender, age or social class, but those which accrued from a childhood and often an adolescent life, of being devalued, unwanted, unloved and with a tarnished self-esteem.

Like all prejudices, ethnic or gender, operated by a dominant culture, the prejudice ultimately includes the oppressors as well as the victims, reflecting Burke's classic notion that, 'If my brother is enslaved, no man is free.' When we take Goffman's (1968) notion of 'spoiled identity', which is the very essence of those stigmatised and ostracised by society, we see that it fuels the self-destructive lowering of self-esteem. We are reminded of Jesus of Nazareth's injunction who said 'What man is there of you, who if his son asks bread, will he give him a stone? Or, if he ask a fish, will he give him a serpent?' (Matthew 7 v 9-10). We will show that yesterday's 'spoiled childhood', is today's 'adult spoiler'. It is the recognition of Dr Johnson's phrase, 'the effects of deforming poverty'.

Whilst rejecting the revolutionary solutions, we are mindful of the great appeal of the ideals of the French Revolution; Liberty, Equality and Fraternity. We seek a Liberty that is full and fulfilling, open and equal to all, but *not* just a liberty from null involvement, or the opportunity to continue unfree, disadvantaged and poor; no, we seek a positive Liberty.

We are concerned with Equality, not just before the law, nor just as opportunity, (and here we would indict the Left) but an Equality which raises up, not levels down in a jealous meanmindedness of spirit. This Equality is one of aspiration, to fulfil and maximise the individual's personal talents.

What is needed, however, to unite Liberty and Equality in a vision of a progressive social justice, is Fraternity. Not a de-humanising, de-individualising, in-human uniformity, but a Fraternity which delights in every person seeking to express themselves in full citizenship, recognising equal rights and responsibilities. This is an aspiration in tune with the highest attributes of Jesus of Nazareth, of loving our neighbour as ourselves, which drives the pursuit of evolving true social justice. Its fulfilment bestows citizenship on every person, irrespective of age, ethnicity, and without distinction of any kind. It is in the practical implications for a search for justice in a Probation Service which is not sentimental, but conscious of its professional knowledge and practice limitations, embracing the Quaker dictum to 'Seek ye the Godhead in every person'.

Perhaps the great philosophical divide in the argument about the nature of the Probation Service rests on the notion of responsibility. Lady Thatcher was fond of quoting Roger Tilling (1982) who said 'There is no direct proof that unemployment causes crime' – which Lady Thatcher rightly castigated as a calumny against the unemployed, and she was right to assert that the vast majority of unemployed people are not criminal, do not neglect their children, nor are they delinquent in any way. However, Lady Thatcher ignored the completion of Tilling's discourse on the causes of crime. He went on to point out that the continued association of unemployment with a whole range of psycho-pathologies cannot be ignored!

We will show that an examination of the antecedents and current life situations of many of Probation's clientele will raise the question of whether they have had equal access to the necessary opportunities to fulfil their citizenship, in terms of their psychological as well as their social development. This is *not* to excuse crime, because we reassert Article 29 of the Declaration, that 'Rights' are only justifiable providing you meet obligations, and that you should not impose upon the freedom and social opportunities of others. In parenthesis, we agree with Judge Stephen Tumim, that whilst a significant proportion of current prisoners might benefit by an alternative mode of societal response, care in the community, a small minority requires containment, possibly for even longer than their original sentences. This is because a small proportion are so damaged and damaging, that we need to protect them, as well as society, from the consequences of their actions, as there is no evidence from current or even the 'best outcome' research (Blackburn, 1993; Howells and Hollin, 1993), that we can reach this small minority of people, especially the psychopathic, safely enough to guarantee other citizens of their rights.

The key question is, however, do or did offenders have the benefit of a full and unfettered citizenship, or are they to some extent, victims of a cycle of deprivation which has marred or impaired their potential citizenship?

What follows is a resume of client-centred research between 1986 and 1993 within the county of Dorset, one of the most affluent areas of Great Britain. We believe our results will raise questions as to Equal Opportunities and perhaps give a pointer towards a style of organisation of the Probation Service that places rehabilitation and re-integrative objectives at the centre as a means of establishing full citizenship.

RESPONDING TO CRIME

Crime, its punishment and prevention, has increasingly occupied the social and political agenda for over a decade, evidenced by the number of Criminal Justice Acts that the British Parliament has enacted (Box, 1982; Howard, 1994; HRH The Princess Royal, 1994)

Broadly, there are three responses to people committing crime.

The first is predominantly concerned with punishment, the protection of society and commitment to prison.

The second might be described as containment and supervision, which takes place in the community, and is predominantly Probation or a Conditional arrangement.

The third, and largest proportion of judgements are, of course, fiscal by way of fines and compensation, which might be described best as purging and a fiscal restoration.

All three broad elements are acknowledged to have a degree of inherent retribution to demonstrate, and this is very important symbolically, that offenders have 'paid their debt to society'. In addition, and only vaguely understood by the general public, is an acceptance of the idea of rehabilitation and reintegration.

Whilst our focus is essentially on the community perspective of Probation, we are aware of the brooding possibility of custody; conversely some may feel that a fiscal disposal would have restored them to total self-direction, and some may chafe at the apparent constraints of a Probation Order.

Crucially, a new theme has evolved in the community disposal of offenders, namely the notion of 'Partnership'. The interesting Home Office document, *Partnership in Dealing with Offenders in the Community* (1993), represents a welcome effort to integrate a range of community interdisciplinary policies to prevent crime and rehabilitate offenders. But one vital element is missing – namely the active involvement of the offender into the scheme of 'partnership'. Unlike the fields of medicine, mental health or child protection where it can be assumed that the sufferer/victim concurs with the legislative and professional objectives of the service provided (which is to avoid illness, or 'manage' symptoms, ensure child safety, and treat mental disorder and/or prevent its re-occurrence) by definition offenders, especially persistent offenders, reject society's laws and mores. Why do they do this? Is it because they are evil, psychotic or have uncontrollable impulses? Or is it due to a combination of circumstances? Offending for them is their only perceived feasible solution to their particular situation, as in effect they take what we define as 'an alternative market response'.

In respect of the concept of evil, we have to disclaim any expertise in this metaphysical conundrum; whilst the interface between psychiatry and offending has always carried, albeit reluctantly, a degree of public acceptance that the person is not culpable in the usual way. We are mainly concerned with the broad thrust of offending behaviour, which causes most concern and implied one of three causations.

First, there is a conscious decision to engage in criminal activity which appears to have no exonerating circumstances whatsoever. This will include the so-called 'white-collar-crime' rather than the more publicised 'blue-collar-crime'.

Second, people commit offences because, for whatever reason, there appears to be a deficit or an inadequate development of their socialisation, so that offences cause them no guilt, unlike the majority of people; or they have no social inhibitions, again in contrast with the vast majority of the population. Such deficits or inadequate development may be innate or due to faulty learning; the extreme example is of a severe personality disorder or psychopathy. However, if this was accepted then such a person would ultimately be dealt with by psychiatry rather than primary criminal legislation.

The third group might be described as a breakdown of the psychological or social inhibitions in people who generally do not engage in illegal behaviour.

This schematic model needs to be placed within an age context so that the 'cognitive decision' group might occur throughout a lifetime, whereas the deficit or inadequate 'development' group have most of their offences in teens and early adulthood, whilst the 'stressed group' appeared to require some form of a psycho-social trigger or precipitant.

The first group within our psycho-social schema clearly merit only minimal consideration, for they appear to have 'consciously' turned their backs on Article 29 of the United Nations Declaration and overtly restrict the freedoms of others, for their own gratification. For such offenders the law should take its natural course until restitution as well as retribution is complete. The Probation Service has only minimal services to offer such offenders because they have the competence, resources and cognition to fulfil their obligations as citizens.

It is the latter two groups for which, for us, Probation was ideally designed. Namely, in the spirit of equity as well as reflecting the pursuit of social justice, to reach and to help the damaged and/ or the vulnerable. How valid is such a sweeping and perhaps controversial view?

NEW TROUBLES COME NOT SINGLY BUT IN BATTALIONS: PSYCHOSOCIAL ANTECEDENTS OF PROBATION CLIENTS

We were led to this position by an analysis of the range of problems facing the ordinary probationer. We will report upon three separate studies, whose implications give us the direction for intervention, and to justify a nil or minimal punitive retributive response.

The original survey involved Social Workers from two southern cities who had completed a self-administered questionnaire on the psycho-social problems of their young adult (18-35 years) clients within the local Probation and Social Services departments (Pritchard and Cox, 1990). The original results quite frankly surprised us, not least the degree of mental health disturbance and we wondered whether it was some form of artefact. So using an improved methodology, the questionnaire was completed on the first consecutive young adult clients allocated to a Probation and Social Service Department's Social Workers in January 1991. We had a response rate of over 70%, which in view of the many pressures upon front line staff, was considered a very reasonable return meriting further analysis.

Our earlier work had taught us the importance of having a data gathering instrument which was user friendly, although the revised survey was still limited. For example, we excluded issues about the client's sexual orientation, or what was their mode of drug misuse, if any. Nevertheless we were able to cover the bulk of their client's current problems from a list of 28, with space for additional other problems, previous difficulties and offences as well as contact with other agencies during the last 12 months. Owing to distribution difficulties, however, we lost a third of our proposed Social Services caseloads; consequently we only published material on Probation clients (Pritchard et al., 1992).

We report here upon both sets of clients but more importantly, for the first time explore a sub-group of 31% of the Probation clients who had experienced some form of being in Care as children. Originally we had thought it unwise to develop this

Table 1
Social Characteristics

	Prob % *(n=214)*	SSD % *(n=120)*	Sample %
Males	86	45	64
Females	14	55	36
<21	41	21	34
22-25	30	23	27
26-30	17	26	20
31+	12	31	19
Married	11	12	12
Single	52	63	56
Cohabit	23	11	19
Sep/Div	14	14	14
Partner <3yrs	37	26	35
Unemployed	74	78	75
Part Time	5	11	7
Full Time Job	21	9	17
Partner Job			
Full Time	14	61	27
Part Time	20	25	22
No Job	65	14	51

aspect as we did not wish misunderstandings to occur, but as will be seen, Probation clients contain a significant proportion of citizens who by all the criteria have had a lifetime of disadvantage and deprivation. This must raise questions as to whether they have been able to enjoy the rights they were entitled to under the United Nations Charter and whether or not this to some extent explains why they could not fulfil their obligations as full citizens.

Table 1 shows the characteristics of the young adult clients in the Probation and Social Services samples.

Important points to note are that Probation clients are predominantly male (86% v 14%) while Social Services are weighted towards females (55% v 45%). Probation clients were slightly younger, the bulk being under the age of 26 whereas the majority of Social Services clients were over the age of 26. Both groups had a significantly high level of unemployment – 74% and 78% respectively – and this in a region where the male average unemployment was at that time 7.5%.

Table 2 shows the multiplicity of problems faced by clients of both services and, whilst we do not wish to dwell upon this too much, it would appear that Probation clients, when allowing for referral bias, not only had more problems but often were more disturbed. They had more severe debt and money problems and slightly but significantly more chronic housing difficulties. Although less mentally disordered, a number had been treated by a psychiatrist; they had a slightly higher attempted suicide rate, but there were fewer with physical disability and education learning difficulties. Nevertheless, it should be noted that 1 in 5 of the Probation clients are considered to have educational difficulties.

Drug and alcohol misuse was, as would be expected, higher amongst Probation clients. Violence against others was a feature which should not be ignored, and 4% of the sample were reported to have engaged in violence against staff. It should be remembered that proportionately over the last decade more social workers died at the hands of their clients in pursuit of their duties than have policemen.

It should also be noted that 31% of the Probation clients had spent some time in Care as children which is perhaps the clearest indication of the lifelong difficulties that these people have had.

Including the non-listed problems, the average Probation client age 18-35 had 6.6 identified problems as opposed to 5.1 amongst the Social Services clientele. It is not to make invidious comparisons, but only to highlight that, so often in the official statistics, only the clients' major difficulty is itemised via the 'administrative' band in which they are dealt with. This fails miserably to reflect the multiplicity of their problems. We can say with confidence, that Probation and Social Services clients are people who have a plethora of difficulties, which goes some way to explain the degree of severe disturbance and disruption that exists in the caseloads of the statutory community services and Probation in particular.

It may be appropriate to point out that studies in other parts of the country have found very similar results to the above (Stewart and Stewart, 1993; Hudson and Roberts, 1993). Taken overall, the findings shown in Table 3 highlight the extensive involvements of Probation clients with other agencies, in particular both

Table 2
Frequency of Clients Problems in Probation v SSD Caseloads

Type of Problem	Probation Clients *%(n=214)*	SSD Clients *%(n=120)*	Total Sample *%(n=334)*
Debt and Money	76	51	67
Jobless 6 Months+	56	50	54
Personal Relationships	64	58	62
Social Relationship	50	53	51
Chronic Housing	24	18	22
Child Abuse	11	10	11
Family at Risk Register	6	4	5
Child in Care	4	4	4
Depression GP Treated	15	13	14
Depression Treat Psychiatrist	10	8	10
Mental Disorder Treated GP	2	7	4
Mental Disorder Psychiatrist	4	13	7
Emotional/Anxiety States	35	37	35
Attempted Suicide	14	7	11
Physical Disability	6	28	14
Education/Learning Disability	22	47	31
Tranquillisers	3	4	3
Amphetamines	14	3	10
Cannabis	30	3	20
Opiates	7	1	5
LSD	5	0	3
Solvent Abuse	2	0	1
Alcohol	46	8	33
Violence v Staff	3	5	4
Violence v Other	28	10	21
HIV Risk	15	14	15
Offence Property	56	3	37
Offences People	33	3	22
Extra Problems			
Abused as Child	3	4	3
Family Sex Victim	2	2	3
Family Violence	5	3	4
Others	29	55	38

Table 2 (cont)

Previous			
Mental Hospital	7	19	11
Prev Custody	45	1	30
Child in Care	4	6	5
Been in Care	31	15	26
Prev Off v Property	73	7	51
Prev Off v People	48	6	34
Other Agencies			
Average Number of Listed Problems	6.4	4.5	5.6
Others Problems	62	67	129
Overall Average	6.6	5.1	6

community and hospital health services. This clearly indicates the urgent need to take a more 'total management perspective' in order to deal effectively with some of society's most disturbed citizens.

As can be seen, there is evidence to support the assertion that Probation is more directly involved with the most damaged clientele than any other community based service. Indeed, the nearest is the Forensic Psychiatric Service and they have far more compulsory and controlled resources. In addition, we compared a recent ex-prisoner group within our caseload study and found few significant differences between those who had served a custodial sentence and those who had not. When reflecting on the success of policy to target serious and persistent offenders, one consequence has been that Probation clients have never been so disturbed, and, in essence, there are no 'easy cases' allocated today. The nearest other services get to the Probation caseload, is the Prison Service, which is more than 17 times more expensive (House of Commons, 1994). Self-evidently, some prisoners would be quite unsuitable for any type of community order, and a significant proportion of prison inmates are rightly 'placed' in optimum security. Nevertheless, taking into account the arguments about the disproportion of prisoners in the UK compared with the rest of Europe, that data suggested that perhaps a substantial proportion of prisoners might have different disposals. Undoubtedly, it can be said that today's Probation Service is in the front-line in the 'battle against crime'.

Table 3
Significant Differences 'Ex Child Care' Clients v Rest

Problem	Ex child % (n=80)	Rest % (n=231)	X2	P. Value
<21 yrs	36	34		
22-25yrs	31	26		
26-30	25	17		
31+yrs	8	23	9.77	<0.02
Debt & Money	85	16	15.96	<0.001
Jobless 6 Months+	68	49	8.25	<0.01
Personal Relationship	74	57	7.26	<0.01
Social Relationships	75	43	24.57	<0.001
Physical Neglect Child	11	2	13.44	<0.001
Misuse Cannabis	33	17	9.37	<0.01
Solvent Misuse	5	0	11.7	<0.01
Alcohol Difficulties	48	28	10.07	<0.002
Violence v Others	34	17	10.76	<0.002
Depression-GP Treated	21	11	5.53	<0.02
Depression-Psychiatrist	23	5	22.11	<0.001
Attempted Suicide	25	7	20.38	<0.001
HIV Risk	29	11	14.63	<0.001
Offences v Property	54	33	10.45	<0.002
On At Risk Register	12	3	7.33	<0.01
Children in Care	12	2	11.77	<0.001
Previous Mental Hospital Admission	19	8	6.95	<0.01
Prev. Custodial Sentence	49	22	21.29	<0.001
Prev. Child in Care	10	3	7.38	<0.01
Prev. Offences v Property	80	41	33.94	<0.001
Prev. Offences v People	52	27	15.9	<0.001
Drug Group	38	28	10.54	<0.002
Alcohol Group	48	28	10.06	<0.002
Jobless Group	84	71	4.76	<0.03
Mental Health Group	33	18	6.01	<0.02
Promiscuity Group	29	11	14.63	<0.001
Housing Group	28	21	1.33	n.sig

From the caseload studies, there were natural sub-groups within sample. These included clients who had been involved in drug misuse, HIV risk behaviour, those with a mental health problem, the unemployed, those with particular drink difficulties, and those with chronic housing problems.

Perhaps we should first note that overall 1 in 4 had problems with drugs and 1 in 15 had HIV risk behaviour, which invariably included drug misuse, casual prostitution or casual sex. This latter feature was found to be higher amongst women than men. Of particular concern was that 1 in 5 had chronic housing difficulties. It is in the area of drugs and alcohol that the Probation clients were more frequently represented. There was no difference between the two agency groups in relation to clients with mental health problems, which included treatment for depression, and/or mental disorder as well as attempted suicide, despite the fact that the Probation Service is not in any way a specialist service for the mentally ill. This latter aspect can not be emphasised sufficiently because it would appear that the concern expressed about suicide in prisons (Dooley, 1990; Gunn et al., 1991) may well be due to the impact of incarceration upon people who already suffer from minor mental health problems, but because they are not 'front rank', may well be missed.

TODAY'S DISRUPTIVE YOUNG ADULTS: YESTERDAY'S NEGLECTED AND DISTURBED CHILDREN?

It is when we examined the 31% of young adult clients who had previously spent sometime in care, that we were forced to ask the question, 'Are today's disruptive offenders, yesterday's neglected and disturbed children?'

Table 3 presents the statistically significant differences between those ex-child care clients and the rest. We only comment on the statistically significant differences, but it should be pointed out that there were greater and more frequent differences along this axis, when we examined our cohort than along any other division.

The ex-child-care clients were younger, which suggests that they come into societal conflict and are in touch with Probation earlier, than those who spent no time in Care.

As their social and personal relationships were more disrupted, their behaviour is more likely to be problematic and classically we found that they were more often physically neglected as a child.

They were more often involved in substances abuse, with a history of depression, and a higher number of attempted suicides, clearly indicative of a lowered self-esteem (Beck et al., 1993; Pritchard, 1995). This theme of low self-esteem was carried over into significantly higher HIV risk behaviour, demonstrating their apparent self-disregard for quite widely known risks (Pritchard et al., 1992; Pritchard and Clooney, 1994) stemming from the apparent life-long disadvantage of these former charges of our Child Care. In parenthesis, we are not being at all critical of the child protection services. Indeed, there is evidence which shows that British child protection has shown the biggest improvement in the Western world from being the third highest 'child killers' in 1973 to the seventh lowest by 1991 (Pritchard, 1992, 1993).

It should be stressed that we are not saying that having been in Care as a child, nor having a minor mental illness, nor showing signs of psycho-social alienation by being involved with drugs and alcohol, nor even unemployment, is a direct cause of subsequent adult offending behaviour. Indeed, all these later adult problems may well be the consequence of their offending behaviour, not the cause of their disturbing behaviour. However, it is an unequivocal fact that almost a third of our sample had a problematic childhood.

However, simple natural justice poses the questions – 'To what extent did their families of origin have 'equal access to public services' (19ii) – 'a childhood entitled to special care' (24ii), and, 'education directed to the full development of their personality' (United Nations 1948)?' When we look at the Declaration's assertion of the inherent dignity and the equal inalienable rights of all members of the human family, a significant proportion of these young adults were not born free and could not take up their entitlements because of the disadvantages involving social origin, and, irrespective of 'blame', their education failed to achieve 'the full development of their human personality and the strengthening of respect for human rights and fundamental freedoms'.

What are the practice implications of these findings within the context of a pursuit of social justice?

The primary purpose of the Probation Service must be to reduce or prevent offences. This accepts the role of protection of society but, equally the duty to rehabilitate and reintegrate the offender/ citizen into the wider community. The long standing arguments about welfare versus punishment, and the issue of care versus control, are over-simplified and a false dichotomy. It is argued that without an adequate welfare service to rehabilitate and reintegrate, there will be no lessening of the propensity of the offenders to re-offend. Equally we may well want to control because we care and visa versa, because within the constellation of client problems are three issues of paradoxically inter-linked concern: namely public order, public health and public cost. Unless all relevant government departments both local and central, take a total management perspective and seek to address public order and public health issues, we are going to be less than effective or efficient and will add to public costs (Pritchard, 1992; Martin, 1993) because, unless Probation and welfare provision can compensate for the disadvantage, there will be little incentive for them to seek rehabilitation or reintegration into citizenship.

MEETING NEEDS AND PRIMARY OBJECTIVES: EVIDENCE FROM CONSUMERS

What do clients need to fulfil their mature adult roles? In an effort to address this issue we turn to our second study which was a consumer survey of probationers' views of the service they received.

During an analysis of single homelessness on the South coast, the consumer views of 153 single homeless people were explored (Pritchard and Clooney, 1994). Based upon a semi-structured questionnaire, it elicited options about the services they had received from various agencies. Almost a third of the sample were interviewed on the street and the rest drawn from every type of hostel in the area which took single homeless people, including a Probation hostel which may have influenced our results. Yet the findings matched surveys carried out in less affluent areas (Scott, 1993; Stockley et al., 1993).

Almost half had been previously homeless, more than a third had had a psychiatric history, and almost two-fifths had previous offences and had spent time in custody. Their current problems, as might be expected, were multiple and included drugs, drink and HIV risk behaviour. However, relevant to this study, more than a third of the respondents had been in contact with the Probation Service during the last twelve months. In comparison with the other 18 various community agencies with which the respondents had had contact the Probation Officers had the highest level of 'helpful' scores. More than 70% of these clients valued their

Table 4
Ex-Custody Probationers v Non-Custody Clients Social Characteristics *(n=57)*

Item		Ex-Custody %	Non Custody %	Sample %
Gender	male	94	77	84
	female	6	23	16
Age	<18 yrs	3	4	3
	19-24	36	34	34
	25-35	36	33	34
	36+ years	22	26	25
Employed	full time	19	12	15
	part time	0	5	4
Marital Status				
	married	11	11	11
	single	47	46	46
	div/sep	19	23	22
	cohabit	19	16	18
Children	1	11	14	13
	2-3	20	7	14
	4+	6	2	3
Live With	self	28	44	38
	parents	17	7	11
	partner	8	7	8
	family	25	21	23
	friend	17	16	16
Live Where	council	31	21	25
	owner/occ	19	4	10
	rent/flat	22	42	34
	bed-sit	8	14	4
	hostel	8	7	8
	bed/break	6	4	4

contact with Probation, only 12% having predominantly negative views. However, one rather surprising finding was that there was some expression of appreciation of efforts of the police to help, i.e. whilst they had the highest negative score, nearly 20% gave examples of individual Police Officers as being helpful.

Armed with these encouraging Probation results, we undertook a randomised, stratified consumer survey on 106 current probationers. In addition to our semi-structured questionnaire, we drew upon the work of Roy Bailey who had undertaken in-depth extensive interviews with offenders (1993). We incorporated a number of statements made by his respondents into a self-administered questionnaire. Of the 106 forms distributed, there was an 88% response rate.

Of immediate practical significance was that whilst four-fifths of the questionnaire required the simplest 'tick and cross' response, there was a page of open-ended questions, and 85% of the sample, despite their relative educational under-achievement, took the trouble to make additional comments about the service, the bulk of which were positive.

The sample was divided into two, the 39% who had had previous custodial sentences, were to be compared with the remainder who had not. Table 4 shows the social characteristics of the two groups which are very similar to the earlier study, the only significant difference being that the ex-custody clients were more likely to be male than female. Again, it was noteworthy that unemployment was the experience of more than 80% of the sample and 16% had a chronic housing difficulty.

Table 5 presents their views on the range of Bailey/Pritchard and Cox statements, both positive and negative about the service. As there were few statistical differences; for ease of presentation we simply show the total sample of those who agreed or disagreed with the statements, and indicate the two significant variations.

Table 6 concerns current probationers' views on the other services, with the exception that the ex-custody probationers were much more hostile to the police, there were no other statistically significant differences.

A brief perusal of the consumer views indicates that there were twelve major issues concerning 'practical' help, nine in regard to 'psycho-social' assistance, six concerned with 'relationship' issues, and four consumer views as to why people get into trouble.

The strongest positive scores were concerned with the quality of the relationship, help with psycho-social problems and appreciating the practical help and guidance the Probation Officer often gave.

Interestingly, a question which might indicate the 'political' orientation of the respondents showed that only 40% agreed with

Table 5
Consumer Views of 93 Probation Clients *(%)*

Statement	Agree	Disagree
Help keep out of trouble	87	13
Find out why people offend	86	4
Help find job or training	71	8
PO is community 'prison officer'	10	67
Give people a chance/last chance	65	15
Help solve housing difficulties	70	11
Help family/personal problems	69	10
If more jobs there'd be less crime	73	16
Jobless I get bored & into trouble	42	41
Want a job, don't admit to record	55	23
Trainings no good, still no job	44	33
Boredom gets u down, probt'n helps	59	13
Family relations not PO business	23	49
PO is a good safety valve	81	2
PO doesn't really do anything	11	57
Daren't take job, if loose, ages before back onto benefit	31	48
PO good helping family problems	58	9
Bottom line PO can't be trusted	5	74
PO listens & tries to understand	86	2
PO helps people take self-pride	74	8
Probt'n soft option: can con PO	14	70
PO not interested: it's only a job	6	81
Usually get fair play from PO	86	3
PO great in court puts your case	63	8
PO accommodation usually grotty	15	32
PO helps you manage money better	36	21
PO often help with job/training	43	15
If PO can't help, finds who can	84	2
PO no help finding accommodation	12	49
Probt'n hostel encourage more trouble	30	29
Benefit system puts you down again	40	25

the statement that the benefit system disadvantaged people and led to crime, the remainder either disagreed or were neutral, reflecting the 'traditional' attitudes so often found amongst offenders.

In respect of employment, two-fifths felt that if they were unemployed they got bored, and therefore into trouble. However,

Table 6
Consumer Views of Agency Helpfulness *% (n=93)*

Agency	(n=)	Helpful	Unhelpful
Current PO	(n=93)	95	5
Friends	(n=85)	92	8
Hospital Staff	(n=74)	92	8
CAB Staff	(n=39)	87	13
Gen. Practitioner	(n=71)	82	18
Relatives	(n=84)	78	22
The Samaritans	(n=25)	80	20
Careers Officers	(n=45)	78	22
Com. Psychiat. Nurse	(n=33)	73	27
Probt'n Hostel Staff	(n=27)	74	26
Priest	(n=37)	70	30
Social Worker	(n=57)	68	32
Job Centre Staff	(n=78)	63	37
Shelter Staff	(n=22)	64	36
Social Security	(n=81)	47	53
Housing Benefits	(n=67)	43	57
Police	(n=85)	39	61

all acknowledged that boredom was a problem which demoralised, and Probation did help to alleviate this.

The suggestion that Probation is a soft touch, only attracted a 14% agreement, with 70% firmly disagreeing. Placed within the context of their previous convictions and their gravity of offence, two-thirds of the clientele had substantial previous convictions and, as one would expect, ex-custody respondents were far higher, although there was little difference between 'gravity', based on the Home Office criteria, as almost half had committed serious offences.

This should be borne in mind when considering outcome measures in terms of societal and Probation objectives. There is little difference between probationers and the majority of offenders in prison, and it is reiterated that Probation is considerably less demanding on the public purse. It was found that throughout the county, 86% of probationers had satisfactorily completed their orders in 1993, which compared with prison and re-conviction rates and return to prison, re-affirms the value not only of Probation to society but apparently the offender as well.

The most important responses were drawn from those open-

Table 7
Best Features About Probation %

Appreciate having some one who you can talk to, who is willing to consider your point of view	71
My probation officer was someone who I felt I could depend upon	10
My probation officer kept me out of prison	5
Valued a range of practical help, including employment, benefits & accommodation	34
Could trust & depend upon the probation officer which boosted their self-esteem by being valued	15
Valued POs accessibility & willingness to respond promptly	8
Other features - career advice, self-understanding, solving emotional problems	13

Table 8
Worst Features About Probation %

Asking too many questions, especially about offences	13
Change of PO, especially without prior consultation	10
Routine & difficulties in travelling to the office to report	18
Hated being kept waiting, especially with poor time keeping POs	9
Being in waiting room, depressing & breaks confidentiality	4
Inconsistency in some probation officers	8
Lack of successful practical help (benefits, job, accommodation)	12
PO had not enough time for me	7
Unsupportive doctors	3

ended questions where clients added their own comments. In response to the question 'What are the best and worst three things about probation?; affirmation was made about the value of the relationship, having someone whom they could rely on, who could guide and give a range of practical help and especially, their accessability and a willingness to consider their particular perspective' (Table 7).

Table 9
Reasonable Income Per Week

Weekly Income	% Response
£50	13
£51-75	34
£76-100	26
£101-125	5
£126-150	11
£151-175	5
£176-200	5
£201+	2

The negatives (Table 8) showed concern about a sense of intrusion, changes of Probation Officers especially without prior notice, the routine, the difficulty of travelling (which was a particular problem in this area) inconsistency in some Probation Officers and a lack of successful help in a practical area.

Table 9 raises a range of issues determined by the respondents. The question was 'It's never easy living on benefit. Realistically in your circumstances if you are on benefit, how much would you need to live reasonably'. One respondent did not answer, one wrote 'a lot', another 'win the pools', but as the table shows, they were modest in the extreme when identifying their needs. If society should ever consider the notion of a 'disability pension' for people with psycho-social 'deficits', this might well be an obvious cost-benefit alternative. In an increasingly competitive socio-economic world, they are less likely to be able to compete, and apart from a humane, just and equitable rationale, such an approach may be financially beneficial to all. Rather than risk them taking up an 'alternative market response' to their plight and adding to the crime figures, mayhem and distress for victims, it may be more productive to provide 'a standard of living adequate for health and well-being' (UN, 1948, 25i)

If we juxtapose the two surveys, we find confirmation of multiple psycho-social problems which theoretically require a counselling-advocacy model of intervention and treatment. In terms of partnership, unless we can engage the disadvantaged, we will fail to include them in society. This seems to match exactly what clients are saying. They require a professional relationship upon which they can rely and go to for guidance and help in dealing with some of the practical problems related to housing, benefits and unemployment difficulties. However, it is not only the psychologically disadvantaged who are our clientele. When we consider the massive socio-economic changes that have occurred in the Western world, people do not have to have had a 'past' to become excluded from society by virtue of being unemployed. They, too, are at risk. There is an accumulative imploding effect, which creates what some have called an 'underclass', others simply the long-term unemployed (Duster, 1994; Lawson and Wilson, 1995). This transforming socio- economic situation, has seen a catastrophic reduction of unskilled and semi-skilled jobs; indeed, because of technology, unemployment is now affecting previously high-skilled people, so that there is an increasing 'army' of long-term unemployed who are showing signs of feeling alienated (Hoover and Plant, 1989; Goldsmith, 1994). This is compounded by economic policies which apparently ignore the psycho-social consequences of long-term unemployment, eschewing Neo-keynsian prescriptions, which certainly in mainland Europe, are beginning to attract bi-partisan support (Michie and Smith, 1994; Doyal and Gough, 1991). Goldsmith (1994) argues eloquently for alternative economic policies which are inclusive of people and which are sustainable in the face of the geo-political pressures upon the planet. He states 'the interplay of market forces is one that is totally blind to all biological, *social*, ecological, aesthetic and considerations of any sort, and which only respond to the shortest term economic consideration' (our italics). If adulthood and maturity is increasingly presented as an ability to be endowed with material possessions, then the 'under-class' and even the average, have increasingly less and less incentive to accept such a vision.

Is this too political? There is a danger that inadvertently the professions are beginning to collude with the government against the citizen by implicitly accepting an a-historical, a-social view of the aetiology of crime and ill-health. It is far too easy to assume a 'technical' stance and argue about different methods, rather than acknowledging that some offenders, in narrow amoral economic terms (which of course we reject), may well be better off being criminally parasitical, than passively living off increasingly inadequate welfare benefits. As one man in the survey stated; 'living only on income support means living under permanent house-arrest.'

The dangers of growing socio-discohesion are not just the nightmare of the fringe Utopians. We are close to a break-down between the haves and have-nots, a position inimical to the Declaration of Human Rights. It is feared that unless a truly 'total management perspective' is taken, sadly we will only respond effectively *after* the disaster.

The Probation Service and the Criminal Justice System are not insulated from the rest of national and international life. We have 'learned' to live with what Hayek (1976) believed were intolerable levels of unemployment for a democratic society. The Probation Service is well placed to raise these issues for wider debate in the search for an inclusive social policy.

If we still have aspiration to be a civilised society in Churchillian terms, and if we take seriously the inter- connections between public order, health and costs, then we must acknowledge that many of our fellow-citizens face a battalion of troubles, without any immediate hope of redress. This is, sadly, a state of affairs which they often reluctantly accept as 'their lot' which will only end in low self-esteem and poor socialisation. Surely this must demand some form of compensatory welfare service to the benefit of all. This is not a comfortable position to espouse. It would be far easier to proclaim, rightly, that the individual Probation Officer can make a positive impact on the life of their clients, but this would be to collude with and accept an unjust social situation. If we are to actualise even the first great article of the United Nations Declaration, then we must stand with Milton who said 'give me the liberty to know, to utter and argue fully according to conscience above all other liberties'. We are developing the research and knowledge base to improve our practice art, *and* inform social policy, which will enable us to honestly confront all citizens, offenders and non-offenders alike, to repeat the great truth that the most effective approach in the reduction of crime is to 'Seek the Godhead in every person.'

Note

This chapter is the personal opinions of the authors' and in no way reflects either the policy or views of the Dorset Probation Service or Southampton University, Department of Social Work Studies.

Seven
'What works': Probation and forms of justice

Peter Raynor

The Chief Inspector of Probation begins the 'overview' section of his 1993 Annual Report with the words 'This is a difficult time to write the report' (Home Office, 1993c). He goes on to explore a theme which has become all too familiar to everyone connected with the probation service in recent years:

> Unfortunately too many users of probation services and the public appear unconvinced that current forms of supervision are either sufficiently rigorous to constitute adequate punishment or sufficiently effective to reduce criminal behaviour.

By 'users' of the service one presumes that he means sentencers rather than clients. This quotation neatly encapsulates the problem which this short paper seeks to explore. If probation is now to be seen as 'punishment', instead of in its earlier guise as an alternative to punishment, how do such punishments fit into the 'just deserts' sentencing models based on proportionality of punishment to offence, which many industrialised countries, including Britain, are adopting? And if 'effectiveness in reducing criminal behaviour' were to be pursued with a little more success than in the past, how would this fit, both conceptually and pragmatically, with a continuing concern for proportionality and justice?

At a strictly logical level, some difficulty of fit is inevitable. A strict 'just deserts' model is concerned with past actions only (Von Hirsch, 1976), whereas the search for 'effective' sentencing measures is primarily a search for interventions that will influence future actions. Roger Hood, among others, argued twenty years ago that sentencing which had forward-looking reductionist aims, whether based on deterrence or rehabilitation, risked injustice through over-intervention and departed from the only morally acceptable basis of sentencing, which he saw as a moral assessment based on the seriousness of the offence (Hood, 1974). Others argued that a return to 'just deserts' models was needed to preserve the rights of offenders not to be coerced into programmes of 'care' or 'treatment' involving intervention beyond the level justified by the seriousness of the offence (for example, the American Friends Service Committee, 1971), while British juvenile justice researchers were beginning to point out that 'welfare' based intervention in the lives of young offenders could prove counter-productive by exposing them to the risk of more coercive and more damaging intervention in the future (Thorpe et al., 1980). Within the probation sphere, it was argued by some practitioners (Bryant et al., 1978) and most cogently by Bottoms and McWilliams (1979) that probation should no longer be seen as a 'treatment' process in which the degree of intervention was determined by empirically dubious estimates of the likely response to treatment, but as a non-custodial penal measure offering a humane alternative to more coercive measures. Such arguments have been highly influential; the purpose of this paper is to re-examine them in the light of current debates about 'just deserts' and effectiveness.

Current experience of what actually happens in penal systems underpinned by a rhetoric of 'just deserts' is certainly not uniformly encouraging. In the United States 'back to justice' sloganising has been associated with a massive increase in imprisonment, particularly of poor and non-white Americans, and the general danger that 'just deserts' thinking can differentially disadvantage the poorest and least powerful has been thoroughly identified by Hudson (1987). In Britain a carefully prepared attempt in the 1991 Criminal Justice Act to enlist 'just deserts' in the service of a rational and decarcerating penal policy has been quickly blown off course by politicians using similar rhetoric to promote a policy of more severe punishment, as in the Home Secretary's speech to the 1993 Conservative Party conference (Howard, 1993). Perhaps a sentencing principle so subjective and negotiable as 'seriousness' is particularly vulnerable to political perceptions of changes in the public mood or of electoral advantage, or even to Ministers' perceptions of their own prospects in party leadership struggles.

Certainly Ministers who deny the existence of socially discriminatory practices in the criminal justice system and of economic influences on crime (MacLean, 1993) are not best placed to integrate the requirements of criminal justice with those of social justice. Quite small changes in the political message seem able to result in quite large changes in practice in volatile criminal justice systems (Zimring and Hawkins, 1994). Perhaps we should not be too surprised that liberal academic criminologists and ambitious but electorally vulnerable Conservative politicians take different public stances about the seriousness of crime.

Strict 'just deserts' models are in fact subject to at least three significant criticisms. They run the risk of failing to take into account morally relevant differences in the social and individual circumstances of people who commit similar offences: are people who have quite different levels of opportunity to avoid crime equally blameworthy if they commit a crime? (Raynor, 1993b). They are also vulnerable on the question of 'dangerous' offenders, where likely future crimes are arguably a proper and necessary consideration, even if difficult to predict (Bottoms, 1977); and the question of whether persistent offenders should be sentenced on the basis of the most recent offence or in a way which recognises a pattern of offending proved to be the Achilles' heel of the 1991 Criminal Justice Act.

It can be argued that these criticisms are not necessarily fatal: for example, the 1991 Act incorporated the elements of a pragmatic accommodation to two of them. By emphasising the role of pre-sentence reports it allowed at least the procedural space for consideration of individual and social circumstance in assessing the seriousness of crime; and it emphasised the need for an explicit basis and reasons when strict proportionality was exceeded on grounds of dangerousness. It is also important to note that none of these criticisms offers support to discredited aspects of the rival 'treatment' model such as one-sided subjective diagnosis, open-ended intervention or the separation of consequences from judgments about the seriousness of the offence. However, the main focus of this paper is on a slightly different problem: when advocates of justice models originally argued against 'treatment', they did so not simply because they expected the abandonment of treatment to lead to a general reduction in the severity of sanctions by putting an end to over-intervention, but also because they could find, and expected to find, no evidence of benefits from 'treatment'. It seems they were sometimes over-optimistic in the first of these expectations; are they still correct in the second? And if there is now rather more hope of using the criminal justice process to provide offenders with opportunities to offend less, how much difference does this make to their arguments?

The influential advocates of 'justice' models during the 1970s were writing in a context which was influenced not only by obvious excesses of 'treatment' (such as the linking of parole decisions in some American states to prisoners' consent to undergo unproven psychosurgical procedures) but also by a consensus among criminologists that 'nothing worked' in the treatment of offenders. In America the terms of debate were set by Martinson and his colleagues in their famously negative review of correctional treatments (Lipton et al., 1975); in Britain the Home Office undertook a similar review (Brody, 1976) with similar results. Years of research on the effectiveness of probation finally ran out of steam with the discouraging IMPACT study (Folkard et al., 1976), after which the Home Office Research Unit virtually abandoned the issue of probation's effectiveness for more than a decade. It became a commonplace of criminological argument that decisions to allocate offenders to any particular programme could not be justified by expectations of benefit, and therefore needed some other justification such as proportionality, or else the diversion of less serious offenders from expensive custody. Bottoms and McWilliams in 1979 took the ineffectiveness of treatment largely for granted, and penal reformers generally based their arguments on diversion or decarceration rather than rehabilitation: the belief that prison did harm proved more durable than the belief that probation did any good. Home Office researchers turned their attention to the evaluation of Community Service as an alternative to custody (Pease, et al., 1977); juvenile justice researchers, alarmed by the consequences of the welfarist 1969 Children and Young Persons Act, concentrated on diversion rather than reconviction (Thorpe et al., 1980); and practitioners sustained their optimism largely by a robust indifference to research. A few unconvinced researchers began local effectiveness studies in collaboration with probation services, but these were not to produce results until after substantial follow-up periods (Raynor, 1988; Roberts, 1989).

Interest in effective practice expressed itself largely in a search for useful techniques (notably those advocated by McGuire and Priestley, 1985) and in the innovative forms of supervision developed in specialised facilities such as Day Training Centres (Vanstone, 1993). A few writers (for example Raynor, 1993b; Harris, 1985) suggested that the requirements of 'welfare' and 'justice' might be reconciled by allowing proportionality to limit the scale of intervention (the 'size of the package' or the degree of interference with liberty), while considerations of potential effectiveness or helpfulness should influence the form of intervention (the 'contents of the package'), but claims about possible effectiveness remained very tentative.

In other countries the position was rather different. Psychologically-oriented correctional practitioners in Canada continued to develop and test programmes (for example Ross et al., 1988) and 'intensive supervision' experiments in America, though largely negative in their results, produced interesting evaluation material (for example Petersilia, 1990; Clear et al., 1987). No doubt they were also aware of Martinson's recantation (Martinson, 1979) which passed largely unnoticed in Britain. By the end of the 1980s and the early 1990s research reviews were beginning to appear which gathered together evidence of effectiveness from a range of programme evaluations, often using the new statistical technique of meta-analysis to identify programme components which seemed regularly associated with positive effects (e.g. Andrews et al., 1990; Lipsey, 1992). This work began to have an impact in Britain through research reviews (notably McIvor, 1990) and through a series of 'What Works?' conferences inspired largely by probation services searching for meaningful programme content to fulfil the enhanced supervision role envisaged for them by the 1991 Criminal Justice Act.

As a result of these and other developments, I believe it is now possible to be a little less tentative about characteristics of effective programmes which command some empirical support. In a paper of this scope it is not possible to do more than summarise these, and some may prove in further research to be more firmly grounded than others. However, the following list is drawn from the contributions of a number of speakers to a recent conference on 'What works: the challenge for managers', and represents some degree of consensus at least among those contributors. (The items relating to programme content are based largely on McGuire (1993) and Lipsey (1992); the more contextual items draw on

Raynor (1988, 1993a), Roberts (1989), McIvor (1990), Petersilia (1990) and Raynor, Smith and Vanstone (1994), but similar suggestions will be found in the work of a number of authors.) In the present state of our knowledge, it appears likely that the more effective programmes are those which:

1. target high risk offenders who are otherwise likely to continue to offend, rather than low risk offenders who may gain little benefit or be harmed;
2. focus on criminogenic need, i.e. those characteristics or circumstances of offenders which have contributed to their offending;
3. are highly structured, making clear and explicit demands and following a logical sequence determined by their learning goals;
4. use a directive working approach, so that participants know what they are meant to be doing;
5. use broadly cognitive-behavioural methods, to provide opportunities to learn new thinking and behaviour;
6. are located in the community;
7. have programme integrity, i.e. are delivered as intended, with procedures to ensure this;
8. have committed and effective management;
9. have appropriately trained staff who believe they can be effective;
10. have adequate resources for continuity;
11. have integral evaluation and feedback.

One of the most comprehensive attempts in Britain to put these principles into practice is the 'Straight Thinking On Probation' programme (STOP) developed by the Mid Glamorgan Probation Service, based on the 'Reasoning and Rehabilitation' programme devised by Ross and Fabiano in Canada (Ross and Fabiano, 1985). While it is important to avoid premature judgments of effectiveness, the findings available so far from interim evaluation reports are broadly encouraging (Lucas et al., 1992; Raynor and Vanstone, 1994a). Readers interested in the full detail are referred to the original reports, but in outline the evidence so far shows that the programme is effectively targeting high risk offenders comparable to those receiving custodial sentences rather than to those receiving traditional non-custodial sentences; that it is feasible for the majority of offenders to undertake and complete the programme despite its quite high level of demand (70 hours of group sessions in eighteen weeks); that completion rates are not worse than for comparable community sentences such as Day Centre requirements; that staff are on the whole supportive of the programme and deliver it with a high degree of programme integrity; that most participating offenders report that they find it helpful; and that there are indications from attitude-measurement questionnaires and from offenders' own comments of some changes in thinking in line with the aims of the programme.

A recent follow-up of 12-month reconviction rates (Raynor and Vanstone, 1994a) covering 107 probationers sentenced to the STOP programme in the first nine months of the experiment and 548 members of custodial and non-custodial comparison groups compares expected and actual reconviction rates for standard list offences, and shows that those sentenced to STOP were reconvicted less than comparable offenders released from custodial sentences. (The predicted reconviction rate based on the Home Office's 'National Risk of Reconviction Predictor' and the actual reconviction rate were both 44% for those sentenced to STOP, while members of the custodial comparison group had a predicted rate of 43% and an actual rate of 49%.) A further analysis of 59 probationers who successfully completed the STOP programme during the relevant period shows a lower reconviction rate (predicted 42%, actual 35%), and members of this group who did reconvict tended to be reconvicted for less serious offences and to be sentenced less severely for them. Readers interested in the detailed figures, and in reoffending by other comparison groups, should consult the report (Raynor and Vanstone, 1994a) which also registers some reservations: for example, the advantages of the programme are less clear for those who fail, for whatever reason, to complete it as planned, and it is suggested that methods of improving completion rates, including better matching to need, might be explored. However, it is fair to say that the majority of findings from the evaluation so far are consistent with the project's aims, and a further planned follow-up should show whether early signs of a positive impact on behaviour are maintained. It is particularly interesting, for example, that those who completed the programme are much less likely to reconvict for a serious offence (defined as a sexual or violent offence or a burglary); 8% of them reconvicted for such offences compared to 21% of those released from custody (see Raynor and Vanstone, 1994b). There were signs instead of a shift to offences less damaging to other people, such as criminal damage or possession of drugs. One of the programme's aims is to promote victim awareness. The reduced seriousness of offending by those who completed the programme is also reflected in the fact that they are the only group in the study who received no immediate custodial sentences on reconviction.

Encouraging results emerging from this programme and others (Raynor, 1988; Roberts, 1989) suggest the possibility that even in Britain we may be moving beyond the era of 'nothing works' into a new period when the question 'what works?' is at least worth asking. We need, of course, to beware of the opposite illusion that 'everything works'; not only is this unsupported by evidence, but it might encourage a fiscally attractive conclusion that further investment in effectiveness is unnecessary. Moreover, for the purposes of this paper we must confront another question: if there are now signs that effectiveness at least might be achievable, how does this affect past arguments about 'just deserts' and proportionality which were based, at least in part, on the perceived ineffectiveness of penal sanctions in influencing offenders' behaviour?

Programmes like 'Reasoning and Rehabilitation' and STOP have in fact run into considerable criticism based on familiar arguments against the 'treatment' model, and these are reviewed in a recent paper (Raynor and Vanstone, 1994b) which seeks to re-evaluate and re-state the 'non-treatment paradigm' in a manner which does not presuppose ineffectiveness. One recent critic (Neary, 1992), for example, argues that attempts to influence (or in his terms 'manipulate') offenders' thinking are reminiscent of *Clockwork Orange*, and that such programmes serve an ideological function in diverting our attention from the social context of offending. Such criticisms seem to be overstated: we all (including presumably Neary) try to influence people's thinking, and helping people to identify and act on more alternative options in the face of difficult social situations can be seen as a form of empowerment rather than manipulation. However, there are some more substantial concerns which require us to think carefully about the place of such programmes within a 'just deserts' model. These direct our attention particularly to issues of proportionality, negotiability, social goals and alternative models of justice.

The principle of proportionality of sentence to offence requires that sanctions are limited to those justified by the seriousness of the offence: one of the strongest arguments against the 'treatment model' was the child faced with years of custodial 'care' for stealing a packet of sweets. However, a 70-hour programme as a condition of a probation order does not easily accommodate the idea that a person whose offence is less serious than the average for the programme might be required to serve only 30 hours, or a particularly serious offender required to serve 140 hours and do the programme twice. This would have absurd consequences for programme integrity. A less pedantic approach to proportionality is required, which ranks sanctions in broadly comparable levels of seriousness (perhaps five, as in the Hampshire 'matrix': Hampshire Probation Service, 1992) rather than in strict arithmetical equivalence. In any case, it is difficult for strict proportionality to allow for different perceptions by different offenders of the severity of the same sanction. (It is interesting and revealing that the most systematic attempt to do this, namely the Unit Fine system, was quickly abandoned in Britain, presumably because it required sentencers to impose fines of the same subjective severity on the rich as they habitually impose on the poor.) Within such a system of broad comparability a reasonable degree of perceived fairness could probably be preserved, provided that one central principle was retained: no proportional sentence should be artificially inflated simply to make even a possibly effective programme available, since this would conflict both with the empirically-based principle of targeting high-risk offenders and with the moral principle of fairness or treating like cases alike. In particular, the presumed benefits of a programme should not be used to justify an increased sentence as being 'good for' an offender, since even where beneficial effects can be shown to be probable, they cannot be guaranteed for a particular individual. A related problem is posed by offenders who might qualify by reason of 'seriousness' but whose needs are different from those the programme is intended to meet: that is, in the language of Home Office National Standards, they are not 'suitable'. A developed system might require a range of programmes at a comparable level of seriousness to ensure reasonably equal opportunity of access to suitable programmes. Similar questions have repeatedly been raised about women's access to appropriate Community Service projects (Dominelli, 1984).

The question of negotiability is potentially more problematic. Ideas about good practice with offenders which grew out of the critique of the 'treatment model' (see particularly Bottoms and McWilliams, 1979; Raynor, 1993b) rightly emphasised the principle of negotiation with offenders and of informed consent to involvement in any process of supervision, particularly if this might make demands for active participation rather than mere passive availability. A 70-hour programme which emphasises programme integrity and follows a particular sequence of modules and learning opportunities presents problems for fully informed consent to every detail, particularly in the context of preparing a pre-sentence report. However, many programmes present the same problem, perhaps particularly those whose content is unclear and which are devised in the light of available resources when the probationer is already under supervision. A more realistic model of consent would focus at least on clear explanation of and consent to the degree of restriction of liberty entailed (i.e. the time demands of the programme), its purpose, the type of participation expected or required, and the consequences of non-compliance. Intended benefits should not be highlighted in such discussions since consent does not guarantee their delivery. Many educational processes (including compulsory ones like school) are influenced but not determined by learners: the choice is not simply between officer-led and probationer-led agendas, since all programmes contain a mixture of these, but between a coercively imposed or openly negotiated initial agreement, backed up by an honest approach to respective roles and responsibilities. The responsibility for content and quality of programme opportunities rests with providers, and for compliance and participation with probationers. In practice, long and complex programmes often represent a continuing engagement with a probationer's partial, conditional and intermittent commitment to the goal of reducing offending. Bottoms and McWilliams' notion of 'unconditional help' is perhaps too simple for the messy world of practice: what is needed is a continuing sensitivity to issues of consent and participation, combined with a commitment to programme quality. This is likely to be facilitated when programmes are seen and delivered as training rather than as 'treatment'; for a fuller discussion of these problems see Raynor and Vanstone (1994b).

The third problem is posed by the actual goals and purposes of such programmes: that is, their intention to be effective in helping offenders to reduce their offending, and their effectiveness, if this can be demonstrated, in achieving this with some offenders. If they are commended to sentencers and, by implication, to offenders on this basis, do they not infringe a basic principle of justice models to which I drew attention at the start of this paper, namely that sentences should be decided with reference to past behaviour rather than expected future behaviour? Does the re-entry of effectiveness as an issue in the sentencing debate undermine a large part of the logical basis of 'just deserts' thinking? Here common sense suggests one answer (of course we want sentencing to reduce crime as well as being fair) but the strict logic of proportional punishment based only on past offending simply excludes such issues from the argument. This problem exposes, in my view, some important contradictions at the heart of fashionable justice models, and requires some re-thinking about the form and content of the justice which these models offer us.

The current rhetoric of 'just deserts' is a curiously abstract, formal doctrine, divorced from social context and from any vision of social objectives beyond 'law and order', which it does not obviously or easily achieve. In this it differs from its claimed neo-classical origins in eighteenth century social theory: for writers such as Beccaria (1764) or Bentham (1789) proportionality had a social purpose and even a clear consequentialist element. Free and rational citizens, equal before the law, needed to be encouraged to make rational decisions to avoid crime, and this required the penalties (the 'cost' of crime) to be proportional, determinate and knowable in advance. If we divorce the notion of proportionate penalties from social context and social purpose, we are left with little more than punishment (or as Christie, 1982 reminds us, the graduated infliction of harm or pain) without any clear vision of what it is trying to achieve. In particular, once we have deprived the offender of liberty or time, the pure justice model gives us no very clear idea about how to use it (again, it may guide us on the size of the package but not on its content). The appeal of formal justice models may lie partly in their rejection of 'modernity' and their capacity for easy linkage to conservative appeals for the restoration of often imaginary traditional values and ways of life; however, their origins lie in early modern society rather than in pre-modern societies, and while they properly alert us to the dangers of positivist social engineering through uncontrolled 'treatment', they offer no new vision of desirable social goals or new bases of social order and harmony. In turning against the excesses of modernity they may even help to invite the post-modern social fragmentation. One of the most telling criticisms of the 1991 Criminal Justice Act and its preparatory White and Green Papers was that they seemed content to attribute crime to individual wickedness and were largely silent on social causes or context. Perhaps this is best understood as a self-denying ordinance necessarily adopted by pragmatic Home Office reformers under a Prime Minister who believed there was 'no such thing as society'; however, the resulting version of 'just deserts' is decontextualised and not rooted in a wider social vision or a network of supporting social policies. When the content of 'justice' is so thinly reasoned and weakly supported, it easily collapses into 'punishment', and the penal policy agenda is rendered vulnerable to political hi-jacking by the Right. The difficulty of incorporating consequentialist notions like effectiveness within such a 'just deserts' model seems more a consequence of the narrowness and abstract nature of the model than of the inadmissibility of effectiveness. So if we want to pursue both justice and crime reduction, and if we want effectiveness without the excesses of coercive treatment or disproportionate intervention, by what standards of justice or fairness should our efforts at effectiveness be judged?

In fact the criminological literature is not short of alternative visions of justice which are more rooted in actual social practices and human needs. Christie (1977) draws his models largely from traditional and rural societies, and sees crime as a conflict or dispute which needs to be managed by a collective process of discussion and negotiation which both clarifies social norms and reinforces social bonds: an important element is the restoration of the offender to full membership of the community once appropriate reparation, whether practical or symbolic, has been made. (This is, of course, the proper meaning of 'rehabilitation': the restoration or recovery of moral status as a member of a community, rather than simply the cessation of offending.) In a more modern-seeming vein, the 'republican' criminologists (Braithwaite, 1989; Braithwaite and Pettit, 1990) argue that criminal justice policy should contribute to the attainment of social policy goals which both respect individual rights and contribute to the common good: crime, they suggest, is controlled by 'reintegrative shaming', which draws on shared values both to communicate disapproval of offending and to offer the offender a route back to normal social status and esteem when the offence is accepted as blameworthy and regretted or repaired. Effective penal sanctions, they argue, are reintegrative in aim and effect, and they point to Japan (which alone among industrialised countries has experienced a long-term decline in crime) as an example of a modern society which relies little on overt punishment of offenders, but very heavily on communication of disapproval and on encouragement to admit guilt and promise improvement. No doubt there are cultural contexts and characteristics in Japanese society which are not readily transferable; however, the principle that penal sanctions should aim at reintegrative effects seems both persuasive and widely applicable. Such ideas also offer a social rationale for offence resolution by mediated agreements and symbolic or practical reparation, as advocated by Wright (1982, 1991) and practised in a number of innovative projects (Marshall and Merry, 1990; Warner, 1992). There are also implications for community sentences: probation itself can be seen as reintegrative, offering offenders an opportunity to take responsibility for offending and to make a practical contribution to the reduction of future offending.

Within such organic models of justice which see penal policy as a component of social policy and a contributor to the cohesion of social life, the pursuit of effectiveness takes a natural place as an integral goal of criminal justice alongside other goals such as fairness, economy, due process and compatibility with social justice. What such models offer is a recognition of offenders as members of communities, and as having much in common with other members: offending is not their only, nor their most important characteristic. Control theories (Hirschi, 1969) also stress the importance of social bonds in restraining us from crime. Such approaches to justice aim at reintegration and inclusion rather than at segregation and stigmatisation. I am indebted to Sue Warner for drawing my attention to the writings of the Lebanese poet Kahlil Gibran on crime and justice (Warner, 1993; Gibran, 1991): here he offers another inclusive perspective:

> Oftentimes I have heard you speak of one who commits a wrong as though he were not one of you, but a stranger unto you and an intruder upon your world.
>
> But I say that even as the holy and righteous cannot rise beyond the highest which is in each one of you,
>
> So the wicked and the weak cannot fall lower than the lowest which is in you also.

Effective programmes have their place within a model of organic justice which aims at compatibility with social justice and communal solidarity. The conceptual problems arise mainly when 'justice' becomes a formal and abstract notion divorced from real human purposes and interests. Effective rehabilitation, if it can be achieved, serves the ends of justice by offering one route to the reintegration of some of our fellow citizens who are in trouble with the law; it also offers an alternative to non-integrative and stigmatising punishments which achieve little change in attitudes or behaviour. The probation service needs to debate and develop its own models of justice and its own conception of its contribution to justice if it is not to be blown off course by the temporary political preoccupations of Ministers. It could then develop a distinctive reforming contribution to a penal policy which is once again drifting towards a sterile preoccupation with ineffective punishment, while parts of our cities drift closer to the post-modern nightmare and the war of all against all.

Eight
Helping offenders as an element in justice

Roy Bailey

Probation practice is becoming standardised, largely on the basis of the perceptions of Home Office ministers, Probation Service managers and Probation practitioners about the protection of the public and the administration of justice. The Government has adopted the notion of punishment in the community as the norm by which to evaluate the contribution made by the Probation Service to the criminal justice system. *National Standards for the Supervision of Offenders in the Community* were first published by Home Office in 1992, but by 1994 ministers were urging that they should be revised, not only to make them crisper and clearer but more ostensibly punitive.

During a decade of government rhetoric directed toward 'more condemnation; less understanding' and punishment instead of rehabilitation, Ministers appeared to be unaware of the subtler exhortation to hate the sin but love the fellow sinner. Nonetheless, the traditional concept of Probation as enshrined in the Probation Rules since 1907 imposed upon probation officers a duty to 'advise assist, and befriend' the people under their supervision. This statutory injunction has not been rescinded but, politically at least, it now appears to occupy an incidental rather than a central place in official thinking, with Probation being presented to the courts as a community sentence characterised by restriction of liberty and the imposition of sanctions.

Although, with regard to many of the defendants appearing before the courts, a monetary penalty or some form of restriction of liberty may be perceived as necessary in the pursuit of justice, the protection of the public in the longer term by the reduction of recidivism is more often achieved by providing the offender with appropriate help, encouragement and supervision than by increasing the punitive sanctions.

During 1990-1992, the elements comprising effective 'help, encouragement and supervision' were among matters considered by the writer in an investigation of what young adult serious offenders aged 16-24 and their supervising probation officers had to say about their experience of the Probation supervisory process, with particular reference to their:

- motivation for entering into the supervisory relationship;
- expectations about what supervision would mean for them;
- understanding of help, and of how it might be provided;
- perception of the other person in the working relationship;
- experience of the ways in which Probation supervision actually works;
- views as to outcome.

A structured interview of about 50 minutes duration, using an open-ended questionnaire, gave each respondent the opportunity to say whatever they wished about an issue without being led toward preconceived answers. Interviews were conducted with each young adult participant, and separately with the supervising probation officer, using virtually the same questionnaire. The interviews were tape recorded, and subsequently transcribed verbatim, on the understanding that the transcripts would be made anonymous without changing significance. After transcription the tapes were wiped.

Thirty-nine 'pairs' (78 persons) were interviewed in five Probation areas in the UK. The interviews occupied about 75 hours and the transcripts ran to some 140,000 words.

The data obtained from this project provide insights into many aspects of Probation practice in 1990-1992, but this paper deals simply with the views and opinions expressed by the young adults about the meaning for them of the kinds of help they received from probation officers, and their perceptions of the operation of justice through experience of Probation supervision.

A review of the interview transcripts revealed that while the sanctions inherent in the Probation Order usually appeared to ensure the relationship between a young adult serious offender and his or her supervisor, it was the *quality of the relationship* which determined the dynamics and interactions – for good or for ill – within it. After quite a brief period on Probation, most (but not all) of the young adult respondents indicated that they were content to continue working in partnership with 'their' probation officer because, as they saw it, they enjoyed the relationship and they could 'see something in it' for them. For example:

> LILY: Without Probation, well, I'd have gone down the hill. I'd still be on drugs. I'd still be committing offences. It's not just the Probation, of course. If it had been somebody I don't like I suppose I'd have come to see him, but I'd still be committing offences. It's only because I feel close to Phil, and he's so good to me. In the time that it took him to do the Social Enquiry Report, I realised that he was the first person I could really open up to about my home, job worries, being in Care, people that I mixed with, drug abuse and things like that. I trusted him, which is really unusual for me: I don't trust anyone. He's always got time for me. If I do things right, he'll say 'well done'. I need praise if I do something right; if I've done it right one week I can do it again. And if I do, or think about doing something wrong, Phil doesn't shout at me, but we sit down and discuss it sensibly. He gives me the support I need.

This young woman exemplifies the great majority of the young adult participants in the study who felt the need to be helped to change. Few of them pro-actively chose to be serious offenders; for almost all, their offences were a re-active response to individual circumstances, often shaped by the peer-group culture of their neighbourhood. Offending behaviour made some sense to them in their situation as they perceived it, but these young adults said that they would prefer to keep out of trouble, to 'act normal' and to achieve an established life-style – usually identified as 'a place of their own' with a partner, and a reasonably well-paid job.

For some, however, that was easier said than done, for example:

> MAX: One part of me wanted to make a go of it. Probation is intended to help you to keep out of trouble, and part of me wanted that, but at the back of my head I knew that I was fooling myself and that I'd be getting into trouble again.

Speaking about his attempts to work with Max, his probation officer said:

> Max was a high risk, status-seeking offender, a 'car addict', with a lot of problems at home. I knew all the negatives, so had no great hopes, but I wanted to work with him positively. Max's family history has been difficult and violent. Father deserted Max and his mother after quite a lot of violence on her and the four young children. Mother suffered from mental illness and as Max and his older brother moved into their teens she found it more difficult to cope and tended to reject them...He was the victim of a serious paramilitary beating, and was then living around various addresses...young people who've grown up in that environment, having had a very poor school and no real way forward in life, so that joy-riding and stealing cars offers excitement and a sort of achievement and a way of getting money...Contact with me was good for 3 or 4 weeks, then it was lost. He returned to his environment and was immediately drawn back into his old circle. I couldn't convince him (inaudible)...But it wasn't just environment, the urge was in him...I'm still in contact with Max, and one day he may himself want to do something about his life. It has to come from him, I can't force him.

Perhaps surprisingly, Max was the only one of the 39 young adult respondents to express such a complete inability to change, but there were others – particularly among those faced with apparently intractable material problems – who wanted to keep out of trouble but despaired of doing so. For example:-

> PETE:...he put me on this course, and I don't like it; It's not helpful at all...it never changes anything. You get in there and they talk about it, talk and talk, but it doesn't seem to come out to anything...I've no money at all, and I can't walk round the streets like that so sometimes I steal it. I don't want to, and I don't like it, and feel afraid that I'd be caught, but what else can I do? That course should deal with things like that, but they just talk and don't seem to understand what it's really like.

His probation officer, Frank, said:

> He was really sunk by having two old motoring charges, on which he got really heavy fines. It was £600 which is,

> on DSS Benefit, virtually a prison sentence ... Money is a problem. He's at home with his parents, but his relationship with his father is not very good. Unless he gets another job, or Benefit is restored, financially he's in difficulty. When clients are vulnerable, and there's no immediate solution to their problems, there's nothing much a course can do except identify the options.

At the other end of the spectrum, however, was Cliff:

> You see, I've been in Care most of my life, for 14 years, and I'm dead against social workers; they interfere with your life, and I thought Probation would be just another social worker, but I now know that probation officers are there to help you, to give you help if you ask for it. On Probation I've been doing some good things. The Project is brilliant – it's fun, but it's about changing as well. Probation is to help me change my life-style, to stop my criminal way of thinking. I get understanding from Dora (his probation officer). She understands any problems I have. My Dad died a year and a half ago and me and Mum wasn't getting on at all well and Dora gave me advice. She helped me to change. And I did have a bad drug and drink problem...If I'd come out of prison and Mum had been the same as she was before and I hadn't got my new girlfriend I'd have gone back on the drugs and – and I wouldn't have cared, nothing to lose. But now I've got some good things and I want to keep them. All the best things have happened since Dora.

Cliff's phrase 'nothing to lose' recurred in other interviews and it points to the sterility of the sort of punishment in which offenders with 'nothing to lose' are forced to lose what little they have – or to gain status by increasingly criminal or deviant means. All too often the notion of punishment entails loss of money, loss of liberty, loss of available options and – essentially – loss of self-esteem.

English law has explicitly rejected the principle of *lex talionis* – an eye for an eye, etc. – but justice may sometimes appear to require some sort of quid pro quo by which the offender suffers personal discomfort, pain or loss as a form of expiation for the suffering he or she caused to others. These are likely to be rare and exceptional cases, and research has indicated that, in the general run of cases, victims are more likely to favour restitution, compensation, reparation and explanation – even, perhaps, apology.

For their part, the young adults made it clear that humiliation – whether deliberate or unintentional – tends to drive persistent offenders deeper into their a-social or anti-social behaviour, and is associated with an unsuccessful outcome. Conversely, where they were able to experience a practitioner's sustained practical interest and concern, and were treated as persons deserving respect, alongside a rigorous challenge to their offending behaviour, there was at the least a basis for a successful outcome.

Custody, as a form of punishment, was perceived as perhaps 'deserved' but as a sort of dead end, devoid of any real hope of re-integration with family or community. For example:

> BARRY: I knew that if I'd got custody again I'd come out and do the same things again. I wanted to do better than that, make a fresh start.

> SEAN: In gaol all they have to do is keep you safe and contained. That's all gaol's for. There's no real rehabilitation and all that – it just doesn't happen ... Whenever I came out of gaol I was just on the streets on my own; nobody you can talk to or discuss things with. You were back to square one.

> TED: Prison's alright; it's what you make it really, but it's no answer.

Somewhat unexpectedly, almost all the young adult serious offenders perceived their present probation officer as a significant source of help. They were able to identify some of the ways in which the professional skills and personality of 'their' probation officer were seen as specifically helpful, and said, for example:

> LUKE: If ever I start to feel like I know I shouldn't do, I can go in and talk to her, and I have done. I feel much better when I'm talking to her because she'll sit there and listen.

> FRED: He's always the same – he's always willing to listen. He listens before he tells you what he thinks. He can tell you what he thinks, though, if you do something silly, but he does it in a nice way.

ROSS: Probation? Well, it's sort of, you know, you get the chance to, sort of, have somebody talking. It's hard to explain...Somebody to get me talking. It was to have a friend, in a sort of a way, like having a friend to turn to...Tracey's very helpful to me, you know, understanding. She's easy to talk to...Somebody to talk to when things are going wrong – you need someone. Some people have no one. Things go wrong and they're on the streets with nobody. Most people have nobody at all when things get on top (inaudible). Mostly people don't really care...Tracey's interested in you and you can talk to her.

BOB: If there's any problems I tell her, and she sorts it out for me. She tells me things, and I listen, and then I understand.

SEAN: A probation officer isn't just an ordinary fellow. He's someone with a bit of authority, and he's with you and not against you. If he asks a question, it's to help you – not like the peelers who only ask you something so's they can charge you.

CLIFF: With Dora, I'm learning a lot more about myself really, and what I'm capable of doing.

BARRY: Helen helps me with the DSS. When there are problems I don't have a clue what to say to them, but she helps me to deal with it.

IVY: At first I found it difficult to talk with Pauline about private things. Now I trust her and I'm beginning to talk with her about things I'd never talk about with anyone else...some awful things...Then I feel better because I've got things out of my system.

ALAN: What am I learning from being on Probation? Well, she's helping me to become independent, giving me confidence to speak out...It's up to me whether I stay out of trouble. In 3 years time I hope to have my own flat, be in work, and be independent.

The qualities to which the young adults referred in these few examples suggest that probation officers may be found helpful to people under their supervision by acting, for example:

- as a safety valve or sounding board;
- as someone who listens;
- as someone to talk with;
- in giving advice and guidance;
- as a supportive authority-figure;
- in helping to develop insight and understanding;
- as representative and advocate;
- by exploring issues of dependency and responsibility.

The 1990s, however, have seen a tendency in the Probation Service toward a fragmentation of the supervision process into a number of discrete specialisms. This sort of development is intended to enable individual practitioners to study, and to offer to clients, professional skills which they might not otherwise be able to acquire or to practice at any depth. This is wholly admirable, but a risk for clients can emerge when virtually every practitioner is required to become a specialist, leaving no one with responsibility for relating to the 'whole client'. For this reason it is essential to retain the notion of the 'key worker' – i.e. a general practitioner – who sticks with a client and knows that client well, building up a relationship of trust. 'Key working' does not imply that the client is denied access to specialist officers or groups, but it does mean that the primary care and supervision of that client lies in the hands of one practitioner, not in a bewildering collection of them. Moreover, each client is able to develop a personal relationship with someone who values that client as an individual, not merely as a member of a group – a group which may be adopting a pre-defined programme into which its members have to be slotted, and with which they are expected to comply.

The *National Standards for the Supervision of Offenders in the Community* (1992) stated that effective Probation supervision 'should generally entail establishing a professional relationship in which to advise, assist and befriend the offender'. This is true, yet the moves of the present government to cut costs and to achieve rapid results – or, at least, a rapid turnover – in the fields of medicine and education suggest that the Treasury might regard the development and constructive use of a good working relationship between a probation officer and an offender as altogether too leisurely and expensive by comparison with the application of timed procedures such as a rigorous course of instruction provided for people under supervision who are compelled to attend or to face the sanctions.

There is, of course, nothing wrong with a carefully devised 'course of instruction' so long as it is designed to be relevant to the needs of the course members themselves and so long as it is an adjunct, not an alternative, to a good working relationship between client and supervisor. There was no doubt whatsoever in the minds of most of the participants in this study about the importance of that relationship as a factor in a successful outcome to supervision. More to the point, the young adult clients did not merely generalise; many of them could identify and describe components of a good working relationship, with particular emphasis upon trust and integrity. Their statements included comments such as:

TREVOR:...then I had Richard Peebles – he was a bit stuck up. When you were talking to him, he'd always got his nose stuck in a book. I felt he never had enough time to try and talk. When he *was* talking, he was doing his work as well and didn't seem to be taking any notice of me...I wouldn't confide in him – Richard wasn't giving me any of his time, so I wouldn't give him mine.

TED: Probation officers aren't just an odd bunch of people to do with the police – they're there to help you. They're interested in you. They're actually concerned about you.

TOM: He's like a dad to me, the way he talks. Nobody's ever talked to me like the way he has. He talks straight to me. He's not like *my* dad, not at all, but he's like a dad.

SEAN: Laurie's straight. He talks to you and you can trust him.

STEVE: Probation doesn't sit and laugh at you if you act stupid. They take you seriously and then you begin to take yourself seriously .. they respect you. I've learned to respect myself and now I can respect others. In fact, you've got to respect others if you want them to respect you.

TIM: Phil treats me like an adult with a mind of my own.

SID: In my personal opinion Harold is a very good probation officer because he has helped me to stay out of trouble. He thinks that I am a person who can make something of my life.

LILY: Phil is really good. He always listens and has time for me. He thinks that I am making a go of things and pulling myself together.

They identified seven of the elements which, in their opinion, underpinned the sort of working relationship in which they might feel it worth their while to listen to their practitioner and perhaps to be influenced by him or her. It is not at all surprising that these constituents of a 'good relationship' were:

1. time and attention;
2. interest and concern;
3. respect and courtesy;
4. purposefulness, i.e, objectives that the client can share;
5. mutual recognition of positive personal features;
6. frankness and plain speaking;
7. trust.

The first six elements point to relatively explicit concepts, but the last in the list is more complex. It is also the essential dynamic at the heart of a good working relationship. In common usage it is taken to mean that when a person A 'trusts' person B, person A believes that person B will do nothing which would harm person A; that is, person B will use his or her strength, knowledge or skill in the best interests of person A – or, at any rate, will do so as far as is practicable. The term is also taken to mean that person B will not intentionally deceive person A.

The young adults expressed their views very clearly. For example:

ALAN: It's taken me time to trust her. Giving somebody trust is hard, and now she's got my trust and I can open up to her.

PETE: If I didn't trust him I wouldn't bother with him and I wouldn't come to see him. There wouldn't be any point, would there? If you don't like him or trust him, what use would he be to you?

TREV: I was in Care most of my life, in various Children's Homes, and when I left Care I didn't have much to fall back on...and at least on Probation I'd have someone to talk to. It's good to know that someone's there...When Penny's not here, when she's down on Court duty, I don't talk to anyone else...I don't want to tell things to strangers.

The element of trust can be the most difficult to transfer from an individual practitioner to others in the Service, though it is not impossible. Much depends on the nature and intimacy of the business to be transacted, and there is no good reason to expect a client to transfer his or her hard-won trust to another practitioner at the outset of a new relationship, or to another officer who is running a particular project, or simply because another officer is on office-duty. Yet that trust must be earned if supervision is to be something more meaningful and effective than simply going through the motions.

It is arguable that as human beings grow towards social maturity they must, as a practical necessity, learn how to discern between people whom they can trust and those who should not be trusted. This process is, of course, complicated by the fact that different people may properly be trusted for different purposes; it is, perhaps, rarely that one person can trust another person absolutely.

The statements made by several of the young adults suggested that in their lives they had had little experience of trusting or being trusted – and yet it was something they valued highly. They valued the trust which they believed was reposed in them by their probation officers, and they recognised that their own trust in their practitioner was an essential element in his or her ability to help them to 'keep out of trouble' and to begin to fulfil their own potential.

People familiar with the normal run of defendants appearing in the courts cannot fail to be aware of the adverse personal circumstances experienced by many of those who offend repeatedly and sometimes seriously. Those factors include homelessness or instability in housing; destitution or very low income; family trauma or breakdown; unemployment; heavy debt; educational disadvantage and failure; and poor physical or mental health.

Of the 39 young adult serious offenders in this study, 16 could be assessed as experiencing 3 or more of these factors (including six with 4 factors and two with 6 factors).

In more detail, it appeared that 70% were unemployed; 64% had experience of severe family problems, including parental loss or neglect; 36% were sporadically homeless, with unsettled accommodation; and over 20% were educationally disadvantaged. Poverty, sometimes accompanied by heavy debt (often in the form of accumulated fines and compensation), was noted in respect of about 25%, while poor physical or mental health afflicted 18%.

The relationship between social deprivation and disadvantage and social justice is a matter for philosophers and economists, but probation officers are all too familiar with a clientele for whom there is little comfort in the current practice of 'social justice'.

In his Annual Report for 1992-1993, the Chief Probation Officer for Devon wrote:

> For many with whom the Service works in such a committed way, the social context is not supportive. The majority are relatively young. They are on the threshold of hope for their future. To many of them that future can look bleak indeed. Employment prospects remain poor and restrictions on income support, especially for 16 and 17 year olds without work or access to an illusory training place, can mean impoverishment or worse. It is too easy for them to feel abandoned by the adult world and those in authority who ought to be giving them all the encouragement possible. Instead they can come to experience the world as lacking in care and reflect that back as lack of care or regard for other people and their property.

Justice for the victims of crime, as well as more abstractly for the wider community, sometimes entails help for the offender so that he or she can make reparation or restitution. Central to this must be the provision of individualised help so that offenders can begin to re-evaluate for themselves the contribution which they might make to the community and to develop their own potential constructively.

As evidenced in my research, by far the greatest part of Probation work is probably of the traditional type in which practitioners concern themselves with helping clients to manage their personal difficulties in ways that take into account not only the offenders own well being but also the maintenance of the existing social order. Is this the best they can achieve? These young offenders' responses also point to latent talents present in many young people under the supervision of probation officers. This has encouraged some practitioners to attempt a rather distinctive approach, either alongside the traditional ways of working or as an alternative. Instead of helping disadvantaged people simply to 'learn to live with' and thereby find ways of coping with an adverse environment which seems conducive to re-offending, the practitioners help them to discover how they – probably in association with others – might attempt to change for the better some of the elements in that *environment,* rather than solely trying to change *themselves.* Such an approach can offer the possibility of a two fold benefit to the community – an improvement for everyone in the general quality of life and the reduction of offending by the re-integration of the former offenders.

Nine
Justice through inequality? The Probation Service and women offenders

Anne Worrall

> To accept that 'justice' and 'equality' are to be achieved by parity of treatment is to collude in the acceptance of the inequalities which co-exist with such 'equal treatment'. To assume that justice for women means treating women like men is to ignore the very different existences which distinguish the lives of women from the lives of men of similar social status (Eaton, 1986, p.11).

> Effective action to prevent discrimination requires significantly more than a willingness to accept all offenders equally or to invest an equal amount of time and effort in different cases. The origin, nature and extent of differences in circumstances and need must be properly understood and actively addressed (Home Office, 1992b, p.32).

It is a salutary reflection that if men committed the same amount of crime as women, the whole criminal justice system would collapse overnight – and most criminologists would be out of work. The crime prevention industry would be bankrupted; house and car insurance premiums would plummet. Tabloid newspaper circulation figures would drop through the floor, 'Crimewatch UK' would be off the air and crime writers would be reclassified as historical novelists. But the world would be a different place in other ways as well. The home would be safe, little girls (and boys) would be safe, old women (and men) would be safe, even multi-national corporations would be safe! Crime would be at a level that any civilised society ought to be able to tolerate.

The inescapable fact is that female crime, as a social phenomenon, is no threat to society. That is not to argue that female crime is not 'real' crime, nor to deny that a handful of individual female criminals are dangerous or greedy or both. Rather it is to make the point (see Carlen, 1990), that if all women's prisons (with the exception of one wing of a closed establishment) were shut down today, it is quite possible that the person on the Clapham omnibus would never notice.

Why, then, do we still find it necessary to imprison little girls of fifteen and teenage mothers with their babies? How have we reached the 1990s without preventing a judge sending a nineteen year old black first offender called Tracey Scott to prison with her ten week old baby saying:

> Would it be right to let young women know that one way of possibly or probably avoiding custody would be to deliberately become pregnant between the time they have been detected committing a crime and the time they were sentenced? One of the ways of discouraging them is to let them know that some others have been dealt with in an unpleasant way? (Judge Pickles, quoted in *The Independent*, 3 January 1990)

The reason, of course, is that it is not women's criminality that is so frightening – it is their *sexuality* and especially their *black sexuality*. When it comes to dispensing justice to women, crime becomes inextricably entwined with race and sexuality. As the case of Tracey Scott illustrates, courts come perilously close to criminalising female sexuality but in so doing, they are merely reflecting wider fears, fuelled by media hyperbole, that an underclass of undeserving, poor (and frequently black) women is set to subvert the peaceful, industrious and law-abiding British (white English?) way of life [1].

Women may commit very little crime *but we can hold them responsible for a great deal of it*. As victims of rape and domestic violence, they ask for it. As partners of child sexual abusers, they collude with it. As lone mothers (or as working mothers) they produce and rear the next generation of its perpetrators. Even when they try to behave responsibly by providing as nurturing a home environment as their straitened circumstances allow, they are blamed for it. As one police superintendent on the Meadowell estate observed after the 1991 riots, 'The women take responsibility and the men are freed up to do what they like' (Campbell, 1993, p.204).

These, then, are the very different existences which distinguish the lives of women trapped in the poverty *created* by a state which then dares to blame them, not for their own offending or offensive behaviour, but for that of the absent or delinquent (or both) men in their lives. What should astound us is not that some women in these circumstances resort to crime themselves, but that so many do not!

The purpose of this chapter is to demonstrate the impossibility of separating criminal justice from social justice when attempting to understand and deal with women who commit crimes. The achievements of the Probation Service in relation to many women offenders will be acknowledged but the continuing problem of women's imprisonment will be identified as requiring a fundamental change in the Service's attitude, both to its own abilities and to its relationship with sentencers.

THE DILEMMAS OF VISIBILITY

The 1980s might well be viewed in the world of criminology as the decade when female crime was rendered visible. It is no longer possible to introduce a book or article on women and crime by saying that it is a contribution to a neglected area of criminology. Over the past decade, interest in the subject has increased exponentially and there is now a well established theoretical literature which challenges the conventional wisdom that female criminals are peculiar and of only marginal interest. Pioneering work by Carol Smart (1976) caught the imagination of an increasing number of women students on criminology courses and CQSW probation options. Collaboration between women criminologists, probation officers and ex-prisoner campaigning groups ensured that the treatment of women offenders was placed on conference and training course agendas. Research projects burgeoned. Anecdotal evidence matured into respectable data (despite the scepticism of some established criminologists – see, for example, Nigel Walker, 1981) and the tide of accusations of sexual discrimination in the criminal justice system became unstoppable. Women offenders, though few in number, were being judged as doubly deviant – as breakers of gender norms as well as of criminal law. They were being sentenced more for the type of women they appeared to be than for the seriousness or otherwise of the crime they had committed. Rendered invisible and mute, they were being written out of the scripts of their own lives by experts in medical and social regulation who claimed to know more about them than they could ever know about themselves (Worrall, 1990).

Sadly, there is now a danger that the study of women and crime has found itself in something of a cul-de-sac. It has exposed itself to criticism by sometimes seeming to adopt an uncritical and misunderstood feminist hegemony which says that women criminals are always treated more badly than men criminals. (For example of the way the Home Office has seized on such simplistic arguments to discuss any accusation of discrimination against female offenders, see Hedderman and Hough, 1994). Apart from the fact that *certain* women are treated leniently by courts, it is also fairly obvious that men criminals do not get such a wonderful deal from the system either. Crude calls for *equality* may simply result (and, some would say, *have* simply resulted) in women being sent 'in their droves to dirty, violent and overcrowded prisons for long periods of time' (Smart, 1990). On the other hand, a line of argument which has been termed the `libertarian tendency' (Carlen, 1992) proposes that female law- breaking should not be regarded as problematic but rather as women's rational response to intolerable conditions of existence. Consequently, any attempt at influencing criminal justice policy or intervening in the lives of women offenders with a view to reducing their offending is seen to smack of 'social engineering'.

Neither perspective has been helpful in offering guidance to probation officers who, whilst trying to avoid viewing women criminals as merely the passive victims of an irredeemably discriminatory system, nevertheless believe that women must be helped to stop offending because it is women themselves who suffer most from their crime.

WHERE HAVE ALL THE FEMALE OFFENDERS GONE?

As Harris (1992, p.98) says, 'part of the problem is that it is unclear what the "better treatment of women" actually means.' In the early 1980s, the predominant concern amongst those probation officers willing to cast a critical eye over their work with women offenders was that *too many were being placed on probation.*

Whilst women represented between 15 and 17% of known offenders, 33% of probation orders were on women. In absolute numbers, that was nearly 12,000 in 1981, compared with 24,000 men (Home Office, 1993e). And far too many of those (36% compared with 17% of men) were first offenders. There was certainly some concern about the numbers of women sent to prison (about 1,300) but there was an assumption (informed by theories of labelling and deviancy amplification) that diverting women from probation would automatically reduce the numbers in prison. The theory worked for juvenile crime in the 1980s but it failed spectacularly for women (although it has to be said that juvenile justice workers demonstrated a much greater commitment to keeping young people out of custody, even at the risk of incurring magistrates' wrath, than probation officers have ever done to keeping women out of prison).

By 1992, the numbers of women on probation had fallen to 7,300 (a mere 18% of all orders) but numbers in prison had risen to 1,600. Additionally, numbers of women on community service orders rose from 1,600 in 1981 (of whom 18% were first offenders) to 2,600 in 1992 (of whom 30% were first offenders). These last figures dealt a blow to another piece of the received wisdom of the 1980s – that increased use of community service for women would help to empty women's prisons. What we now have to face is that the size of the female prison population appears to be largely uninfluenced by changes in the numbers of women serving non-custodial supervisory sentences. To put it crudely, sentencers continue to send a certain number of women to prison despite there being more than enough vacancies for them on probation and community service orders. Those women are disproportionately black, poor and/or first time offenders.[2] A high proportion of black women in prison are there for drugs-related offences but that by no means accounts for the total race discrepancy. In any case, female foreign prisoners suffer particular privations in the British penal system and are rightly considered a proper concern for the Probation Service (Abernethy and Hammond, 1992).

WHATEVER HAPPENED TO WOOLF AND THE CRIMINAL JUSTICE ACT 1991?

An optimistic view of the Criminal Justice Act 1991 was that the principle of 'just deserts', on which the Act was based, would result in a fairer deal for women criminals. If sentencing was to depend predominantly on the seriousness of the current offence, the implication *should* have been that fewer women would go to prison for relatively minor offences, however frequently committed. It did not automatically follow that women who commit serious offences would be given the chance of 'high tariff' community disposals –probation centres and community service. Nevertheless, it did enable such sentences to be argued for on the basis of a different logic – namely, that refusal to give such opportunities amounted to discrimination as defined in Section 95(1)(b).

In creating the Youth Court, the Act also opened up the possibility of more flexible treatment for 17 year old young women (and young men). Given the government's earlier courageous proposal to abolish imprisonment for young women under 18 years (Home Office, 1990a), ironically thwarted by appeal to equal opportunities discourse, it is not unreasonable to think that someone, somewhere, at some time, was hoping that courts would send fewer women – and certainly fewer young women – to prison.

Although, as several writers have pointed out, Lord Justice Woolf did not consider women's prisons in his Report on the 1990 Prison Disturbances (1991), the implications of his principles for women's prisons have been discussed creatively (NACRO, 1991; Player, 1994). In particular, one interpretation of the concept of 'community prisons' has been a proposal for a large number of locally based houses, 'set aside for the purpose' where women would reside (possibly with their children), making use of community facilities and resources to provide their daily regime (NACRO, 1991). One wonders how this would have differed from a hostel, but if it had resulted in the demise of most women's prisons as we know them, the name would probably have been a small price to pay.

But all this is now in the past. The 1993 Criminal Justice Act restores to courts the right to take previous convictions into account indiscriminately. (As we know, the 1991 Act never removed the right absolutely – it just made courts think twice before doing so). The so-called 'flexibility' of the Youth Court appears to have resulted in 16 year olds being treated routinely as adults, rather than 17 year olds being treated routinely as juveniles. Given the discriminatory nature of the guidelines for assessing maturity and stage of development, this is perhaps not surprising. But the impact may prove to be particularly great on young women, who tend to be regarded as 'more mature' than young men of comparable age. And it seems likely that a 16 or 17 year old mother will be regarded, by definition, as an adult. Whilst the resulting pressure on accommodation may lead to an expansion of the female prison estate, it now seems unlikely that the political climate is right for experiments such as hostel-prisons.

WHO IS TO BLAME?

The Probation Service has tended to blame the communication skills of its officers for failing to keep women out of prison. The primary fault has been thought to reside in discriminatory language in Social Inquiry and Pre-Sentence Reports. Rigorous gatekeeping exercises have exorcised from reports 'irrelevant' information and the (mis)representation of women in ways which are perceived to reinforce stereotypical gender and racial expectations. The process seems to have been very successful in persuading courts that (white?) women who commit relatively minor crimes are not necessarily doing so as a 'cry for help', nor do they necessarily need someone to talk to about their problems – no more so than any law-abiding woman, that is! But the message that the Probation Service can offer something to women who, for whatever reason, are deemed to be at risk of losing their liberty, is not being heard.

Her Majesty's Inspectorate of Probation (1991) and the Association of Chief Officers of Probation (1993) seem to think that what is needed is the right strategic policy, marketed in the right way. *If only* our service delivery was truly informed by anti-discriminatory practice, *if only* our quality assurance procedures were really effective, *then* we would be able to persuade sentencers that women offenders are *safe in our hands*. There is an assumption that the Service can 'get it right' and that, once it has put its own house in order, courts will not fail to be convinced about what is on offer.

But the problem is both more complex and more simple than this. It is more complex because, whilst overt use of discriminatory sex-role stereotyping is no longer common-place in reports, there is still a belief that the concept of 'tariff' is gender-neutral and impacts equally on men and women. In other words, the belief that men and women are 'at risk' of custody at the same stage of their criminal careers and for the same type and seriousness of offence is tenacious. Consequently, there remains considerable confusion about the kind of probation centre and community service provision which is most appropriate for women (Dunkley, 1992). One report writer may refer a woman because her life-style places her 'at risk' of custody whilst another report writer may refuse to refer the same woman on grounds of 'net- widening' because her offence is insufficiently serious to warrant custody. And who is to judge which of the two is behaving in a more discriminatory fashion? There now seems to be some evidence (Denney, 1992) to suggest that report writers who, for the best of anti-discriminatory reasons, argue that black women do not need to be placed on probation, are contributing to the likelihood of a custodial sentence, regardless of the seriousness of the offence. There is a danger that a blinkered adherence to consistency and equality discourages the creative thinking and intellectual dexterity necessary to tackle these conundrums and, perhaps more crucially, the maturity and wisdom to live with the uncertainty they generate.

On the other hand, the problem may be much simpler than this. True, the service is far from perfect. It is certainly not being suggested here that probation officers should stop worrying about what they write in reports or that they should stop deliberating about what constitutes appropriate provision for women at probation centres, in hostels or on community service orders. But humility and sanity demand an acknowledgement that there is a limit to the influence that such introspection will have. If the events of 1993 teach us anything, it is that all the money and time invested in training the Probation Service for the challenges of the new world of the 1991 Criminal Justice Act count for nothing when votes are at stake. When it comes to getting 'back to basics' the most vulnerable groups in society will always be sacrificed – and women offenders are amongst those groups.

The communication of a message depends on both a sender and a receiver. No matter how sophisticated the sender believes the message to be, it will be ineffective unless the receiver is predisposed to hear it. Recently, a female magistrate was heard to say, 'We don't listen to anyone. We just do what we think is right'. At first sight, this may appear an appalling admission. But perhaps the Probation Service could learn something from such naive confidence. Drakeford, in an excellent article about the dangers of becoming a 'breach enthusiast', exposes the obsequiousness underlying the drive for 'credibility' and the 'folk-horror that exists within the service at being singled out by sentencers as "unrealistic"' (1993, p.294). He argues for the reaffirmation of a minimalist approach to breach proceedings and, amongst other things, claims that anti-discriminatory practice demands more (not less) flexibility and sensitivity to the differing circumstances of disadvantaged groups. He concludes:

> Strong arm tactics in probation are a sign of weakness in the thinking of the service. Less coercion and more consideration are the ingredients ... for a defensible as well as a successful future (Drakeford, 1993, p.301).

Mary Eaton (1993) interviewed women ex-prisoners who had somehow managed to turn their lives around. The factors which enabled them to do this may offer insights to probation officers working not only with women ex-prisoners but with all women offenders – and perhaps all offenders. Women offenders will only change their lives if and when they have access to the structural pre-conditions of social justice – housing, employment and health facilities. Without these things they have no chance of reconstituting their own lives and those of their 'families' – however they choose to define that term.

But structural factors alone are insufficient. The women Eaton interviewed had all made a conscious decision to re-direct their lives – they wanted things to be different. In Probation jargon, they were motivated to change. But such motivation was not something which just happened. In order to make that decision, they had to feel confident that change was possible. And to feel confident, they had to achieve both self-recognition and recognition by others. They had to feel that they were people of worth who had something to contribute.

The key to recognition was reciprocal relationships. For many women offenders, their only experience of relationships is subordination, exploitation and abuse. Whether in personal or official dealings their expectations have been of hierarchical relationships in which they are told what they *should* do and how they *should* behave in order to please other people:

> Both inside and outside the prison, women frequently found that they were patronised and infantilised by official agents of social control. Most of the women were

> dismissive or resentful of the supervision offered ... Few singled out such an experience as a significant factor in their movement towards autonomy and self-direction (Eaton, 1993, pp.95-96).

Women offenders often demonstrate a healthy scepticism for 'contracts' that appear to restrict their already limited choices and offer no obvious benefits (Worrall, 1990). They will rarely be openly hostile and will usually give the impression of wanting to please but that is a survival response borne out of the need to placate people who are more powerful than they are. When it comes to it, appointments will be missed (except in times of crisis) because evasiveness (even with the risk of breach proceedings) is preferable to the perceived injustice of one- sided, oppressive 'contracts'. Anything which contributes to the breaking down of those expectations and the development of *mutuality* in relationships will help to motivate women towards change. Probation officers who listen and encourage and avoid judging are more likely to motivate women to re-direct their lives than are those who insist on hierarchy and the strict application of National Standards.

Perhaps it is time the Service said, 'We just do what we think is right'. There is a great deal of imaginative work being undertaken by probation officers with women offenders, characterised by *democracy* and *empowerment* and focusing on the experiences that unite rather than divide women. Some examples will illustrate the point.

In prison, probation officers are struggling in a hostile environment to work alongside some equally committed prison officers to help women offenders come to terms with and survive their experiences both inside and outside prison. Individual and group work in women's prisons now routinely acknowledges that many women in prison are survivors of sexual abuse. Prison probation officers have also taken the initiative in equipping themselves to undertake assertiveness training with women, which is often the key to helping women negotiate fair and non-oppressive relationships.

Research by Julian Buchanan and others (1991) in Merseyside indicates that women have viewed the Day Training Centre as a 'haven where they are regarded as individuals of worth and potential.' In contrast to the drab exploitation of their daily existences, the Centre has provided opportunities for personal growth and personal choice (and this despite the authors' uneasiness that the women's offences were insufficiently serious to warrant the recommendation in the first place).

In an attempt to accommodate the reality of the requirements of 'punishment in the community', Marian Jones and others (1991) devised the 'Miskin Model' of groupwork with women offenders, which combines formal activities to address offending behaviour with informal activities designed to empower women and promote personal growth. Such an approach seems to have secured the commitment and enthusiasm of middle management, so crucial to the success of such experimental ventures.

Tara Mistry (1989) describes and evaluates the benefits of a 'feminist model' which enabled women to negotiate with probation officers about the structure and content of groups. Claiming to adopt a feminist perspective in work with women offenders is frequently perceived by the organisation as threatening, but when its principles are itemised as they are by Mistry, there can be little to which any moderately self-aware and reflective officer or manager can take exception. They are principles which accord closely with the traditional social work values of respect, acceptance and self-determination. Those principles include starting from the material and emotional place where women are, viewing their offending in its social and economic context, encouraging women to take control of their lives and treating them as equals. Nor is the philosophy of self-help – the acknowledgement that women have the inclination, skills and resources to help each other – in any way exclusive to an approach labelled 'feminist'. Yet the idea of a group run *for* women *by* women remains an emotional obstacle for many men. This seemingly atavistic fear of exclusion has to be recognised for what it is by men themselves, who have much to contribute to helping women offenders, *by working with men.* This is not to argue that women should not work with men or vice versa – that is happening all the time. Rather, it is to voice exasperation that the value of making some 'all women' provision is still disputed.

CONCLUSION

In this chapter I have attempted to argue that:

1. There is a need for a fundamental shift in the Probation Service's thinking towards a celebration of the *low level of*

women's offending and away from collusion with statements and policies which criminalise women's poverty, colour and sexuality or hold them responsible for the crimes of men;
2. Given the low level of women's offending, the Service (and, indeed the criminal justice system as a whole) can afford to experiment and take risks with radical non-custodial provision, from which lessons might also be learned about provision for all offenders;
3. Justice for women offenders will not be achieved through conventional equal opportunities policies alone without a recognition of the particular social injustices with which many have to contend.

Ten years ago, Andrew Scull (1983, p.165) argued that 'tinkering around with the criminal justice system in a radically unjust society is unlikely to advance us very far towards justice'. The Probation Service, however, has a long and hitherto honourable tradition of trying to do precisely that. It is not large or powerful enough to do anything more than tinker, but it has no reason to be ashamed of some of the ways in which it has tinkered towards justice in the past. The problem now, though, is that it is in danger of placing obstacles in the path of justice. And one of those obstacles is an inflexible adherence to the doctrine of 'equal treatment'. Of course, 'equal treatment' does not mean 'same treatment' but it is this very lack of precision and clarity about the term that allows it to be misappropriated by social control discourses of widely differing political hue.

The Probation Service has demonstrated that a commitment to equality of treatment can help many, predominantly white, women who have committed minor offences to be diverted from the unwarranted intrusion of probation orders. This is an achievement of which it can be proud. Nevertheless, it is perhaps time to acknowledge that this commitment is insufficient to keep many other women offenders out of prison. Justice for these women will only be achieved through *unequal* treatment – through a conscious Service decision to target resources for special provision for women who, for whatever reason, are likely to be considered by the courts for custodial sentences. In order to do that effectively, however, the Service will need to overcome its current squeamishness about being criticised occasionally by sentencers. Campaigning (as opposed to politely 'marketing a strategic policy') to keep more women out of prison will teach the Service a great deal about its own strengths. It will help to revive the dormant commitment to social justice which still motivates the majority of students who enter training for the Service. It will not change a world in which women are held responsible for far more crime than they will ever commit but it is an honourable piece of tinkering that will help the Service regain its self-respect. It is not unrealistic. It is an achievable goal.

And finally.....

On 26th November 1993 *The Guardian* reported the following story:

> A pregnant mother of six about to start five days in jail was saved when solicitors held a whip-round in court to pay her fine.
>
> Sharon Jones – due to give birth to her seventh child in two weeks – was sentenced by magistrates at Ebbw Vale, Gwent, for failing to pay a £55 fine for TV licence dodging.
>
> Mrs Jones said 'It was the first time I've ever been inside a court and I was terrified. I pleaded guilty by letter and the court fined me £55 to be paid off at £5 a week. But I just couldn't afford it. A fiver a week is a lot of money when you've got six kids and no job.
>
> The chairman of the bench said, 'All the magistrates sitting that day are very pleased this lady has been saved from jail. No magistrate likes sending anyone to jail, especially a woman in Mrs Jones's condition'.

But to jail is where he would have sent Mrs Jones, claiming he had *no choice*, if her solicitor (coincidentally(?), a woman) had not had the humanity and sense of justice to intervene and put him to shame. I wonder what would have happened if it had been the court duty probation officer who had organised the whip- round?

On the following day, Roger Levitt, found guilty of misleading a City watchdog body to cover up debts of £34 million, was ordered to do 180 hours community service. The judge said, 'the restriction on his liberty is commensurate with what he has done' (*The Guardian,* 27 November 1993). I wonder what his pre-sentence report said – if there was one.

Notes

1. The government's recent attacks on lone mothers are an excellent example of indirect institutional racism. Whilst 14% of all mothers are classified as lone parents, the proportion rises to 51% in the Afro-Caribbean community. However, the proportion of those who have an earned income (as opposed to 'scrounging' on the state) is much higher than for other ethnic groups (*The Guardian*, 9 November 1993).
2. 26% of the female prison population is non-white. 70% of women's crimes involve theft, compared with 40% of men's. 29% of women in prison are there for non-payment of fines, compared with 24% of men. 33% of women in prison are first offenders, compared with 11% of men (Home Office, 1992a).

Ten
Justice: Do they mean for us?
Black probation officers and Black clients in the Probation Service

Marcia Francis-Spence

I had the pleasure of meeting John Pendleton on one occasion during my social work training at Nottingham University. My memory of him is that his presence and his personality filled the room. He struck me as someone who would be equally comfortable in both academia and in practice.

At the time I was an anxious student unsure that I would complete the course never mind practise as a probation officer and eventually progress to training probation officers (in fact, do what John was himself doing at that very moment). Social work courses are intensive, with a range of visiting lecturers participating in the teaching; consequently only a few make a lasting impact. The impact that John made on me was such that two years later whilst practising as a probation officer and overhearing a colleague lament his death I could immediately recall this man. It was an honour to be asked two years later to contribute to a book dedicated to John.

INTRODUCTION

My motivation for joining the Probation Service arose out of a determination to make some contribution, however small, to the elimination of the injustices endured by certain groups in society who come into contact with the criminal justice system. Of particular concern to me was the disproportionately high number of Black people in the criminal justice system, at the same time being aware that there were very few Black probation officers. A placement in the Probation Service further reinforced my impression that Black clients were indeed disadvantaged by the Probation Service as well as the wider criminal justice system.

There has been some documentation charting the experience of Black clients in the Probation Service. Black probation officers and their role does not however appear to be a topic considered worthy of in-depth discussion. In this chapter my intention is to offer what amounts to a personal perspective on some of the dilemmas surrounding the treatment of Black clients and Black probation officers within the Probation Service. I will be focusing on Justice – the definition I would like to adopt is that used by the Collins Dictionary, that is, *'moral and legal fairness'* (*Collins Dictionary*, 1990) and examine whether it applies to Black people involved with the service. If we are to believe the media that Black communities distrust the criminal justice system then clearly there must be consideration given to where and how Black probation officers fit in.

LIVING WITH OPPRESSION—WHAT CHANCE JUSTICE?

The interests of the oppressor and the oppressed are very different. Consequently in 'an oppressive social system, one's identity is either that of the oppressor or that of the oppressed' (Cress-Welsing, 1991, p.240).

Black peoples' presence in Britain is not a new phenomenon as at the time of the Empire all British subjects were free to move within it. Hence White subjects travelled to the colonies and some Black subjects travelled to Britain.

The invitation from the British government to Black people during the 1950s was therefore a special one above and beyond that right of movement. Unfortunately the government failed to give consideration to, or make provision for any children individuals might have. The short term and temporary measures adopted then were a precursor of what lay ahead for Black people in Britain. They came, settled, and tried to adapt to a system which accepted no real responsibility for adapting in turn to their needs. An analogy can be drawn between this situation and that of a family inviting a relative to stay. The guest accepts the invitation on the basis of close family ties, unaware, however, that the host has hidden agendas. On arrival, the guest, realises that he or she is expected to provide not only their own food and shelter but also to make no demands whatsoever on the host. This lack of preparation is apparent in every British institution.

The outcry from Government supporters is likely to be 'why should anything change in Britain?' and 'why should Britain change its institutions to accommodate foreigners?' This has resulted in Britain still holding fast to the concept of White superiority and the existence of White British culture, thus failing to acknowledge that Britain is now fully enmeshed within a variety of cultures, a result of Britain's imperialist policies. British institutions continue operating as if whole sections of society are invisible.

Cress-Welsing (1991) suggests that: '...a White racist social system is completely incapable of providing total equality of opportunity to Blacks. Such a system must, for its maintenance, produce differential levels of functioning for White and non-Whites' (p.240).

Attempts made by the state to enact legislation which counteract racism in the form of various Race Relations Acts have to be viewed in the context of racist immigration legislation being passed simultaneously. Gordon (1992, p.192) asserts that Britain makes it explicit that there is still no place for Black people and offers little pretence that they are here '...on anything but sufferance and on condition that they accept their subordinate status in British society without complaint'.

BLACK AS A COLLECTIVE TERM

'Black' is commonly used to describe people of mainly African, Asian and African-Caribbean backgrounds who suffer discrimination on the grounds of skin colour. Black communities however are still going through a process of self identification, having initially adopted the word Black to describe themselves collectively and to serve as a political statement in the fight against racism experienced by them on the basis of skin colour. However, the move to self-identification has been used (by both Black and White people) to create division between the Black communities. The psychological effect on Black people resulting from 'Black' being defined in entirely negative terms and the fact that racism is endemic in language, art and culture should not be underestimated. Historically, Black people have frequently been encouraged to fight each other for the small piece of cake that has been made available to be divided between the various groups rather than combining forces to ensure the system divides the cake in a more equitable way. In using the term Black to define such a varied group, it is important to acknowledge that African, African-Caribbean and Asian people have different histories and consequently different experiences of the criminal justice system. Whilst the Asian population make up a higher proportion of the population of Britain than those of African-Caribbean origin, national figures indicate that they are less likely to be involved with the criminal justice system as defendants or as offenders (NACRO, 1991b).

The different experiences however do not mean that the experience of one group is necessarily any less severe than for others as racial attacks and stereotyping take on different forms. What is of concern as Gilroy (1987, p.13) states is that 'the fact of Black people breaking the law is offered as proof of their incompatibility with Britishness'.

CRIMINALISATION OF THE BLACK COMMUNITY

I must make it clear that in no way do I wish to deny that there are criminal elements within the Black communities like any other community, who of course, deserve to be dealt with in the Criminal Justice System. Overwhelming evidence however suggests that a large number of those within the system are there because of injustices at the various stages of the Criminal Justice system; injustices which can and must be eradicated if there is to be any peace for Black and White people.

There is in my view nothing special about crime committed by Black people. However, a community which is continually being told that they are intrinsically deviant and that crime and violence are part of their very being, surely has to question whether it has the same choices that are open to others and whether the laws of that society apply equally. Intrinsic in abiding by any rules is a belief that they apply to you and that you have something to lose by not adhering to them.

For an entire community to be labelled as 'a problem', and its members told that they do not belong, and that they have no stake, in society (nor will they ever have), to be treated as visitors who have outworn their welcome, even though this is the only home most of them have ever known, surely has a devastating effect that can lead to self destruction:

> If Black people are increasingly convinced that the criminal justice system is discriminatory and won't give them a fair deal, they are increasingly alienated from the rule of law. As they become alienated they will not see why they should abide by the values of a system which discriminates against them (Cavadino in Upshall, 1989, p.3).

The Black community has little or no representation with regard to the decision-making process of the criminal justice system. Black people however are over-represented as recipients of that system. In view of this it is necessary to ask whether one of the cornerstones of the criminal justice system, which is being judged by one's peers, is being fulfilled and why clearly this does not apply to Black people. Owing to the very serious racial, social, economic, political and cultural oppression that Black people have to deal with daily, they are not allowed the comfort of dealing with their problems as are other sections of the community. Criminalising young black men, in particular, can be viewed as a move which directly undermines the structure of Black families.

It is not my intention to romanticise or excuse criminality within the Black community, neither do I expect a lower standard of behaviour from Black people than White people. Nevertheless it has become increasingly difficult to deny that many Black people are in the system because they have refused to endure and accept the treatment meted out to them by various institutions ranging from school, to employers, to the police. The problem lies with British society which has built into its structure a belief system that makes it possible for one group to see themselves as deserving better treatment in all areas than others. Black people, and Black men in particular, are repeatedly labelled as anti-authoritarian or irresponsible. It should be unsurprising if this is substantiated given the treatment meted out to them by those in authority. Cress Welsing argues that it is not accidental that Black men in particular are treated so harshly, as the '...males represent the major potential threat and challenge to male oppressors' and therefore the '...racist social system can survive only if Black manhood is destroyed' (Cress-Welsing, 1991, pp.246-47).

This is not to deny that other groups in society are disadvantaged – but to profess how racism compounds any disadvantage that Black people suffer. However most offenders

(Black and White) do not commit serious offences. Nevertheless there are an increasing number of serious offenders emerging from both groups. If punishment is to be used as a deterrent it should be applied regardless of the colour of skin.

I have no reason to believe that the majority of Black people would find any of these statements contentious. However, if justice is to prevail, the criteria used to inform decisions need thorough examination. In the case of a Black offender, the focus of attention should be on how he or she was processed through the criminal justice system and on what basis they entered. These are fundamental areas that need to be addressed if Black people are to receive justice in the criminal justice system.

The Home Secretary in the Foreword to Section 95 of the Criminal Justice Act states that :

> The aims of our criminal justice system are to prevent and reduce crime, to dispense justice fairly, to protect the public, to punish the guilty and to acquit the innocent. It is vital that management practices in criminal justice processes are, and are seen to be, devoid of any improper discrimination (Home Office, 1992d, p.2).

The criminal justice system nevertheless is still experienced as oppressive to various groups in society on the basis of gender, social class, skin colour, heterosexism and mental illness, which Section 95 of the Act is aiming to address. I do not in any way wish to dilute 'race' by bringing in other oppressions but like Sivanandan (1991, p.44) I believe our oppression must open us out to the oppressions of other people. 'Race' is so immediately identifiable and the impact so severe that it compounds all the other oppressions and thus casts doubt on the legitimacy of British laws and their ability to offer justice to Black people.

In order to comprehend why racism persists, a full understanding of other oppressions is necessary. Only by doing so can we discern why racism is upheld not only by those in power but also by other oppressed groups in society. Whilst other oppressed groups are targeted for discrimination they do not experience the prejudice derived from the historical conditioning which views Black as bad and therefore undesirable. Here in Britain, other oppressed groups are *marginalised* whilst Black people are actually made *invisible*. In effect 'the Black community is becoming both a wasteland and a combat zone' (Hooks, 1991, p.107).

A FORCE FOR CHANGE?
BLACK PROBATION OFFICERS AND THE SERVICE

Very few outside of the Black communities can be persuaded to attend to, let alone accept as credible, the plight of Black people within the criminal justice system. This emanates from the fact that Black people and their struggle are viewed as external to the criminal justice system; racism, therefore, is assumed to be individual rather than institutional. There is little to convince us that the Probation Service is exempt or indeed any different to other parts of the criminal justice system in relation to racism. The whole system is considered to have the same ethos in that '... racism permeates the Probation Service and the criminal justice system' (Denney, 1992, p.147).

In fact the criminal justice system has been described as a series of decision points, with some decisions being made independently in the system and others resulting directly from previous decisions (Harris, 1992). If this is indeed the case then this might account for the apparent lack of impact of training designed to raise awareness and sensitise criminal justice practitioners to the injustices meted out to sections of this society on the grounds of 'race'. If training is to have any impact it will need to take place independently and yet simultaneously with strategies to ensure all parts of the system receive similar training but which is at the same time agency specific. The difficulty in implementing change in the criminal justice system is due in part to the fact that it presents not one, but a whole network of institutions. In view of this, it is therefore of no surprise that '...even despite a will for change and new awareness of the problem, there is a long way to go before the Black person caught up in the criminal justice system can expect 'justice' rather than 'criminalisation' (Upshall, 1989, p.3).

Probation work is largely determined by the behaviour of stronger players and groups in the politics of criminal justice. The Probation Service has nevertheless been instrumental, as a player within the criminal justice system, in developing policies and making attempts to address practice in order to ensure more equitable and sensitive treatment of Black offenders. These policies were however implemented only at the convenience of the service and as a result tended to be responsive rather than be pro-active in implementing change. The service can take some credit for significantly influencing other players within the criminal justice system as well as enhancing the awareness of racism within their own profession. The police and magistrates, although still some distance behind, have been left with no alternative but to respond. Judges have finally succumbed to the pressure to undergo training in an attempt to raise their awareness of racism. The majority appear to have done so reluctantly while others like Mr Justice Brooke appear to need no convincing. In a recent lecture he stated that he had 'not the slightest doubt that there is something going on, at each stage of the Criminal Justice process, which tips the scales on some occasions against some Black people' (Brooks, 1993, p.10).

Black staff have been part of the Service for the past 20 years though it was not until the mid 1980s that we began to see a noticeable increase in the number of Black probation officers. The Probation Service can claim to have achieved a degree of success in attracting Black officers to the Service; the retention level however needs addressing. In discussions with Black colleagues from the Probation Service there is a general feeling that Black officers entering the Service quickly become disillusioned and many are not staying beyond their confirmation year and thus, though there is now a visible pool it does not appear to be an increasing one. This may be a result of the lack of a clear structure within the service for Black staff. In my view the fundamental error is the failure to value diversity let alone manage it; there is still adherence to an assimilation model. The Probation Service has indeed attempted to move away from its White middle class image by adjusting recruitment strategies. It is nevertheless debatable as to whether the presence of Black probation officers in the Service has significantly influenced the middle class image for which the Service has been renowned. As far as I am aware there has been no close examination into the social class status of the relatively new professional groups in the Black communities in Britain. Nevertheless Cress-Welsing argues that:

> ...'class' does not refer to income alone but to actual existing power. And since Blacks across the board are oppressed and powerless under White supremacy, none of us have power. Therefore, there are no classes among Blacks (Cress-Welsing 1991, p.156-57).

I have no doubt that some readers will disagree and assert that they are aware of Black people whom they consider to have power.

However, what Cress-Welsing is alluding to is the degree of actual power, '...the power to protect one's life and the lives of one's group members in the framework of an existing power system' (Cress-Welsing, 1991, p.158).

The Probation Service, like the British government in the 1950s, neglected to give any consideration as to why it was recruiting Black officers. In my view the expectation was that they would enter the Service and fade into the background leaving the Service to absolve itself of any criticism. Black probation officers would focus on working with Black clients. Consequently recruitment was influenced by the number of Black clients as well as the areas in which Black recruits lived. This practice has effectively amounted to no more than a tokenistic gesture, in effect marginalising Black probation officers, which many have been fighting. Another consequence of such ill-considered recruitment of Black officers is that they can unwittingly become directly involved in reproducing and perpetuating racism, because their training often amounts to little more than absorbing traditional professional values and in turn using their closeness to and knowledge of the Black communities to keep them from reacting against the system.

It appears that the employment of Black probation officers was the Probation Service's anti-racist strategy. If this was indeed the case, with the expectation that Black people's presence would be sufficient to eradicate or halt racism, then clearly such an ill thought out strategy could only operate at certain times and in certain areas.

The Association of Black Probation officers (ABPO) was set up in the early 1980s; its function was to act as a support group and to promote appropriate Service delivery to the Black community. The early 1990s saw the creation of Black staff support groups in Probation Services wherever there were enough Black staff to make such a group viable. The fact that Black people within the Service sought to organise themselves into self-help and support groups is surely an indication that the support systems within the Service have failed them.

Whilst there is no doubt that major Black influence is required within the Probation Service if change is to occur it is evident that it has to be more than a numbers game. There is still proclamation from some quarters for an increase in the number of Black probation officers. Though I would not disagree with that, I believe that unless it is taken a stage further it will be a pointless exercise.

My vision of the next stage is of the Service demonstrating clarity as to the possible roles of Black probation officers, that it acknowledges how the Service disempowers Black probation officers regardless of whether they are managers or at main grade. Both groups complain of their isolation and marginalised status within the Service. Many are of the opinion that though they are welcomed initially, they subsequently find that their views are ignored and their experiences devalued. This treatment is not unlike that meted out to Black people when they entered Britain in the 1950s.

The high turnover rate of Black probation officers in the Service has numerous implications. For example, it leads to a dearth of experienced Black officers. As a result it is not uncommon to see one of two things occurring: either inexperienced Black officers are encouraged to take on responsibility they are ill-equipped to deal with, which then ensures they are not as efficient as they could be, or alternatively, the few experienced Black staff that are available are pressurised into entering areas they might not be interested in, or are under such stress that they also cannot work to full capacity and thus run the danger of appearing inefficient. The repercussion is that, if they fail, it is not only a reflection on the individual but the ability of other Black staff is also questioned. The above issues are rarely recognised as contributory factors. The reality is that to survive and get ahead, individuals depend on informal networks of co-operative relationships. Friendships, help from colleagues, even 'customers', are seen as the keys to success (Jones, in Whiting, 1992). Black officers are disadvantaged in this area.

Though the majority of Black probation officers have an interest in the uplifting of Black people, not all yearn to play a part in the struggle against racism in the Probation Service, a factor which has to be acknowledged. Like any other group, Black people make choices and not all Black people are affected by racism in the same way. Consequently some will prioritise other factors as being more important. Some will feel they have far more to lose than gain by becoming involved and are not therefore prepared to take what they consider to be risks. This is not intended as a criticism but rather acknowledgement that people need and have the right to make choices. Nevertheless we cannot ignore the fact that many Black people will succeed 'on the backs of', or because of the plight of Black people.

Black probation officers are working in a system where they, although agents of that system, are viewed as peripheral. To be effective therefore Black probation officers individually as well as collectively need to be candid about their role. This involves being aware of who placed them there, as well as for what purpose, and to assess the rewards they derive from being part of the system:

> The role of black staff...is qualitatively different to White in an agency. That indeed should be built into job descriptions and job specifications. That does not mean to say black people should only deal with black people. The agency therefore must be clear why it wishes to recruit black staff and convey clearly and directly to prospective black staff what tasks the agency envisages being performed by black staff. At present hidden agendas prevail (Divine, 1991, p.126).

Roles however need to be distinguished from 'tasks'. Whilst the former are developed over a period of time the latter are given. Black probation officers enter the Probation Service with a clear understanding of what their tasks will be but their roles are laden with ambiguity. The majority of Black officers may welcome the opportunity to work from a Black perspective, that is, starting from a perspective which reflects, is informed and is defined by Black people's experience. Instead most are forced by circumstances into a position whereby they are in fact doing little more than attempting to manage an anti-racist perspective which is in effect a response to racism and in reality should be White people's responsibility. Black probation officers' potential strengths and diversity are rarely acknowledged.

Anti-racist practice requires proactive strategies, listening to the people who need Services, finding ways to value people both as providers and users and above all to create alternatives which are not oppressive. If Black staff in the Probation Service are to make lasting impact there is little point in them being only at the bottom rung of the ladder where the amount of power they have to implement change is negligible. Where Black staff are employed by the Probation Service solely to work on issues pertaining to 'race' or to work only with Black offenders, it will prevent individuals from gaining the wide range of professional experience they require if they are to achieve promotion. It may also push 'race' issues into the margins. However, the steady growth in the number of Black qualified staff has brought a challenge to the Service. One consequence is that a White institution is being faced for the first time with the possibility of sharing power with Black people.

It will however take far more than simply employing Black probation officers to provide solutions to the problem of racism in the Probation Service. Being Black carries no automatic guarantee that officers will possess the skills to work with Black clients. Power relationships between officer and client will inevitably be present irrespective of colour, for example in terms of social class, gender, sexual preference or culture and of course the authority of the job.

In seeking solutions commentators on the injustices suffered by Black people in the criminal justice system have ventured only as far as anti-racist strategies, stopping short of accepting or attempting to comprehend the perspectives of Black people. This is not surprising as it merely reinforces what most Black people already know, which is that 'White people only deal with Black people from a position of power' (Madhubuti, 1978, p.187). Instead the predominately White Probation Service must cease talking *at* and *for* Black people and start talking *with* them on an equal basis, respecting what they have to say.

TRAINING AND DEVELOPING OF STAFF

Social work training has been going through a process of change. It began with the introduction of the DipSW in 1991, a main feature of the DipSW being a national requirement that anti-racist and anti-oppressive practice must be central. An anti-oppressive perspective in social work education is a new phenomenon. Though CCETSW offers no clarification of the terms 'non-discriminatory', 'anti-discriminatory' and 'anti-oppressive' practice as cited in Paper 30, 'It can be argued that anti-discriminatory practices tend to reflect equal opportunity policies whereas anti-oppressive practices attempt to link in with notions of equality and justice' (CCETSW, 1991, p.25).

There is a real possibility that the Home Office will return to the pre-1972 situation and remove probation training from social work in an attempt to enable probation trainees to focus more on probation work or that it will allow a mixed economy of training to develop. Some probation officers welcome this as they believe that probation is not, and never really has been, social work. Educators and practitioners however should strongly oppose this trend. If we agree that the criminal justice system is oppressive for many groups in society and that the Probation Service is the only part of the system showing real commitment to making any meaningful attempt to address this, then probation officers must acquire the skills, knowledge and values to equip them to challenge this. A move to exclusive training would endanger the value base of the service which includes a belief in the worth of every individual, the capacity of individuals to change and their right to self-determination: 'Recognising and working to change oppressive power relations is a necessary starting point for probation work which confronts the ramifications of racism' (Denney, 1992, p.164).

If the Probation Service is committed to the notion of justice then clearly there needs to be recognition that anti-racist and anti-oppressive practice within the Service cannot be promoted without an infrastructure which makes this possible. Such an infrastructure includes ensuring that a prerequisite for probation officers entering the service is that they undergo training which enables them to recognise and understand racism and other oppressions and to develop strategies to work from anti-racist and anti-oppressive perspectives. These are areas in which the Probation Service could attempt to bring about change in the criminal justice system through leading by example.

It is essential that a commitment to work on issues of equality and justice as it relates to Black people be secured at the most senior levels, at the same time ensuring that it is fully understood by staff at all levels. Black probation officers have little alternative but to continue to fight for justice for themselves as members of the profession as well as on behalf of Black clients. There is no room for complacency. Particularly if we subscribe to the view that '... White control has been the most pervasive manifestation of racism in the system, the source of its greatest dysfunction's, and the most effective barrier to change' (Naik, in Denney, 1992, p.165).

The Service must be committed, demonstrating a commitment that ensures that Black practitioners' skills are utilised and results in their promotion to positions where they can begin to influence change. It is paramount that Black officers be treated as professionals rather than being marginalised in the Probation Service whereby they are viewed by others as being employed solely because of their colour and, consequently, only to work with Black clients. As Singh states:

> ... recruitment of Black workers had only a marginal impact because their ability to effect change was blocked by the prevailing power structures and practices into which they were placed' (Singh, 1992, p.25).

The Probation Service was not prepared for the consequences of employing Black probation officers. The many difficulties now facing them needs to be recognised as anti-racist statements have done very little in bringing about positive changes. All that they do is give Black people the illusion that change is on its way yet it never seems to arrive. These statements encourage expectations of justice from what is in fact an unjust system where racism merely takes on different guises. Central to the issue is that to the majority of White people, Black is synonymous with problem and this hinders them from seeing the individual. Clearly we need workforces which reflect the population and thus it follows that we need to see Black people as professionals in the criminal justice system. The last decade has made it clear that recruitment by itself may be exposed as merely window-dressing. There are now examples of teams with Black managers and, or, with anything up to 50% Black staff. Close examination however reveals that nothing has changed because there has been no process.

MOVING FROM FINE WORDS TO ACTION: ADOPTING A 'PROCESS'

Most institutions appear to be unaware of the fundamental differences between the term anti-racist and non-racist. Clarity and consensus in defining anti-racist practice is therefore urgently needed if we are to ensure it is not only obtainable but also has meaning and relevance. The Probation Service in moving forward should review its current stance and exercise clarity as to whether its aim is to be non-racist or to adopt an anti-racist stance informed by Black perspectives.

Section 95 of the 1991 Criminal Justice Act for the first time in the history of the criminal justice system, represents an attempt to implement positive steps towards good practice in relation to oppressed groups. Awareness of racism – non-racism – is insufficient unless complemented by action at both personal and institutional levels. Anti-racist training is vital. However, whilst most Services appear to be taking this on board, the training lacks structure and has a tendency to be grounded in paternalism, failing to move beyond sympathising with Black people and dealing with them only as victims.

Change is usually advocated as an attempt to offer greater sensitivity towards Black people, developing a greater understanding of their cultures and lifestyles. Training is accompanied by a call for recruitment of more Black people throughout the criminal justice system. The central question of racism however is not addressed, i.e. the institutional practices of a society based on unequal social, economic and power relations (Gordon, 1992, p.191). A one or two day workshop can only serve as an introduction to the process.

Managers have a responsibility to ensure that staff are made aware of why they are undergoing training. There appears to be very little recognition of the need for individual and team preparation prior to training as well as individual and team evaluation. Training is of limited use unless it is maintained in order to sustain good anti-racist practice development. Strategies used should not be about inducing guilt as this only leads to immobilisation, not about anger which in turn leads to denial, but should instead be directed towards 'touching the minds' of White people: 'Touch the mind and you touch the situation; put something on the mind of the receiver and you force him or her to confront the condition' (Madhubitti, 1978, p.128).

Anti-racist practice is not a fixed process and therefore will need refining and developing with regular review to gauge the effectiveness of training and practice. 'It requires flexibility and responsiveness to the changing nature of racism in the criminal justice system and society as a whole' (Kett et al., 1992, p.28).

CONCLUSION

The Probation Service must demonstrate clarity as to its motivation for employing Black staff. Clarity will ensure vision which in turn would enable every employee to contribute their fullest to the Service. A long term perspective is required as change is never immediate but takes years. The Probation Service has a responsibility to educate as well as train its staff in order to begin to change the mind set. Crucial to all this is that line managers are trained to manage diversity. They need to recognise that Black officers as well as officers from other oppressed groups will be influenced in their practice by the perspective they bring from their particular group.

Increasing the numbers of Black probation officers in the Service, while White staff undergo anti-racist training, is not sufficient to elicit trust in the Black communities or ensure justice for Black clients and Black probation officers. That alone will do nothing to change a system where racism and oppression is so endemic. If Black probation officers entering the Probation Service continue to be trained only by White people (and in some cases by Black people but who have themselves only been trained by White people), in institutions using methods which only consider Eurocentric viewpoints and, where they do consider Black perspectives, do so only very superficially and thus as inferior, then clearly we are in danger of moving in circles.

The pervasive and endemic nature of racism within the criminal justice system ensures that more pro-active measures have to be adopted. These are necessary to combat the inbuilt explanations which abound, distorting Black people's development and denying them justice, be they practitioners or clients. It is after all not the intention that counts, but the effect.

Note

The author acknowledges personal access to ABPO minutes of meetings and attendance at AGM.

Eleven
Towards justice in probation work with prisoners

Brian Williams

Probation officers have only limited room for manoeuvre in the face of the radical and confusing changes being imposed on the criminal justice system by central government. Although there has been some scope for progressive innovation during the early 1990s, penal policy is confused and contradictory, and prisons are among the most difficult institutions to change. Nevertheless, there are opportunities for the Probation Service to exert a positive influence through its presence in the prisons.

How can we learn from experience (of both the British and other more punitive criminal justice systems) ways of working more justly and more effectively with prisoners? This chapter will review aspects of that experience, point to some trends and suggest some possible future strategies for injecting greater justice into probation work with prisoners. The concept of justice has been put to very different uses by the Woolf Report, the government and the penal reform lobby: the potential for reconciling these theoretical conflicts in practice will be considered.

JUST DESERTS OR JUSTICE?

The 1991 Criminal Justice Act was based upon the New Right criminology of 'just deserts'. The implications for prisoners were mainly negative: the notion of 'twin track' or bifurcated sentencing led directly to longer sentences for offences connected with drugs, violence and sex,[1] while the new parole arrangements meant longer periods of incarceration for many prisoners sentenced previously. Commentators on North American prisons have noted that the bifurcation philosophy also seeps into prison regime planning, so that less restrictive prison environments are always complemented by harsher, dehumanising regimes which can be used to punish those who do not respond (Lowman and MacLean, 1991; Christie, 1993). As Barbara Hudson put it:

> The more we succeed in realising a bifurcated response to crime, the greater become the problems for the prisons. As the incarcerated become more and more concentrations of the difficult and the dangerous – this time in reality as well as in public mythology – the greater the emphasis is bound to be on security and control (Hudson, 1993a, p.145).

Other writers have eloquently described the contradictions inherent in the just deserts model of sentencing policy. How can it be just to sentence offenders without reference to their individual needs and circumstances? The philosophy is a powerful one, however, appealing to commonsense ideas about measured retribution. For a time, it was attractive to both left and right, partly perhaps because it included an attack upon the abuse of professional discretion. It is fundamentally based upon individualism, stressing as it does the rationality and moral competence of each offender, but it lacks humanity and it is discriminatory in effect. It emphasises formal rights, but not remedies for injustice (Hudson, 1993a; Christie, 1993).

The 1991 Act did, however, include some of the positive elements of the just deserts approach, not all of which were repealed by the 1993 Act. For the first time in British criminal justice legislation, there was a provision in s.95 for monitoring – if not actually redressing – improper discrimination, reflecting a commitment to formal equality before the law. Breach proceedings for ex-prisoners who do not comply with the conditions of their release for community supervision are now dealt with openly in the Magistrates' Court, replacing the previous, bureaucratic, discretionary recall system. The Carlisle Committee's recommendations on openness in the early release system were implemented (spurred on by a European Court of Human Rights judgement), and the anxieties caused by the secrecy of the parole system were to some extent reduced. Greater openness in reporting may improve practice in other parts of the system, particularly in the light of Woolf's recommendations on adjudications and the appointment of a prisons Ombudsman, although this appointment was delayed on political grounds until 1994.

The National Standards dictating the way in which probation officers should work with prisoners under statutory supervision similarly combined positive and retrograde approaches. While the first National Standards (those governing Community Service Orders) certainly led to a higher breach rate, and thus to more offenders in prison, the early signs are that this may not be happening with throughcare cases, where the supervising officer retains considerable discretion in interpreting the acceptability of missed appointments – although mechanistic application of the National Standards[2] could make breach much more common.

EXPOSING INJUSTICE

It is clear, then, that recent changes have made it generally more difficult to work towards just treatment of prisoners, but have also opened up some specific possibilities of doing so. There were plenty of conspicuous injustices in the way prisoners were treated prior to the 1991 and 1993 Acts, and some of these will be briefly reviewed before we move on to consider the opportunities presented to the Probation Service by the legislation and the Woolf Report, and the nature of the Service's response.

Probation work in recent years has been characterised by rapid, and sometimes barely comprehensible, change. This has not been good for morale, and probation officers have had to cope with developments which most have found distasteful. Some have worked to redress injustice through their everyday interactions with individual clients, some have campaigned collectively on wider issues, but many have grumbled and got on with the job. There is a danger that one can become insensitive to injustice, accommodating to change and thereby passively or implicitly supporting it. It therefore seems important at this stage to review some of the injustices of which all probation staff working with prisoners are aware: is the Probation Service colluding with these injustices, or is it engaged in trying to end them?

Space does not permit a full examination of the injustices of the prison system in England and Wales, but a few examples will suffice to illustrate the argument.

Life Sentence Prisoners

Since 1981, lifers have had recourse to the European Court of

Human Rights on several occasions, and the 1991 Act had to be amended in response to concerns expressed in the House of Lords about its failure to comply with European law. The rights of most discretionary lifers were significantly improved as a result (see Richardson, 1994, pp.88-89)[3] – but serious injustices remain. As in other jurisdictions, lifers who continue to maintain their innocence post-sentence remain inside for disproportionately long periods, and a minority seem unlikely ever to be able to satisfy the requirements of the Parole Board. The Home Secretary retains the right to veto the release of prisoners at the expiry of their tariff, and recent ministers have been keen to appear tough on serious offenders, to such an extent that a former Lord Chief Justice has criticised political interference in release decisions.

Writing in a report of the work of a committee he chaired on the implementation of the life sentence, Lord Lane described changes in practice as a trespass by the executive on the discretion of the courts, and argued for 'taking such decisions on the liberty of the subject out of the hands of politicians' (Committee on the Penalty for Homicide, 1993, p.18). The then Home Secretary responded the same day, rejecting the committee's recommendations.[4]

Apart from its injustice, this situation has explosive potential in an already volatile prison system, and the prisoners involved find it hard to maintain a cooperative attitude towards a system which shows every sign of having forgotten about them. They may initially be content to keep themselves busy with constructive activities, but when this receives no recognition the 'personal struggle' of adjustment to indefinite imprisonment can turn into outwardly-directed anger (Lowman and MacLean, 1991, p.142). Field and prison probation officers are faced with a dilemma in working with such clients: do they campaign for legal changes, do they try to help individuals to improve their parole prospects, or should they reinforce the official line? (Such prisoners are usually defined as immature or subversive, and campaigning is taken as further evidence of inadequacy).

Probation officers' work with such prisoners has too often been bureaucratic and reactive (Mitchell, 1992; Williams, 1992), an approach which is unlikely to succeed with people who may feel considerable anger towards the prison system, although Mitchell attributes it largely to financial constraints and lack of appropriate staff training.

HIV Positive Prisoners

Throughout the 1980s, the prison medical service colluded with the abuse of HIV+ prisoners' right to confidentiality and with their effective segregation from other inmates. The use of Viral Infectivity Restrictions (VIR), originally devised to deal with other, more infectious diseases, meant that prisoners known to have HIV or AIDS had no right to keep the diagnosis confidential, and in practice they were unable to associate with the rest of the population (see Williams, 1991, pp.102-6).

These abuses of HIV positive prisoners' rights have officially been brought to an end by a Circular Instruction to governors,[5] but in practice individuals remain isolated. Once confidential information has been divulged, it cannot be re-protected, and despite a substantial education programme, prisoners and prison officers remain suspicious of official reassurance about the safety implications of working in everyday contact with people with HIV (Padel et al., 1992; Dolan et al., 1990). Even some supposedly enlightened writers have supported New Right ideas for reducing the prison population by introducing electronic tagging, including 'left realists' who have argued that:

> ...it may well be in relation to the spread of HIV infection and AIDS that electronic monitoring and house arrest could have their greatest value. Managing the growing number of prisoners who are seropositive is likely to become a major problem for prison authorities (Berry and Matthews, 1989, p.131, cited in Sim, 1991).[6]

Meanwhile, prison numbers in England and Wales rose inexorably from the beginning of 1993 in response to the 'prison works' philosophy behind that year's Criminal Justice Act, although a reduction was achieved in Scotland by releasing minor offenders early under the Prisoners and Criminal Proceedings (Scotland) Act 1993.

There are clear guidelines available, indicating what good social work practice involves (for example, ACOP, 1990a), but these are useless in isolation. The Probation Service has not been particularly influential in this area of prison policy, but it may be able to use its position on Criminal Justice Consultative Councils and its knowledge of individual clients' circumstances and feelings to prevent similar abuses in future.

Probation officers working with prisoners clearly have a

particular responsibility to provide confidential counselling to HIV+ clients – although their official responsibilities make it difficult for them to undertake this themselves. There is perhaps scope for volunteer associates to take over the 'befriending' part of the probation role in such cases, and it is likely that specialist voluntary organisations can play a part in all but the remotest prisons' work with these clients. Groups like the Terrence Higgins Trust and Scottish AIDS Monitor tend to combine counselling with campaigning, and this may sit uneasily with some governors' attitudes towards outside involvement, but their expertise is needed and prisoners are more inclined to trust them than the Prison Medical Service.

Parole

The secrecy and uncertainty of the parole system have caused considerable discontent ever since its introduction in 1967. The 1991 Act and Court of Appeal judgements have considerably increased the openness of the parole system, and the Act diminished the degree of discretion involved in the decision to release shorter-sentence prisoners.

Some probation officers took up their right to consult lifers' prison files, and many must have been appalled by what they saw: prisoners were labelled early in their sentences, and the repetition of the views of former governors, prison probation officers, medical officers and so on, could be traced through the words of their successors down the years. Only rarely did officers challenge such material, although prison probation officers have been willing to ask colleagues and members of other disciplines (such as medical officers) to reconsider prejudicial comments in confidential, written reports. Opening prison records to the scrutiny of their subjects (not yet the prison files, but at least the parole reports) must improve the quality of what is written, as it has done in other fields.

Selective Service Provision

Although one or two Probation Services set up pilot schemes providing court reports and throughcare for particular groups, the Service as a whole has an abysmal record where foreign offenders are concerned (see Tarzi and Hedges, 1990; Williams, 1991; Cheney, 1993). The Middlesex experiment shows that it is possible to engage in effective anti-racist work with prisoners from abroad.

The provision of court reports for people remanded in custody when arrested at the airport of entry on suspicion of drug-smuggling has made a substantial difference to sentencing in one area, and collaboration with voluntary organisations to provide effective throughcare has been shown to be possible in a number of Services and prisons (Abernethy and Hammond, 1992).

Nor are foreign nationals the only group to be excluded from the services of probation officers. It was always difficult in some areas for released prisoners to obtain help with accommodation and other practical needs after serving short sentences (Monger et al., 1982), and a side-effect of the bifurcation philosophy is that prisoners serving less than 12 months are now released without statutory supervision.

THE WOOLF REPORT AND JUSTICE FOR PRISONERS

The publication of the Woolf Report was clearly important, although commentators have differed as to how radical its implications are. Despite all its limitations, it opened a window of opportunity for the Probation Service and for everyone else interested in justice for those in prison.

The London prison reform groups have been united in their desire to keep Woolf's agenda alive, but successive Home Secretaries have been at best ambivalent and at worst hostile to the Report's prescriptions. For nearly two years after its publication, there was some hope of progress being made on them, but the intervention of a politically weakened Prime Minister in the latter part of 1993 led to the spectacle of Home Office ministers claiming, in all apparent seriousness, that 'prison works' (*Prison Report*, 1993, p.3). Attention returned to the prison-building and privatisation programmes and to reducing the rights of the accused and of prisoners, and the momentum was to some extent lost. Nevertheless, there is a good deal of mileage in implementing Woolf yet, and it offers an agenda around which there is some consensus – in itself a tribute to the political skills of Woolf and Tumim.

The Report's weaknesses should not be overlooked, however. To fail to point them out would be to fail to analyse properly what justice for prisoners means.

Woolf's notion of justice is (perhaps not surprisingly) a limited and legalistic one. There is no doubt that it appeals to commonsense: obviously, prisoners ought to be treated like people rather than as simply the ingredients of some 'toxic mix' (to use Cavadino and Dignan's vivid phrase) or as inactive, deteriorating livestock or like 'vegetables that go off if they are not eaten soon enough' (Stern, 1994, p.246).

But justice is more than an adherence to legal guidelines (although what Hudson calls 'the jurisprudential frame of reference' is in danger of gaining complete ascendancy; Hudson, 1993a, p.123). It is part of Woolf's strategy for getting his recommendations implemented that he uses the language of just deserts, but this is fraught with danger, as Nils Christie has pointed out:

> The idea of just deserts makes it possible to streamline the system, and particularly to disregard all other values than the gravity of the act... What was a system of justice is converted into a system of crime control. The classical distinction between the judiciary, the executive and the legislature has to a large extent dissolved (Christie, 1993, pp.172-73).

This is precisely the danger that Lord Lane was pointing to in his report on life sentences. The logic of limited, mechanistic notions of justice is to use what Christie calls 'the Sentencing Table...an order from above' (p.139), 'completely controlled by the politicians' (p.145) and, as he goes on to remind us, mindless obedience to orders encourages totalitarianism.

It is this kind of reliance on bureaucratic methods that has prevented imaginative work by probation officers with prisoners in the past (see Williams, 1992). Woolf wisely exhorts the different criminal justice agencies to make more effort to understand and liaise with each other, but pays little attention to the role of probation officers (or any of the caring professions) in prisons, concentrating instead on the undeniably important issue of job satisfaction for prison officers (see Roberts, 1994).

When Woolf considers race, he rightly pinpoints the implementation gap between the prison service's good race relations policy and its limited impact on black prisoners' experience – but the Report frames this partly in terms of administrative inconsistency in monitoring racial incidents, which rather misses the point – although it does also call for greater energy to be put into promoting what it calls 'non-racial policies'

(Woolf and Tumim, 1991, pp.304-5). In practice, little seems to have changed in recent years, with 'racial discrimination (and stereotyping) intrinsic to the social organisation of prisons' (Genders and Player, 1989, p.131), and Woolf's terminology suggests that, like that of the prison service, his 'definition of the problem is wrong' in failing to see that racism is a matter of injustice and of differential levels of control and punishment (McDermott, 1990, p.227).

It is important that probation officers have opportunities to negotiate the terms of their throughcare work with clients. There is clear evidence that clients regard such negotiations as a fair and just way to engage with them (Monger et al., 1981; Williams, 1992), and that this approach makes it easier for workers to communicate their preferred 'personal style and concern for the client's rights and welfare' (Williams, 1991, p.80). This kind of discussion can be framed in the language of contracts if the political climate so dictates, although many in social work have reservations about the misleading implications of offering clients contracts (see Hudson, 1993a; Day, 1991; Simpkin, 1979).

Woolf gave only limited credence to the views of prisoners and, as Joe Sim has shown, qualified any statement quoted from a prisoner if it was critical of the staff or the inhumanity of the system (Sim, 1994). In contrast, the Report displays an 'uncritical acceptance of staff benevolence' (p.36) and of uniformed staff's evidence – except where it was given through the Prison Officers' Association, when a note of scepticism appears. Yet the abuse of power by uniformed staff is a crucial obstacle to securing just treatment of prisoners:

> ...no number of formal rules will secure justice unless the prison officers deliver it in their daily rounds, in their intimate relationships with those over whom they exercise great and sometimes regrettably unyielding power. About how to persuade officers to deliver justice in this sense, the Report has very little to offer' (Ryan, 1992, quoted in Sim, 1994, p.37).

As Sim argues, the whole apparatus of contracts or compacts between prisoners and the system depends upon justice being dispensed by maingrade prison officers, and the Report does not address how to bring about the necessary change in uniformed staff attitudes.

As a number of commentators noted, the Report is also extremely weak in its awareness of gender (Liebling, 1991; Player, 1994). Woolf is careful to explain and justify the exclusion of women's perspective, but this will not lessen its impact on women prisoners, since changes to the whole system are likely to be made on the basis of its recommendations and assumptions. As Elaine Player suggests, a separate enquiry is needed into the radical changes which are required in women's prisons consequent on Woolf's recommendations and the policy responses: there is no evidence that anyone in the prison service has given this issue any systematic thought (Player, 1994). Justice is not gender-blind or colour-blind, although just deserts tends to emphasise formal equality at the expense of the political effects of difference.

INNOVATIVE PROBATION PRACTICE

To some extent, the Probation Service has seized the opportunity presented by Woolf. It has largely been distracted, however, by its pursuit of a particular model of managerialism, and by the need to respond to a constant stream of new initiatives and demands from the Home Office.

Life Sentence Prisoners and Parole

Probation officers are not in a position to do much about the policies applied by the Parole Board and the Home Secretary, but they have been involved in campaigning, in collecting evidence for and supporting other campaigners, and in staying with the victims of political policies, the prisoners themselves, and helping them to make their cases for release and against inaccurate labelling.

The Probation Service has not done much to encourage litigation by prisoners, or to publicise relevant cases to others who might be affected. It may be that the development of combined bail and legal aid schemes in many prisons and more joint working between prison and probation officers, encouraged by some of Woolf's proposals, will make it possible for prison-based probation officers to become more involved in this kind of work in the future.

Probation staff have quietly assisted many prisoners who maintained their innocence, including some whose cases have become famous examples of miscarriages of justice, and many have been involved in the running of groups such as Liberty, but this has been an individual rather than a systematic endeavour. It may be that it would be politically impossible for the Service to take up such injustices officially, although there is certainly scope for closer liaison and greater trust to be developed between probation and the relevant campaigning groups.

Through professional associations such as NAPO, ABPO and ACOP, probation officers have collated evidence of injustices affecting lifers and other prisoners. The associations have become increasingly effective at publicising issues, and have begun to coordinate this work with some of the penal reform groups, although there is considerable and understandable suspicion in NAPO of some groups, such as NACRO, which seem to be in competition for probation jobs.[7]

The introduction of contracts, and greater consistency in providing sentence plans, make it possible for probation officers to play more of a part in examining and meeting prisoners' needs. If there was better liaison between probation and the other services working with prisoners, it would be easier to help long-term inmates construct their own regimes, as they have tried to do in Canada.[8] Innovative work by some education departments with women prisoners could be extended if probation staff became involved in them, although the women's prisons will have to change fundamentally before contracts can be anywhere near as meaningful for women as for men (Player, 1994). Prisoners' families could also be usefully involved in sentence planning in some cases (Padel, 1993).

The *National Framework for the Throughcare of Offenders* calls for 'clear and systematic throughcare', but it remains to be seen whether the resources necessary for its implementation will be made available (Prison Service, 1994).

As far as the new arrangements for prisoners to have access to official reports affecting their chances of parole are concerned, the Probation Service has a clear responsibility to monitor the impact of these changes, and to ensure that prisoners are able to take full advantage of them. There has, until recently, been considerable uncertainty as to whether prisoners are entitled to copies of their Home Circumstances Reports: surely the new arrangements make it possible to involve clients to a much greater extent in recording their own progress, where they are willing to take part.

HIV Positive Prisoners

Like the prison service's race relations policy, the probation service policy on confidentiality and HIV is good on paper. It has hitherto been frustrated by the problems outlined above. Probation officers need to regain the trust of HIV+ prisoners, and it will not be easy. It seems likely that more cooperation with the voluntary organisations already mentioned is the way forward.

This is another area where the Home Office has taken a narrow, legalistic line, in this case concerning not only the availability of condoms but even official willingness to admit that drug use and sexual activity go on in prisons. Research has been suppressed and prevented, although the illicit activities are informally used as 'containment activities' (Thomas, 1990, p.4). It may be that there is a role for probation officers in sponsoring research, an activity already begun in a limited way through NAPO. They should also be involved in challenging discrimination and misinformed comments on AIDS in prisons, pressing for more constructive policies and spreading existing good practice. Some prisons, for example, have found ways of making condoms available to inmates, supposedly as part of 'home leave packs', and probation departments' efforts to run groups for drug users and to provide information on HIV should be better-resourced by the Service.

Selective Service Provision

Because of the gradual implementation of sentence planning, beginning with long-term prisoners, and the reliance of the National Framework for Throughcare upon sentence planning for its implementation, it seems likely that short-sentence prisoners will continue to be neglected by the probation service. The Framework advocates routine intervention with remand prisoners, but this has considerable resourcing implications and the necessary increase in funding seems unlikely to be made.

Alison Liebling's research noted that young prisoners attempting suicide were amongst those least likely to be receiving regular contact and support from the outside probation service. They are also less likely to perceive this contact as useful (Liebling, 1992, p.156).

This has sobering implications both for resourcing priorities and for the kind of service provided to vulnerable young people. It seems clear that probation could and should be doing more to identify these prisoners and to engage with them during and after their sentences.

Effective intervention to protect the rights of those suspected of immigration offences could also be undertaken, in partnership with existing voluntary organisations, but here it will be the Probation Service which has to swallow its reservations about taking sides politically: most immigration aid organisations are quite rightly not content to individualise immigration problems, they want to publicise individual cases and campaign to change discriminatory laws.

Overall, there is considerable room for improvement in the Service's dealings with prisoners from abroad. They are not a group which commands much public sympathy or political clout, but their exclusion from the arrangements for throughcare simply cannot be justified. The rhetoric of s.95 of the 1991 Act will be expensive and complex to put into action: prisoners who speak little or no English will need interpreters present at every interview, and probation officers will have to liaise with families and services in the home countries of the clients. Some expertise has been developed in Middlesex, and it should be shared as a matter of urgency with colleagues in provincial throughcare teams and in prisons. Now that overseas prisoners are included in parole and conditional release arrangements, they must be given an equal opportunity to participate.

VOLUNTARY AFTER-CARE

Without arguing for intrusive intervention for its own sake, it seems that some short-sentence prisoners may need social work help during the immediate post-release period, and there is a danger that the official preoccupation with high-risk parolees and the exclusion of short-termers from National Standards may lead to a neglect to assist the relatively few short-term prisoners who would welcome some help with resettlement. Official agencies do need to be proactive in offering such help, because people who have been in prison are cynical about official agencies' willingness to help them and take some convincing.

Shortage of resources may mean that this traditional area of activity is simply abandoned by some probation services. This would be short-sighted, given that the over-arching aim of the Service's work with prisoners is now meant to be: 'To assist prisoners before and after release to lead law-abiding lives' (Home Office, 1992b).[9]

There is a danger that the abolition of statutory supervision for those sentenced to less than twelve months' imprisonment will reduce the scope for probation officers to befriend prisoners as an activity in its own right. Befriending will have to be justified in terms either of a statutory supervision period or of preventing reoffending. The same offenders will presumably be ignored each time they are sentenced to further imprisonment, until they are subject to statutory supervision by virtue of receiving a long sentence. This does little to help vulnerable groups like people with learning difficulties. Evidence is accumulating that minor offenders who might at one time have been hospitalised are increasingly being imprisoned (see Hudson, 1993a, chap. 3).[10]

Voluntary agencies are willing to become involved in partnerships to sustain voluntary throughcare (NACRO, 1993d), but there is understandable suspicion from probation officers fearful of losing other statutory roles to the 'independent' sector.[11]

CONCLUSION

Unfortunately, competition between the Probation Service and the voluntary and private sectors is being encouraged by government policy, and the outlook for future cooperation is not good. Some writers have been optimistic (Stern, 1994; Smith et al., 1993), but it is hard to see how this will prove justified.

Probation officers have traditionally been more concerned with practical matters than with the application of abstract concepts like justice. At a time when the values of the Probation Service are under attack, the rights of marginalised groups, including by definition all prisoners, will need defending in a careful and determined way.

Woolf's jurisprudential idea of justice is limited, but it may be useful in defending the status quo. To advance prisoners' rights will require a more radical definition of justice and a determined rejection of just deserts in favour of a more positive justice:

> We must think. That may not be the worst alternative when the other option is the delivery of pain (Christie, 1993, pp.184-85).

Notes

1. De Haan has noted the same effect in Dutch penal policy (De Haan, 1990, quoted in Hudson, 1993a, p.35).

2. The Standards are set out in Chapter Eight of Home Office, 1992b.
3. The British courts have also gradually become more willing to intervene in prisoners' rights cases: for example, the High Court has twice ruled on prisoners' access to records affecting their classification and parole reports. According to the Prison Reform Trust, these judgements imply that all management decisions in prisons are now potentially open to judicial scrutiny (Travis, 1993).
4. Ironically, in his response, Michael Howard also used the legalistic argument about the separation of the powers of the executive and the judiciary, saying that 'Sentencing is for the courts, not politicians. If the courts decide that imprisonment is appropriate in a particular case, then they should be able to pass that sentence, and it is the government's job to provide the necessary prison to send them to' (quoted in Shaw, 1993, p.12).
5. CI 30/1991, 'HIV/AIDS organisation and procedures at establishment level', doubtless published in response to criticism of existing arrangements in the Woolf Report and in reports by the Chief Inspector of Prisons (see also Ralli, 1994).
6. Similarly Elaine Player has argued that 'Requiring a woman to wear a monitoring device is unlikely to violate her respect and dignity more seriously than remanding her in custody' (Player, 1994, p.216) and that implementation of Woolf's notion of community prisons may require such innovation if it is to work where women's prisons are concerned.
7. At Feltham Young Offender Institution, for example, NACRO has established a pilot scheme counselling and advising young offenders. NAPO has boycotted this, and argued for similar schemes to be provided throughout the young offender system by the Probation Service itself (NAPO, 1993).
8. See Lowman and MacLean (1991) on the activities and official obstruction of the Infinity and Joyceville Lifers' Groups.
9. This has not gone unchallenged: see for example Whitehead et al., 1991, chap. 5.
10. Similarly, remand prisoners command few resources despite their vulnerability and difficult conditions – and it seems unlikely that this will change substantially under the *National Framework for Throughcare* (see NAPO, 1993).
11. see note 7.

Twelve
Justice in an unjust context: Implications for working with adult male sex offenders

Malcolm Cowburn and Panna Modi

> *...the prophetic concept of justice was formed at a time of great inequality and social injustice. The prophets strongly argued that justice should be towards the poor and oppressed. They did not mean that the poor and oppressed should receive any different treatment from the rest of the community...They held that there should be one law for all..*
>
> *In practice this notion of justice did not operate. The rich, the aristocrats and the businessmen sold out the poor, building up their own estates and fortunes within the law as administered. The poor had no redress, for the influence of the wealthy held sway over the administration of the law. It was against this that the prophets spoke* (Pendleton, 1987, p.3)

This chapter will examine the operation of Justice in relation to adult male sex offenders within the Criminal Justice system and in the context of offence-focused work. British society is dominated by white middle-class, professional, heterosexual, physically and intellectually able men. It is this group that dominates political, economic and intellectual activities, to the detriment of other groups. Prevalence studies indicate that sexual violence is common to all groups in society, yet what is known about the adult male sex offender is based on information obtained from convicted sex offenders. As such it gives an unbalanced perception of the sex offender often drawing from prejudiced views particularly in relation to convicted Black and Gay offenders. The paper articulates an anti-oppressive value base for practitioners, and discusses implications for practice.

Thus in this chapter we are concerned primarily with issues related to the treatment of Black[1] and Gay[2] men, convicted of sexual offences, by both the Criminal Justice and the Penal systems, although we recognise that developing an anti-oppressive value base has implications for all work with sex offenders. Central to our discussion are two interwoven features: the notions of cultural hegemony, and personal identity.

CULTURAL HEGEMONY AND IDENTITY

Cultural hegemony is the dominance, the ascendancy of one particular culture over other cultures. In Britain today the dominant culture is that of the white middle-class intellectually and physically able, heterosexual man. The dominance is sustained by personal and structural oppression. The National Association of Probation Officers (NAPO, 1990) defines racism thus:

> Racism is a systematic form of oppression and in Britain it is black people who are the victims of racism and its perpetrators are white. In our multi-racial society racism is a problem created and maintained by white people. NAPO therefore defines racism as a combination of power and prejudice exercised by white people and white institutions the effect of which is to systematically oppress black people. In short, therefore, racism is the systematic oppression of black people (p.3).

NAPO defines 'oppression' as:

> ...the application of prejudice and discrimination by people or institutions in positions of power the effect of which is to subjugate a person or a group of persons and to deny them access to equal and fair treatment (p.3).

However, oppressed groups are not homogenous and exclusive entities, and people can experience a number of different forms of oppression, as Brown (1993) comments:

> I have heard it commonly stated that racism is just another form of oppression. The argument goes on to say, that if one grasps an understanding and general concept

> of oppression then one will gain an understanding about all the forms of oppression, including racism. I am unsure about this theory, but one thing I can say is that racism, by its nature, can act as a vehicle to carry and promote all other forms of oppression. I would argue that racism is in a class of its own...
>
> the issues for Black women remain far more complex than those of their white counterparts. As well as experiencing racism they are still subject to sexism and combinations of the two. The sexism that Black women face is compounded even further because of racism. Black women are often placarded as unfortunate, willing brainless sexual non-entities by the media and white society. Being Black and disabled carries with it all the prejudices of disabilities, but also comprises the racist dynamics, that still have to be faced by the individual. The same of course could be said about sexuality. Black Gay and Lesbian people are discriminated against because of their sexual orientation, but still have to suffer racism because of their skin colour (p.6).

Hegemony is both embodied and sustained in the various products of our culture that describe some identities as positive whilst denying others. For example, in television advertising, there is a preponderance of White heterosexual images: disabled people are rarely shown except to persuade the viewer to donate to 'worthy' organisations. The few images of Black people are generally either in a sporting or a sexual context. There are no positive images of Gay men or Lesbians.

Similarly with language, the dominant grouping will often seek to suppress or eradicate languages that represent a different and, perhaps subversive, culture, whilst also using and approving pejorative terms to describe people not in the dominant group. The attempts of the British Government, at different times, to suppress the various Gaelic languages in the 'British' Isles both by legislation and by 'educational' programmes are but one example of this process. To a lesser degree until relatively recent times the accent with which a person spoke would either gain or restrict their access to employment particularly in public office, thus perpetuating the power of one particular class.

Groups have responded variously to these attempts to define them and control them. A common element in their resistance has been their attempts to assert their own self-definitions – their own language, names, culture and identity. The Women's Movement, the Civil Rights movement in the USA, the various groups of Black and Asian people, Gay rights and Disabled people's movement from the 1960s onwards have embodied this resistance. June Jordan (1989) suggests Black people in the United States of America define, develop and take pride in 'Black English' and their 'Black' identity. Debates within the Lesbian and Gay community reflect similar responses (Smith, 1992) .

The hegemony in which any therapeutic work is located constantly influences and affects it. This is seen most sharply when we consider the concept of identity.

Recognition of the importance of identity-work, particularly in responding to the needs of abused children has been the subject of important discussion in the last ten years (Maximé,1991; Ahmed, 1988; Modi and Pal 1992; Kennedy et al., 1993) and is relevant to the present discussion. The core components of identity that are commonly identified are gender, race, and sexuality. For instance, the Children Act states that 'due consideration should be given to the child's religious persuasion, cultural, racial, and linguistic background' (cited in Kennedy et al., 1993, p.30), and the Government guidance accompanying the Children Act 1989 adds that 'The needs and concerns of gay young men and women must be recognised and approached sympathetically (cited in McCaughey, 1993, p.28).

Maximé (1991) however, describes how in white dominated society some Black people deny their race and culture and have a low self-esteem. She describes a five stage model of the process necessary to enable an individual to develop a secure and confident black identity (pp.53-56). These stages are:

1. the *pre-encounter* stage where the person is unaware and has adopted a 'eurocentric' world view, and often denies that racism exists;
2. the *encounter* stage, where the person encounters racist circumstances which force them to begin to reinterpret their world view;
3. the *immersion* stage, where the person attempts to remove all aspects of their previous identity whilst developing an intense sense of their Blackness. Often at this stage the new identity is negatively based – i.e. in reaction to White oppression;
4. the *internalisation* stage where the individual has separated

from their old self and has moved to a new sense of self, positively defined, as Black;

5. the *internalisation-commitment stage* where the individual grounded in a positive sense of identity begins to be involved in Black groups and community issues, thus making an outward statement of their sense of identity.

Similar stages – from unawareness to aware integration have been described by a range of writers in relation to the formation of Gay identity (Ford, 1993 provides an extensive review of the literature).

We have described this process at length here both because we believe it applies to the development of positive identity for people in *all* oppressed groupings, and has particular relevance to working positively with adult male sex offenders. Indeed Maximé concludes her paper with both a warning and some guidance that are very relevant to the issues of this chapter:

> Of importance is the warning and message from Comer and Poussaint (1975). 'A positive identity...must be built on an inner core of pride and positive feelings...or it may fade away under the harsh light of realities'

and for workers to assist in the development of positive identity they:

> ...may be required to change (their) ideas and perhaps be involved in a re-education process which requires sensitivity and receptivity to race (p.56).

We will return to the implications of identity work with sex offenders later in this chapter. First however we look at White heterosexual constructions of sexuality and understandings of sexual violence.

WHITE HETEROSEXUAL CONSTRUCTIONS OF SEXUALITY AND UNDERSTANDINGS OF SEXUAL VIOLENCE.

In March 1989 42.1% of sentenced adult male sex offenders in the prisons of England and Wales were convicted of offences of rape. When the proportion of each ethnic group was examined in relation to this offence it was discovered that 37.1% of the White group of sex offenders were convicted of rape whilst the majority of Black sex offenders were convicted of rape including almost 80% of the

West Indian, Guyanese, African group (Cowburn, 1991, pp.21-22).

Understandings of black male sexuality as predatory and dangerous have pervaded common, clinical, police and judicial responses to sexual crimes for many years. For example, of the 455 men convicted of rape and executed in the USA between 1930 and 1967 405 were black (cited in Davis, 1981, p.172). La Free (1980) studied the inmate population of a maximum security prison in the USA. In relation to issues of race and racism he found that Black rapists did not receive longer or harsher sentences than their white counter-parts unless they had raped a white woman in which case their sentence was significantly longer and was served in harsher prisons. Davis (1981) argues that North American society manufactured the myth of the Black rapist to sustain and legitimise racial oppression and this prevents us from developing adequate theories of rape:

> The myth of the Black rapist continues to carry out the insidious work of racist ideology. It must bear a good portion of the responsibility for the failure of anti-rape theorists to seek the identity of the enormous numbers of anonymous rapists who remain unreported, untried and unconvicted. As long as their analyses focus on accused rapists who are reported and arrested, thus on only a fraction of the rapes committed, Black men and other men of colour will inevitably be viewed as the villains responsible for the current epidemic of sexual violence. The anonymity surrounding the vast majority of rapes is consequently treated as a statistical detail – or else a mystery whose meaning is inaccessible (Davis, 1981, p.199).

For more recent examples of collusion with this myth see Ellis (1989) who after long exposition cites 'evidence' to prove that Black men are more prone to rape than White men or 'Orientals'. Although he acknowledges that there is no evidence relating to 'Orientals', he does quote seven sources that, he claims, prove that Black men are more likely to rape than White men. At least three of the sources he cites only use official conviction data and thus the 'corroboration' for his racist theory may only indicate that White systems of criminal justice are racist in their operation.

The most influential of the sources quoted is Amir (1971). Amir's data was statistical information obtained from the police and related to all cases that they considered to be 'founded'. Ellis fails to recognise, or acknowledge the strong possibility that a white police force may be racially biased in how it responds to black and white men accused of rape. Also Ellis does not acknowledge that Amir's study was undertaken in a predominantly black area. Brownmiller (1975) notes:

> Since Amir was studying a large Northern city with an extensive black ghetto population, the sociologist's proportion of black offenders was higher than the national average...The FBI...records that 47% of all rapists are black. Amir in Philadelphia found that 82% of his rapists were black (p.182).

Just as Black sexuality is constructed by White society in such a way that it is perceived as predatory and dangerous and thus requiring strict control, so has the sexuality of the Gay man been similarly described by heterosexual dominated society. Ford and Robinson (1993), having considered the two principal heterosexual schools of thought concerning the aetiology of 'homosexuality' (social learning, and biologically determinist), comment that:

> ...underlying both of these positions is the concept of unrestrained and uncontrolled male sexuality but especially male homosexuality. This not so well concealed discourse feeds the myth of gay men as paedophiles who prey on young boys and may feed into the conceptions of practitioners in their work with sex offenders (p.12).

And they highlight the legal restrictions on the expression of Gay male sexuality which do not also apply to heterosexual behaviour- i.e. the age of consent, the fact that a third party allowing two consenting Gay men to stay together overnight could be guilty of procuring homosexual acts; two men kissing or cuddling in public can be charged with 'Indecency', etc.. All of this additional legislation further reinforces the idea that Gay male sexuality is predatory and in need of external control (Ford and Robinson, 1993, p.12).

Not only is the framing of legislation homophobic but the policing of Gay sexuality is discriminatory:

> In 1989, 31 men were sent to prison for consenting sex with men aged between 16 and 21, there were 3,500 prosecutions for consenting homosexual relations between men over the age of 16, with 2,700 convictions and 380

cautions. 30% of all convictions for sexual offences were for consensual gay behaviour, but this represented only 13% of recorded sex offences; men who commit consensual gay offences are four times more likely to be convicted than men who commit heterosexual and violent sex crimes (Tatchell, 1991; Stonewall, 1992, cited in Ford and Robinson, 1993).

In reviewing data relating to sex offender recidivism Barker and Morgan (1993) comment on the differential rates of re-conviction:

> Such studies are generally in agreement in finding the very highest recidivism amongst exhibitionists: rates between 30 and 71 per cent...Next in order of magnitude are: non-familial child molesters of boys, between 13 and 40 per cent; non-familial offenders against girls between 10 and 29 per cent; incest offenders 4 and 15 per cent; and rapists between 6 and 35 per cent (Barker and Morgan, 1993, p.15).

They urge caution in drawing conclusions from recidivism studies, because of a range of methodological inconsistencies across the studies (pp.12-14). This is echoed by both Quinsey (1984, p.101) in his review of recidivism studies of rapists, and also by Furby and her colleagues (1989, p.25) in their wider ranging review of the literature. However, in considering the 'landmark' study of Abel et al. (1987), Barker and Morgan (1993) note:

> One further anomaly is that the study revealed the highest rate of victimisation by offenders against boys. This is discrepant with findings from victim surveys...which identify girls as far more likely than boys to be sexually abused. The explanation may be a higher prevalence of men in the community who tend to abuse girls than was found in Abel's sample (p.8).

We would suggest another factor in the explanation: that statistics reflect the homophobic policing of consensual sexual activity.

IMPLICATIONS FOR PRACTICE

In this section we consider the necessity of adopting an anti-oppressive value-base and perspective for planning programmes of work with adult male sex offenders and the implications for practice. All people convicted of sexual offences, belong to one heavily stigmatised group i.e. the 'sex offender', but many also may belong to other stigmatised groups because of their race, gender, sexuality, mental or physical ability, age or class. These powerful stigmas, and in this paper we are focusing on race and sexuality, when they come together are very strong inhibitors to engaging in therapeutic or offence-focused work. If work with perpetrators is to empower them not to commit further sexual offences it must not only confront their offending behaviour by de-constructing the cognitive frameworks which support and nurture their offending; it must also actively address the nature of oppression in their lives and help them to develop a different and positive sense of their identity. To do this programmes need to consider centrally the various 'core components of identity' which we identified earlier. However, stigma and experience of oppression are also the common experience of many workers and thus must also be considered. We begin by looking at issues for workers.

Worker Issues

The individual worker

> Social work confrontation of social work profession precedes social work confrontation of black clients at least in the early stage (Ahmad, 1992, 35).

Exploration and examination of workers' own experience of oppression is necessary before undertaking any therapeutic work and especially before undertaking any joint work – i.e. the pairing up of colleagues of same race, different race, of same gender or different gender. Examination must take place of both how as individuals workers they may be oppressed and how they may inappropriately use their power to oppress. A male probation officer who contributed to the *Changing Men* practice manual (Cowburn et al., 1992) commented:

> In working with sex offenders, the male worker initially may find himself having difficulty in coping with the emotional demands of the task. Once he begins to work intensely with sex offenders there are two main influences which shift him from the safe ground he has previously practised on. The first is the style of the groupwork...based

> on feminist theory. The second, is that the abuse of women and children is emotive, and in order to work effectively he will find that there can be no safe withdrawal into the safe collusive ' boys will be boys' attitude...often adopted by male probation officers in relation to other offending, e.g. car thefts (p38).

Issues for women are also summarised in *Changing Men*:

> Sex offenders are expert at victimising children and women, and women workers do not escape their attentions. It is essential for women workers to be enabled to retain a sense of their gender identity whilst undertaking this work. Workers are often routinely exposed to material that could undermine them (p.34).

For Black workers the above situations are exacerbated significantly by racist responses from both offenders and other workers:

> Black workers have to work very hard to prove to their white clients that they are as good as, or better than their white colleagues. Black female workers have to work twice as hard in the engagement process, compared to their white counterparts (p36).

Gay men and Lesbian workers whether or not they have declared their sexuality similarly experience negatively attitudes and behaviours from both offenders and other workers.

Identifying and confronting oppression

Dominelli (1989, pp.12-13) in discussing white workers' responses to examining their own racism identifies a number of strategies that are commonly adopted to deny or deflect from the issue. These strategies involve both acts of omission (for example 'decontextualisation' as a strategy enables white workers intellectually to acknowledge the existence of racism whilst treating Black people as though they were white) and acts of commission (for example 'dumping' the responsibility for challenging racism on to Black workers; Dominelli notes that 'this can often mean referring all black clients to a black worker'). Such strategies are used similarly in relation to other forms of oppression. Identifying them in both individual and agency practices are essential prerequisites to developing practice that does not deny other peoples' identity and experience. Identification of oppressive practices and commitment to changing them are key elements in developing strong working relationships.

Joint and co-working

The distinction that we would make between joint and co-working is that in the latter the workers are physically working together – generally at the same time with the same client or client group. Joint working can involve different workers working with related clients to a common aim – e.g. a probation officer working with a perpetrator of sexual violence and a social worker working with a victim of the perpetrator: both sharing an overall aim of victim protection but working to different objectives with their specific client.

Both forms of work ideally should require workers to share and agree a common value base, aims and objectives. In a context of anti-oppressive practice this will involve a discussion of power dynamics and differing personal experiences. Mistry and Brown (1991) have highlighted many of the issues to explore in relation to Black/White co-working: we suggest that other areas of oppression are similarly examined. They describe how personal idiosyncrasies coupled with being Black can be used – in predominantly white groups – as a vehicle for negating and dismissing Black workers. They also note that the interaction between a Black/White worker pairing is often interpreted by clients as a relationship between the powerful and the powerless. Obviously these comments are relevant to other worker pairings, and essential for workers to address. Mistry and Brown state that:

> If both workers share a common understanding of the structural and political context of racism they are likely to be able to demonstrate a consistent model of working (p.107).

It is important for workers to discuss these issues before they start work together, but also recognise that issues of power and oppression in a working relationship are never finally resolved but require regular review and adjustment.

Supervision and support

The terms 'supervision' and 'support' relate to different processes that serve different needs and objectives. These processes may occasionally overlap. According to what is required, supervision and support may be provided by different people according to their grade, role, race, gender, sexual preference and physical ability. The table[3] below lists some workers' needs and suggests how they might be met. Where we stated 'support group' this specifically refers to groupings of workers based on race, gender, sexuality, and disability.

Workers' Needs	**Function**	**By Whom**
Management of feelings	support	Peers, support group, SPO
Consistent quality of work	supervision	SPO, peer pairing
Accountability	supervision	SPO
Values Check	supervision	Peers, support group, SPO
Anti-oppressive practice	supervision	Peers, support group, SPO
Equitable allocation of work	team management, supervision	SPO
Identifying training needs	supervision	SPO, team
Career development	supervision	SPO
Awareness of stresses	support	SPO, peers, support group
Individual practice issues	support/supervision	Peers, co-worker, support group, SPO, consultant

However, whatever the purpose or focus of a supervisory relationship both parties need to recognise and acknowledge the power differentials within it, and how these effect both workers, and offenders(s). For example, is it appropriate for two white workers – one supervising the other's work – to be working with a Black sex offender, without any Black consultancy? Perhaps expediency, based on a scarcity of agency resources, will find justifications. However, even if both white workers had received and internalised anti-racist training, it is our view they would still be unable to offset the implications of the substantial power differences adequately enough to undertake work with the Black sex offender, which is not oppressive.

STRUCTURED APPROACHES TO WORK

Work with sex offenders almost always passes through four phases: selection, assessment, work, and evaluation. These phases are however, not always recognised and acknowledged.

Selection

The decision to undertake a piece of work with an offender is most often statutorily determined (reports, conditions in court orders and statutory licences). However when offenders have the option to volunteer for work on their offending behaviour their experience of oppression may affect their willingness and ability to do so. Wilson and Shine (1990) in their study of Aylesbury Young Offender Institution noted that Black sex offenders were unwilling to participate in programmes of groupwork intended to examine their offending behaviour. In the light of the fact that the Black young offenders were otherwise as willing as their White counterparts to engage in other activities of the institution, it would appear that Droisen's (1989) explanation of why Black families do not report familial abuse may be relevant in this instance. She suggests the following explanation for this phenomenon: to be Black in a white dominated racist society is to feel and to be stigmatised; being known as a victim of sexual abuse is also experienced as a stigma. This potentially double negative experience, Droisen argues, effectively inhibits many Black victims from reporting their abusers to White authorities. Additionally she notes that such reporting would possibly be seen by a betrayal of their own racial group.

It is also noteworthy that Cowburn (1991) found no Black workers working (within the Prison Service) with sex offenders on their offending behaviour.

Assessment

There are a number of different types of assessment: risk, and treatment/work needs assessments are what concern us here. Assessment is the process that precedes a period of planned intervention: whether the intervention is a programme of work, a child protection plan, or the re-call of a dangerous offender to secure accommodation. The process involves the gathering of relevant information and systematically analysing it and then formulating a plan of action on the basis of the analysis. The main areas about which information is gathered are: life history, including sexual life history, pattern and type of offending, level of responsibility accepted, attitudes to children, women and acts of violence (such as rape), history of other convictions, patterns of substance and alcohol abuse, current support networks, issues related to sense of self – sexuality, racial and gender identity, and level of social skills. Identifying areas in this way is helpful insofar as it highlights the many issues that need to be considered but there are also potential dangers if an anti-oppressive perspective is not explicitly included. For example, in looking at a person's life history and support network, Salter in her list of information required in an assessment (pp.182-83) specifies that attention should be given to 'strengths and problems in marriage'. To assume a marriage (in Britain at least) is to assume a wife and to assume a wife is to assume heterosexuality: such an assumption may prevent a full and adequate assessment of a Gay man who has committed sex offences. In relation to giving information, some Asian languages do not have the vocabulary to describe the detail often required in offence accounts – this may well inhibit certain offenders' ability to describe their offence and this in turn may be considered to be a kind of denial. Speaking of work with sexually abused boys from the Bangladeshi community, Neate (1991) noted the difficulties experienced by Nadira Osmany, the Bangladeshi worker:

> There was no language for her to use. Sex, and homosexuality in particular, is taboo for discussion outside marriage. The language is either academic or the equivalent of four-letter words. She had to hint at what had happened, then use graphic language to describe the acts (p.4).

Additionally she identified a gender dimension to the work that was potentially problematic in this sensitive area:

> The children...were all boys, and Osmany is now convinced, albeit against conventional wisdom, that a male worker should handle disclosure work with Asian boys. She says: 'I did get the information from the boys but the whole thing was very, very embarrassing and distressing for them' (p.4).

The experience is similar in other Asian languages (Neate, 1991, p.4).

Deciding what is relevant and how it is interpreted is not value-free and generally embodies the 'world-view' of the dominant group. Owusu-Bempah (1990) has described the white-dominated /Eurocentric family assessments that occur in British social work practice:

> Set in a European framework, professional training 'pathologises' or at best ignores black people's needs, values and culture, including even their family or kinship patterns. Black people are expected to conform to white middle-class needs and values in order to receive a professional service. Those unable to do so are therefore pathologised by practitioners...

An identical process occurs when the assessment occurs within a heterosexist framework: sexual behaviour between mutually consenting adult males is often both pathologised and criminalised (Tatchell, 1991).

However, merely to adopt a culturally sensitive – what Sharma Ahmed (1988) has described as '...the celebration of saris, samosas and steel bands' (p.9) – fails to take account of the effect of negative discrimination and oppression in daily experience:

> The important point is that for black clients the centrality of racism needs to be more centrally acknowledged in the assessment process, and cultural explanations need to be considered in the context of racism (Ahmed, 1988, p.9).

Ahmed (pp.16-17) argues for a radical re-think of standard assessment procedures which recognises the specific experiences of oppression which the person being assessed will have experienced. She notes:

> ...The crux of the problem seems to be that to use a model drawn from one system to talk about, or measure another will produce a distorted picture which hardly aids understanding...

Although she is speaking specifically about assessing Black children her words are also pertinent to the assessment of Black and Gay sex offenders. She also comments:

> Good intentions are not enough. Political beliefs and value standpoints have to be operationalised. There is a need not only to say, but to do something different. In other words, there is a need to transform principles into practice. This can begin with the assessment process. Developing guidelines for practice which incorporate the *centrality of racism* (all forms of oppression) is one disciplined approach to avoiding simplistic explanations (our addition in parentheses).

To obtain a full picture all assessments should find out how individuals view themselves in terms of race, gender, sexuality and ability – such understanding may provide important information for areas of future work. What sense of self a person has about themselves will crucially effect their response to any programme of work. This issue is developed further below.

PROGRAMMES: STYLE AND CONTENT

In their report on probation and other programmes for sex offenders in England and Wales, Barker and Morgan (1993) comment:

> Treatment philosophies vary little from one programme to another, whether delivered over weeks, months or years. This lack of variation is partly due to the overwhelming influence of one or two training organisations. It is also the result of a growing belief in the effectiveness of the cognitive-behavioural approach with sex offenders. ... treatment in this vein concentrates initially on improving the offenders' motivation to change through increasing their empathy with victims, and through identifying their cycles of offending. The later stages of this treatment approach attempt to build on this increased awareness and provide offenders with behavioural methods of controlling their impulse to offend (p.45).

By 'treatment philosophies' we assume Barker and Morgan to be referring to the theoretical approaches embodied in a treatment programme. Whilst cognitive-behaviourally based programmes appear to be the most successful in reducing recidivism (Marshall and Barbaree, 1991), there is little discussion of the philosophical or ideological value base(s) which underpin the programmes, and how they inform and influence both the exercises and the group dynamics. Without a clear anti-oppressive value base it is likely that race and sexuality will either be ignored or assumed to be white and heterosexual, thus the unintended consequence of some programmes may be both racist and heterosexist. In these circumstances programmes will be oppressive to Black and Gay men.

GROUPWORK

The inequalities of power and the potential for abuse from the dominant group – white heterosexual men – constitute a substantial challenge to workers planning groupwork (and particularly with sex offenders- where the potential cost of discussing offending behaviour is already very high). Most groupwork programmes are cognitive-behavioural in their theoretical orientation (Barker and Morgan, 1993). It is likely that such programmes, focusing as they do on 'social learning', may carry implicitly in their content Eurocentric, and heterosexist assumptions: thus making it additionally difficult for Black and homosexual offenders to participate in anything other than a nominal manner.

We have already noted that Wilson and Shine (1990) found that an otherwise active group of Black offenders did not volunteer for groupwork programmes intended to look at their offending behaviour. Ahmad (1992) adds weight to our concerns about minority Black participation in white dominated groups:

> One of the major problems of 'multi-racial' groupwork has been that 'groups' are predominantly White, with one or two Black members. As a result, Black members, instead of gaining support and strength, instead of sharing common feelings and aspirations have found themselves even more isolated and sometimes in threatening situations...even in those groupwork settings, where there is numerical parity between Black and White members, there may be different perceptions about common issues that are difficult or impossible to share; there may be group dynamics that undermine Black members' experience and contributions, there may even be a clash of interests and priorities between Black and White members. 'Multi-racial' groupwork needs to be prepared to deal with these shortcomings and pitfalls. Otherwise, groupwork, however inadvertently, will just collude with the social control of Black clients even though in the disguise of groupwork (p.62).

It is not surprising that currently few Black sex offenders are involved in groupwork programmes (Barker and Morgan, 1993).

We are aware that there is debate amongst Black workers about whether or not Black offenders should attend White dominated groups. Whilst the position articulated by Ahmad and ourselves may be considered to be an ideologically 'pure' position, it is pointed out that in the present economic and political climate such a position may effectively deny Black sex offenders any groupwork experience. The situation is further exacerbated when a Black offender is required by a court order, or condition in a licence to attend a programme.

Ford and Robinson (1993) point to the impact on Gay men of such sex offender programmes, noting that not only is there the issue of safety within the group dynamics, but that certain exercises in programmes may have a significantly higher cost to the Gay man- exercises, relating to sexuality and sexual history for example may put the Gay man in a position where he either lies and assumes a heterosexual mask or he potentially jeopardises his safety. They suggest that much work, particularly on issues of sexuality should occur in all Gay groups or individually.

THE WAY FORWARD

In developing a programme of work for sex offenders that operates from an anti-oppressive value base and yet does not collude with the offenders' denial, there are two main areas to consider: the composition and style of programmes and the underlying values of the work.

The Composition and Style of Programmes

Following her review of twelve treatment projects for sex offenders in the United States of America, Knopp (1988) noted what she called the formation of a ' new sex-offender discipline' (p.27). She identified 'six comprehensive goals for the new sex offender discipline.', amongst which were:

1. Each sex offender needs a complete; individualised assessment and treatment plan; effective initial and ongoing assessments are prerequisites for successful treatment.
2. Each sex offender needs to (a) accept responsibility for the offence(s) in which he has been involved and (b) have an understanding of the sequence of thoughts, feelings, events, circumstances, and arousal stimuli that make up the 'offence syndrome' that precedes his involvement in sexually aggressive behaviours.

3. Each sex offender needs to learn how to (a) intervene in or break into his offence syndrome at its very first sign and (b) call upon appropriate methods tools, or procedures he has learned in order to suppress, control, manage and stop the behaviour.
4. Each sex offender needs to engage in a re-education and re-socialisation process in order to (a) replace anti-social thought and behaviours with prosocial ones, (b) acquire a positive self concept and new attitudes and expectations of himself, and (c) learn new social and sexual skills to help cultivate positive, satisfying, pleasurable and non-threatening relationships with others...(pp.28-29).

Treatment programmes must include a range of treatment/work approaches '...psycho-dynamic, behavioural, cognitive and biomedical elements and incorporate a wide range of educational and training components' (p.27).

Most sex offender programmes in England and Wales concentrate on the second and third features listed by Knopp – those directly addressing the analysis and changing of offending behaviour. The most common means of doing this is in programmes of groupwork. Currently most programmes appear to be concentrating on the de-construction of offenders' denial – particularly of responsibility, and harm to the victim.

Barker and Morgan (1993) note:

> ... it is on the early phases of the treatment process that most of the probation schemes concentrate, in part because many of them are too short to have time to address the other issues. *The technique of 'confronting offending' is commonly used by probation officers with all types of offenders, and this experience clearly translates to the confronting model of working with sex offenders* (p.45 our emphasis).

Although, it may have been that the confrontational skills developed by probation officers in working with sex offenders were generalised to other offending behaviours, it would be generally agreed that 'confrontation' is a prime focus in many programmes of work with sex offenders. Challenging the offender's initially passive account of his behaviour and helping him accept full responsibility for his offending behaviour is a core component of many of the current programmes.

There is clearly a place for confronting offenders' minimalist view of both their own responsibility and the harm that their actions have caused. However for such confrontation to be effective in reducing the risk offenders pose it needs to be experienced within the context of a relationship that is not oppressive and does not deny the offender some positive identity. Pithers et al. (1988, p.147) note:

> Rather than *beginning* therapy with confrontational techniques designed to 'break through the denial system' and *force* the client to admit responsibility for his crimes, the RP (Relapse Prevention) therapist encourages responsibility on the part of the client by fostering an atmosphere of co-operation. This *firm, but nonassaultative, approach* has several goals. By encouraging the client to serve as his own co-therapist, a sense of objectivity and detachment in the client's consideration of his own behaviours is created. Further, an atmosphere of openness is established in which the client and therapist mutually may begin to explore the problem behaviour without the extreme defensiveness that might otherwise he engendered. The absence of a *condemnatory confrontation* and the focus on the client's behaviours enable the client to see that sexually aggressive behaviour is an unacceptable act that he has performed rather than an indication of something he is and will always be a sex offender. Finally this non confrontational introduction encourages the client from the beginning of therapy to play an active part in determining pace and content of his programme (our emphasis).

Confrontation itself is not a value-free activity, and may be experienced differently by both worker and offender according to the gender, race, sexuality, age and ability of both parties: it, therefore, requires the worker to examine her/his own value system. Ahmad (1992, p.35) states that confrontation in an aware and anti-oppressive manner 'requires social work confidence and competence.'. This, she argues, can only be gained when workers are continually 'aware of their own perceptions and values' that have oppressive connotations. A prerequisite for this is 'an ongoing programme of self evaluation', and an essential prerequisite of an ongoing programme is self evaluation, self confrontation.

Whilst confronting offending behaviour is an important component in a comprehensive programme for sex offenders, it is not enough and by itself may, in fact, be harmful. If offending sexually allows offenders to feel power and consequently a strong sense of self, to de-construct that self without replacing it with a positive, non-harmful alternative will not allow them to develop non-offending ways of finding self-affirmation. Considering how this can be done is essential for all offenders but appears particularly crucial for Black and Gay sex offenders whose core identity may be completely ignored by current provision.

At the beginning of this chapter we described the relationship between oppression and identity – oppression denies or marginalises identities that are not part of the dominant group in society. Apart from the implications, already discussed, for group work, we suggest that understanding of this relationship needs to be at the core of all programmes for sex offenders. Work needs to enquire into (assessment) and help to develop a person's positive sense of identity as a firm base from which knowledge, skills and understanding about offending behaviour can be brought together to avoid re-offending.

Underlying Values of the Work

Of particular importance is how workers understand sexual violence and how they understand the links with oppression in wider society. Below we suggest a value base for work with sex offenders that incorporates an awareness of oppression.

Understandings of sexual violence within western societies

1. Sexually abusive acts are a use and abuse of power.
2. People who commit sexually abusive acts can be of either gender, any race, culture, class, sexual preference, and learning ability. They can be of most ages. Some people who are physically disabled may also commit acts that are sexually abusive.
3. People who have been abused sexually should define if and how they would describe themselves in relation to that experience. They can be of either gender, any race, culture, class, sexual preference, physical and learning ability or age. We believe that they are always harmed by the experience, whether or not additional physical violation occurred.

4. People who have been abused sexually are never responsible for being abused.
5. People who abuse other people sexually are always responsible for the abuse.

Implications

All offence focused work in the area of sexual violence must consider and address how perpetrators of sexual violence have used their power to harm their victims. However, assessment and programmes of work must consider how oppression in British society has affected the lives of the offenders themselves. Any work that ignores structural oppression in British society cannot be successful in helping reduce offending behaviour. Programmes of work should particularly consider the following issues:

1. Most dominant understandings of the sexuality of people in oppressed groups are negative. They are often viewed as being 'over-sexed and under-controlled'. These understandings provide the 'justification' for oppression disguised as social control.
2. The sexuality of people in these groups is more seriously policed and punished.
3. The pervasive presence of oppression may make it impossible for people in oppressed groupings to participate in groupwork programmes dominated by white heterosexual men.
4. Exploration and examination of workers' own experience of oppression should be a prerequisite to undertaking any therapeutic work and is essential before undertaking any joint-work.

CONCLUDING REMARKS

Knopp's (1988) first requirement of a sex offender treatment programme is that all sex offenders receive a full individualised assessment and treatment plan. If this were to happen, taking into account issues of oppression, it would become apparent that only to provide groupwork programmes for offenders is inadequate not only because some pieces of work are more appropriately addressed individually, but that groups have the potential to inhibit the participation and contribution of people from oppressed groups.

In this paper we have concentrated on the Black and Gay male sex offender, however, in considering these issues there inevitably develops a critique of White male heterosexuality, which may also be incorporated into programmes of work with all male sex offenders. We suggest that programmes adopt and develop an explicit value base that informs the choice and application of appropriate theories and of methods of practice. This should help confront offending behaviour whilst enabling offenders to develop a positive sense of their identity not constrained or defined by the cultural hegemony of the white heterosexual intellectually and physically able middle class man. This is essential if all sex offenders are to receive equal but different and just treatment by the criminal justice system.

Notes

1. The term 'Black' is used to denote people of African, Asian, and Caribbean descent. Whilst it is acknowledged that this group is in most ways far from homogenous, in Britain they do have one thing in common – namely that they will suffer racism.
2. Similarly, Gay men and Lesbians are not a homogenous group – only sharing homophobic abuse. We are aware that there is much dobate about language and naming (see Smyth, 1992). In this chapter we use the terms Gay men and Lesbians.
3. This table is a development of a similar table featured in Cowburn, Wilson and Loewenstein (1992, p.39) and was originally the work of Jo Thompson a Senior Probation Officer in Nottinghamshire.

Thirteen
Mental disorder, justice and censure

Rob Canton

> All other things being equal, though obviously they are not, it seems to be a plausible hypothesis that the greater the amount of information on the totality of the life of the relevant system members, the less useful (and needed) are generalised concepts such as 'sickness', 'madness' – and 'crime'. The system members come to know so much about each other, that the broad concepts in a way become too simple. They do not add information, they do not explain (Nils Christie).

Theories of justice and just punishment presume that people are *responsible* for their behaviour – and so may justly be punished – and sufficiently *rational* to respond to the threat of punishment by conforming their conduct to the requirements of the law. All theories must therefore give an account of the principles that should shape the appropriate response to people who are not (or not fully) rational or responsible. Our moral intuitions are troubled by the idea of punishing people who do not understand the nature of what they are doing or, in some way or another, cannot help themselves. Children and mentally disordered defendants[1] have been taken to be the clearest examples of people who ought not, on these grounds, to be liable to punishment and for whom treatment might be thought to be appropriate instead (Walker, 1983).

In relation to young offenders, the 'treatment model' found its most complete legislative expression in the Children and Young Persons Act 1969. The treatment ideal, which may not in any case have been realised in practice, soon began to come under strong criticism (Morris and Giller, 1987). Not only was treatment not seen to be working, this approach disregarded a child's rights to justice – in particular, the right not to be punished beyond desert. Treatment appeared to allow or even to require a disproportionate imposition in the name of the young person's welfare. The principles of the Act were gradually eroded during the next two decades and the Criminal Justice Act 1991 now requires the Youth Court to determine sentence in the same way as an adult court: in accordance with just deserts.

By contrast, there has been no sustained campaign for justice for mentally disordered people appearing in criminal courts (though see Bean, 1986). On the contrary, it is settled government policy that mentally disordered offenders should wherever possible be diverted from the criminal justice system: treatment, not punishment, is what is required.

After sketching this policy and the ways in which it is intended to be given effect, I shall suggest that, by at least one significant measure, it is failing. I shall consider Part III of the Mental Health Act 1983[2], especially section 37, and try to show that the statute itself contributes to this failure of policy, as well as denying justice to mentally disordered offenders. I shall argue that Part III reflects – but also *legitimates* – culturally embedded attitudes towards mentally disordered offenders which influence decisions at different points in the criminal justice process and work against the interests of these defendants. Throughout I shall be submitting that the structure of the law allows discrimination and shall adduce some evidence that discrimination is taking place. The position is made worse by inadequate resource provision and the difficulties that many vulnerable people experience in trying to get the care that they need. I shall also be noting the strongly censured and evocative language of mental disorder and crime and considering its effect on people who take decisions. Although this is primarily a critical enterprise, I shall conclude with some specific proposals for practice, particularly the practice of the Probation Service.

THE POLICY TO DIVERT

The consolidating Home Office Circular 66/90 states that:

> It is government policy that, wherever possible, mentally disordered persons should receive care and treatment from the health and social services.

This policy has been repeatedly endorsed by government ministers, by circulars, regulations and codes of practice (for instance, the Code for Crown Prosecutors) and now has the authoritative support of the recently formed Criminal Justice Consultative Council (CJCC, 1993). The *Review of Health and Social Services for Mentally Disordered Offenders*, chaired by Dr John Reed, is premised on this policy and the difficulty of realising its implementation is the principal concern of the review.

The Home Office Circular identifies several points in the criminal justice process, from arrest to sentence and punishment, at which diversion of mentally disordered people might be effected. The police can take someone (who may, but need not, have committed an offence) to a safe place (Mental Health Act 1983, s.136). If a person is arrested, there are, in some parts of the country, facilities for psychiatric assessment in police custody. The police may choose to administer a caution. If the police conclude that a prosecution is appropriate, the Crown Prosecution Service should consider 'discontinuing' if the person is mentally disordered.

Some courts enable psychiatric personnel to undertake assessment to divert defendants from the process at that stage. If there is to be a remand and bail is refused, the court is empowered to remand to hospital (instead of prison) for assessment (MHA 1983, s.35). If a mentally disordered person is remanded to prison custody, the Secretary of State may authorise transfer to a hospital (MHA 1983, s.48). There are certain sentencing powers available to the courts specifically for mentally disordered offenders. If a serving prisoner is believed to be mentally disordered, the Secretary of State may approve transfer to hospital (s.47).

It is to be noted that in no case does this Circular, any statute or Code of Practice *require* diversion. It is always understood that other considerations (defined imprecisely if at all, but often associated with the seriousness of the allegation) may supervene and require the criminal process to be continued. Discretion remains with the decision-taker, who is encouraged to be mindful of the particular vulnerability and needs of mentally disordered people. The effect of the Home Office Circular, then, is to heighten awareness of and sensitivity to mentally disordered people in their relation to the criminal justice system: it does not (and is not intended to) take away discretion.

Is the Policy Working?

How the success of this policy is to be assessed is a complex question, but one measure, presumably, might be the numbers of mentally disordered people in prison. It was, after all, a concern about the numbers of mentally disordered people in prison that led to the formulation of the policy in the first place. And by this measure, the policy cannot be said to be succeeding.

Coid has commented on the numbers of mentally disordered people being held on remand (Coid, 1988). Gunn and his colleagues found that 37% of males and 56% of females serving prison sentences of six months or more may have a medically identifiable disorder (Gunn, 1991). If their sample was representative, then more than 9000 prisoners may be suffering from a significant mental disturbance.[3] Although this study and its implications must be interpreted with care, Prins aptly comments that: 'The numbers give cause for considerable concern and merely serve to flesh out the anecdotal evidence of unsuitable detention and of suicidal behaviour in prison' (Prins, 1992, p.434). There are plainly grounds, then, for thinking that the policy is not working.

Failures of policy and other malfunctions are often scrutinised as problems of implementation and remedies consequently sought in a redistribution of resources or in training initiatives or system management. Doreen McBarnet, however, has urged close attention to the character of statute and regulation in seeking an understanding of the way in which the criminal justice system operates (McBarnet, 1978, 1983):

> ...a good many of the practices in criminal justice described as informal perversions of the formal rules are in fact allowed, facilitated or upheld in the formal rules of statute or precedent (McBarnet, 1978, p.30).

It is with the legal framework itself, then, that inquiry should begin.

Sentencing Powers

Just as mental disorder may or may not be a decisive consideration in diverting a person from the criminal justice process, a criminal court is able to use its full range of sentencing powers in dealing with mentally disordered offenders. There are, however, certain specific measures that are available to the court.

Hospital Order (Section 37)

Where the court is satisfied on the evidence of two medical practitioners that a defendant (who need not be convicted) is suffering from mental illness, psychopathic disorder, severe mental impairment or mental impairment of a nature or degree which makes it appropriate for him (sic) to be detained in hospital for medical treatment (and in the case of psychopathic disorder or mental impairment, such treatment 'is likely to alleviate or prevent a deterioration of his condition'), the court may commit the defendant to hospital for a (renewable) period of six months. The court must be of the opinion 'having regard to all the circumstances including the nature of the offence and the character and antecedents of the offender, and to the other available methods of dealing with him' that this is most suitable.

If the requirements of a Hospital Order are made out but it is not believed that admission to hospital is warranted the court may make a *Guardianship Order.*

At the same time as making a Hospital Order, a Crown Court may, if satisfied that this is necessary to protect the public from serious harm from the defendant, additionally impose *restrictions on discharge,* with or without a specified limit of time (s.41).

Psychiatric Probation Order

Before a Probation Order can be made, the court must be satisfied that the offence is serious enough to warrant the making of a community penalty (Criminal Justice Act 1991, 6 (1)). If further satisfied that the probationer's mental condition requires or is susceptible to treatment (and that this is not such as to require the making of a Hospital or Guardianship Order), the court may include a requirement in the Probation Order that the probationer undergo such treatment. (Powers of Criminal Courts Act 1973, Schedule 1A as created by Criminal Justice Act 1991, Schedule 1 Part II). What this entails varies considerably. An Order with this requirement may be supervised with no more (and perhaps less) rigour than any other Probation Order. In some cases, though, the imposition is substantial. In about 13% of all such orders, there is a residential requirement. HM Inspectorate of Probation noted that 'often the restriction on liberty was extremely high' (HM Inspectorate of Probation, 1993, p.2.3)

Use of Psychiatric Sentencing Powers

None of these measures is common. In 1991, 677 hospital orders without restrictions were made. (In each of the preceding 10 years the figure was between 520 and 760.) Additionally, the courts made 140 Hospital Orders with restrictions on discharge. (Home Office, 1993f, Table 12). 913 people commenced Probation Orders with a condition of treatment (of whom 119 had a residential requirement) representing about 2% of all probation commencements (HM Inspectorate of Probation, 1993, p.1.8).

The table shows the categories of offence for which the Hospital Order is used.

Admissions under Section 37 Mental Health Act 1983 in 1991

Offence Type	Number	%
Violence	163	24
Sexual	46	7
Burglary	59	9
Robbery	32	5
Theft	74	11
Fraud	7	1
Criminal Damage[1]	114	17
Other Indictable	56	8
Summary	126	19
Total	677	101

(From Home Office, 1993f)

The proportion of s.37 admissions for *summary* offences is to be remarked on. Over the last decade, the proportion of summary offences occasioning s.37 receptions has never been less than 15% and has often been higher than one-fifth. Summary offences are offences that may only be tried in the Magistrates' Court: there is no right of jury trial. Although by no means necessarily trivial, they are, almost by definition, among the offences that are least seriously regarded. In 1991, 84% of summary (non-motoring) offenders were fined and just 1% sent to prison (Home Office, 1993a). Section 37 requires that the offence in respect of which the order is made must be 'imprisonable', but this is not at all to say that a sentence of imprisonment would otherwise have been imposed. The summary offences which lead to s37 admissions are likely to include especially offences against public order and some vagrancy offences. Some of these will be serious instances of their type; many will not. Nor is it to be assumed that the offences in the other categories are necessarily serious. There is evidence, then, of 'occasionalism' (Walker, 1985, p.348) – the opportunity of the court appearance being taken to require people to undergo treatment.

The Prison Statistics include a high number of 'other' offences and cases where the offence was not recorded. This precludes any detailed comparison between s.37 admissions and prison receptions. So far as can be told, though, there is a greater proportion of violent and sexual offences than among prison receptions as a whole (only about 14% prison receptions are convicted of these offences) and a much smaller proportion of theft and burglary, (which accounted for more than one-third prison receptions in 1991).

Comparable figures for people made subject to Psychiatric Probation Orders are not available. The recent Home Office Thematic Inspection considered 138 Orders made in five areas and found that, despite local variation, 'overall they were not markedly different from those expected among probation cases generally: theft, burglary and car crime, but also with a slight bias towards indecency, violence and criminal damage'. These Orders had been made before the Criminal Justice Act 1991, but, applying the criteria of the new framework, HM Inspectorate concluded that between one-half and three-quarters would be considered 'serious enough' to warrant a community penalty (HM Inspectorate of Probation, 1993, p.3.5).

The figures suggest (although it could not be said that they demonstrate) that s.37 admissions include both serious offenders (the high proportion of violent and sexual offences) and minor offenders (the high proportion of summary offenders). The same pattern is suggested by the observations of HM Inspectorate on psychiatric probation orders. Psychiatric disposals, then, are used both for people who might otherwise have gone to prison and, at the other end of the scale, for people who would otherwise have been fined or discharged.

Bean has argued that, as a sentencing measure, s.37 is an aberration, entirely disconnected from – and at odds with – the framework of sentencing which is applied to other offenders (Bean, 1986). This anomaly has been made the more acute by the enactment of the Criminal Justice Act 1991. Before then, sentencers had a range of different (often incompatible) principles to draw on to determine sentence (Walker, 1991). The Act attempted to replace this eclectic approach with a coherent statutory framework within the tradition of just deserts:

> Punishment in proportion to the seriousness of the crime has long been accepted as one of the many objectives in sentencing. It should be the principal focus for sentencing decisions. (Home Office, 1991, p.2.2)

Seriousness was to be determined by assessing the wrong done and the defendant's responsibility, then imposing a commensurate loss of liberty. Almost the only sentencing power unaffected by the new legislation – and certainly the only power involving a real and immediate loss of liberty – was the Hospital Order. The principles of just punishment, it seems, are not to guide the court's response to mentally disordered offenders. It is as if justice and desert are not predicates that can be ascribed to the conduct or treatment of mentally disordered people.

An additional juristic anomaly is that mental disorder which, if relevant at all, should make an offender *less* responsible (and so deserving of a lesser punishment) becomes the grounds for the imposition of a *greater* loss of liberty than might otherwise be deserved.

This rather confusing position can be elucidated by an examination of some of the background assumptions of the legislation and, in particular, the status of mental disorder as an explanation of offending.

MENTAL DISORDER AS EXPLANATION

Section 37 does not require there to be any connection between the crime and the mental disorder. If mental disorder is to remove or diminish culpability, or indeed to contribute to an explanation, it might be supposed that a causal connection would need to be established – even if, in practice, the nature of this connection might be difficult to establish.

When the court is considering the issue of a defendant's innocence or guilt, this connection has to be demonstrated. The M'Naghten test states that:

> ...to establish a defence on the ground of insanity, it must be clearly proved that, at the time of committing the act,

> the party accused was labouring under *such a defect of reason*, from disease of the mind, *as not to know* the nature and quality of the act he was doing; or, if he did know it, that he did not know that what he was doing was wrong (quoted Prins, 1986, p.15, my emphasis).

The not-knowing must be a *consequence* of the defect of reason. The judges who answered the House of Lords in these terms may have recalled the way in which Thomas Erskine had set himself his task in his famous defence of James Hadfield, who had shot and wounded King George III:

> I must convince you, not only that the unhappy prisoner was a lunatic ... but that the act in question was the immediate, unqualified offspring of the disease (quoted Porter, 1987, p.116).

If, but only if, this connection can be made out, the defendant is entitled to an acquittal (the 'special verdict').

If Murder is to be reduced to Manslaughter on the grounds of diminished responsibility, a similar connection has to be demonstrated:

> Where a person kills or is party to the killing of another, he shall not be convicted of murder if he was suffering from *such abnormality of mind ... as substantially impaired* his mental responsibility for his acts or omissions in doing or being party to the killing (Homicide Act 1957, s.2).

By contrast, once a defendant has been found to be liable to sentence, there need be no association at all between the offending and the mental disorder for a hospital order to be made. The same indifference to a causal connection is apparent in the legislation relating to psychiatric probation orders. Here the instructive contrast is with another type of additional requirement that a court can include in a probation order. The court can require a probationer to undergo treatment for drug or alcohol dependency, but the court must be satisfied 'that his dependency *caused or contributed to* the offence in respect of which the order is proposed to be made' (Powers of Criminal Courts Act 1973, Schedule 1A as created by Criminal Justice Act 1991, Schedule 1 Part II). There is no comparable requirement when a psychiatric requirement is being considered.

It might be objected that section 37 is a part of mental health law and considers the medical needs of the patient at the time of sentencing, rather than the culpability of the offender at the time of the offence. The causal connection between disorder and crime is therefore irrelevant. This, however, is what is at issue. The criminal law assumes that a convicted offender has *some* responsibility: how is the priority between medical need and commensurate desert to be settled? And if the need for treatment is to take precedence, is it appropriate for a criminal tribunal to make the subsequent adjudication?

A background assumption of s.37 is that the causal association between the disorder and the offence is not so much irrelevant as *self-evident and unproblematic*. In trying to understand human conduct we ask for reasons. If these reasons are not forthcoming – or are not reasons that make sense to us – we may invoke a psychiatric approach. Once disorder has been identified it becomes a *dominant explanation* that puts an end to further (forensic) inquiry and suppresses other explanations.

For defendants who are believed to be not mentally disordered, courts accept accounts of conduct across the broad range of reasons that influence or motivate people. These might include hardship, greed, poverty, selfishness, homelessness, abuse, racism, anger, drunkenness, arrogance and despair. The possibility of a mentally disordered person invoking this kind of explanation seems ruled out: the attribution of mental disorder closes down the eligibility of other reasons. Madness is the cause of their conduct. Reasons are not to be found – indeed not to be looked for – because these are people who are not reasonable or rational. This is the basis of their being not responsible. If reasons are expressed, they are interpreted in the context of the disorder. Mentally disordered offenders are, in a strong sense, taken to be incapable of meaningful action.

Mentally disordered offenders can and do act for any and all of the reasons that influence others. The denial of this possibility, which seems to me to be an assumption embedded in section 37, sustains and legitimises an attitude to mental disorder which marginalises and, by setting them outside the domain of meaningful human conduct, literally dehumanises mentally disordered offenders. Historically, the censure of mental disorder has often been used in this way to deny meaning and significance (including political significance) to human conduct.

In giving its authority to a stereotypical view of mental disorder, the law not only denies meaningful action to mentally disordered defendants. It also obscures the associations between crime and social deprivation and oppression. Connections between crime and indices of oppression like poverty, homelessness and racism are obscured by censuring the conduct as a manifestation of individual pathology (compare American Friends Service Committee 1971). Having a mental disorder is not incompatible with experiencing poverty, homelessness, racism or oppression – on the contrary, these experiences are often associated – and the attribution of mental disorder does not mean that political and structural factors are not part of an explanation. Nor is being mentally disordered incompatible with having a legitimate reason to be angry (Prins et al., 1993).

A further effect of the law's assumption is to *over-normalise* by contrast the behaviour of people who are taken not to be disordered. This is part of the function of a stereotype: in stereotyping 'the Other' we bring 'the Self' into high relief (Gilman, 1985). The stereotype of mental disorder sharpens the image of the legal person as self-controlled, perceiving accurately and making judgements without impairment. In truth, not only do mentally disordered people act for the complete repertoire of reasons: the conduct of people not disordered is often much less calculated, premeditated, purposeful and rational than the law will accommodate.

MENTALLY DISORDERED OFFENDERS AS PATIENTS

The observation that mentally disordered offenders are treated as patients under Part III of the Mental Health Act and so denied the rights of other offenders against excesses of punishment risks missing another important aspect of their position. They are also denied the protection extended to other mentally disordered people against unwarranted intervention.

Part II of the Mental Health Act 1983 provides that mentally disordered people who have *not* committed a criminal offence can only be deprived of their liberty in the interests of their own health or safety or with a view to the protection of others (s.2, s.3, s.4).

Part III imposes no such restriction. It is enough for treatment in hospital to be considered 'appropriate' and 'most suitable'. It is as if the offence itself is taken to be a sufficient demonstration that their interests or the interests of others can only be met by compulsory detention – despite the indication that many of the people admitted under section 37 are convicted of quite minor offences. Here the law trades on a stereotype of offenders. Considered as offenders, they are taken to be unpredictable and irrational; considered as patients, they are taken to be dangerous.

It might be supposed that identifying people as 'mentally disordered offenders' would involve assigning to them the rights of both groups: instead they are denied the rights of either. Patients rather than offenders, they are made subject to mental health legislation and lose the protection against excessive penal imposition accorded to all other defendants. Then, offenders rather than patients, they are denied the normal protection against compulsory admission to hospital.

THE 'RACE' DIMENSION

There is an increasing awareness of the way in which Black people are discriminated against by the existing arrangements. There has long been an awareness of the differential experiences of Black people of psychiatry (Littlewood and Lipsedge, 1989). There is also a well established concern about racism in the criminal justice system (Fitzgerald, 1993b). Not untypically, the position of mentally disordered offenders has been rather slower to be uncovered. There is now an emerging literature that demonstrates the particular vulnerability of Black people dealt with under Part III of the Mental Health Act, as well as showing that courts are more likely to assess Black defendants in psychiatric terms (Cope, 1989; Browne, 1990, Department of Health / Home Office, 1992). Cope (1989) maintains that Part III admissions (including s.47 and s.48 admissions) of Afro-Caribbean people are at 25 times the rate for white people, while Browne (1990) shows the much greater propensity of courts to seek psychiatric assessments on Black defendants.

It seems probable too that other groups are over-represented in this respect. Allen has explored the tendency of courts and psychiatrists to look for psychiatric accounts of women's behaviour (Allen, 1987; also Showalter, 1987). Murphy (1994) has found reason to think that Irish people may well be punished more severely within the criminal justice system, while their over-representation in mental hospitals, especially when detained compulsorily, makes it likely that they are also strongly represented in Part III admissions.

If there is injustice in Part III of the Act, this injustice is amplified by discrimination. In her authoritative review of the literature on race and the criminal justice system, Fitzgerald suggests that it would be appropriate to speak of *indirect discrimination* where 'criteria on which actions and decisions in the criminal justice process were based a) affected ethnic minorities in a disproportionately adverse way *and* b) were not essential to those actions and decisions' (Fitzgerald, 1993b, p.8). The first requirement has been shown to be satisfied by Cope and others. It is part of the purpose of this paper to show that the second condition is also satisfied.

MENTALLY DISORDERED PEOPLE IN THE CRIMINAL JUSTICE PROCESS

Three key decision points within the criminal justice process will next be examined. It is suggested that the inadequate parameters within which decisions are to be taken and background assumptions about mental disorder tend to undermine the policy to remove people from the criminal justice process. Indeed, the shortage of relevant resources often results in the policy's inversion.

The Crown Prosecution Service and the Decision to Prosecute

The Code for Crown Prosecutors affirms that the Crown Prosecutor must consider 'whether the public interest requires a prosecution' (CPS, 1992, p.7). As Ashworth has shown, this sets up a *presumption against prosecution* (Ashworth, 1987). The Code goes on to identify groups of people whose prosecution might appropriately be discontinued, diverting them from the criminal justice process, and reviewing the considerations that are to be taken into account.

When the Code turns to the position of mentally disordered suspects, it begins by endorsing 'the spirit and objectives of the Home Office Circular': when an accused appears to have been suffering from a mental disorder at the time of the offence, 'prosecution will not be appropriate in the circumstances unless it is over-ridden by the wider public interest, including in particular the gravity of the offence'. But this, as we have seen, is no more than the Code prescribes for *all* accused people. The Code goes on:

> Other material considerations will include the circumstances of any previous offences, and such relevant information concerning the nature of the person's condition, the likelihood of his further offending, and *the availability of suitable alternatives to prosecution as may be provided*' (CPS, 1992, p.7(v)(a), my emphasis).

These 'suitable alternatives to prosecution' are usually understood to be psychiatric facilities. These may not exist at all. If they do exist, doctors may be unwilling to accept such troublesome people (Cope, 1989, p.354). In any case, the CPS has no control over such facilities and could have no more than an informal assurance that they would be taken up. The resulting dilemma is very well put by a Chief Crown Prosecutor interviewed by Rutherford:

> It does not make sense to have the power to decide to discontinue or not to commence proceedings in the public interest unless you can also say: 'It is in the public interest for this potential defendant to be diverted to a particular agency'. On a small number of occasions, when we want to divert people away from prosecution to enable them to get help, we have no way of guaranteeing that this will actually happen...The Crown Prosecutor's Code declares that it will not be right to prosecute a juvenile solely to secure access to the welfare powers of the court. In general terms I believe the same principle must apply to adults also. However there are occasions when the public interest may justify taking a person to court, since, unless we take proceedings, a person may not seek or be obliged to obtain the help they really need. It is in this area that I would like to see the powers of the CPS extended (Rutherford, 1993, p.146).

What has happened is that the emphasis on diversion *from* has been translated into a concern to divert *to*. This shift of emphasis is apparent throughout the Home Office Circular and it is easy to see how the effect might be to include people who might otherwise have been diverted. As facilities become less available, CPS could construe it to be their duty to prosecute mentally people *more* readily than other people.

The Bail Decision

Before a court can make a psychiatric disposal, it must seek a medical assessment. This entails a period of adjournment and the court must decide about the granting of bail.

Mentally disordered defendants have the same entitlement to bail as anyone else. If bail must be refused, the court has a power to remand the defendant to hospital instead of prison (Mental Health Act, s.35). Nevertheless, there is some evidence that among the first consequences of invoking the possibility of mental disorder at this stage is to increase the chances of a remand to *prison* custody. In Browne's sample, 47% of defendants remanded for psychiatric assessment were sent to custody. This is considerably higher than would be expected[5] (Browne, 1990). Although HM Inspectorate found very large local variation, in some areas as many as half of people made subject to psychiatric probation orders were remanded to custody for their assessment – even though all of this group received non-custodial sentences and between one quarter and a half had been convicted of offences that were not, in the Inspectorate's opinion, even serious enough for a *community* penalty (HM Inspectorate of Probation, 1993, p.3.10).

Coid looked at 334 mentally disturbed men remanded in prison custody. Finding that many (122) were charged with burglary and theft, he wrote:

> Many of these, however, were minor incidents involving hungry and destitute men, such as shoplifting food and stealing pies and bottles of milk from private houses. 28 men were charged with fraud or deception: virtually all of these had eaten meals in restaurants without the money to pay or had been caught after bilking taxi fares. The second most common charge was damage to property (84 cases). Although there were a few bizarre attacks on public property or that of their neighbours by men with acute psychosis, most of those charged had broken windows. Of 73 offences of [other] violence, most constituted minor assaults, often on the police who had attempted to move the man on when he had been found asleep or acting bizarrely in a public place. Only 32 men had committed offences primarily for gain or in a professional context.
>
> 106 offences seemed from the case notes to have been committed primarily to obtain food or shelter. In 197 cases the men were of no fixed abode on arrival in prison, and in 136 cases the prison doctors considered the men to be incapable of

> caring for themselves independently in the community at the time of their arrest (quoted NACRO, 1992).

Although there are resource aspects to this, it is also, as Grounds points out, a *system* failure:

> There has to be a recognition of the incentives that make the system work the way it does and that bring the mentally disordered into the remand prisons. Remanding in custody rather than to hospital for assessment is easier for courts, cheaper for health authorities, helpful to NHS staff, and provides prison doctors with the psychiatric assessment work in which they take a traditional pride (Grounds, 1992, p.292).

Part of the doctors' reluctance to accept people under this section may be that it gives no power to treat. Whatever the reason, section 35 is not seen as a functional equivalent to a remand in custody.

None of this explains why bail is refused in the first place. The Butler Report, which originally proposed a power like s.35, envisaged that most mentally disordered defendants should be assessed on bail (Home Office / DHSS, 1975, p.12.10). It might be instructive to research the reasons courts give for refusing bail to people in these circumstances and comparing these with general refusals of bail. Reasons are likely to include: seriousness of offence and possible method of disposal, failure to answer bail, problem of obtaining assessment if bail were granted. The Home Office Circular notes that: 'Mentally disordered persons may be at particular risk of being remanded in custody, because their circumstances and way of life may be unstable' (HOC 66/90: Paragraph 18) – instability, incidentally, which was tolerated until the commission of the offence.

Again, there is a clear possibility that the system's apparent concern to identify mentally disordered people – professedly in order to divert them from the criminal justice system – has the effect of involving them in it even further. A heightened awareness of the predicament of mentally disordered offenders collides with a lack of availability of the relevant resources.

The Reed Report proposes the creation of specialised bail hostels, recognising that existing hostels may be reluctant to accept people who are believed to be mentally disordered (Reed, 1992, Recommendation 11.6). As with the working of section 37, there are signs of the unusual jeopardy of this group: hospitals will not accept them as offenders, hostels will not accept them as mentally disordered.

Apart from the intrinsic damage of remand to penal custody, it is necessary to note Moxon's finding that the denial of bail has an independent effect on the likelihood of a custodial sentence eventually being passed (Moxon, 1988). It is also to be noted that Black defendants already have a greater risk of a custodial remand than do white: Fitzgerald cites Hood's finding that 'black men were 16% more likely to be remanded in custody than white men charged with similar offences and with similar antecedents' (Fitzgerald, 1993a, p.44).

Outcome of Assessment and the Sentencing Decision

Since a just punishment is determined by an evaluation of the harm done and the defendant's responsibility, at court it is the defending solicitor who will normally raise the possibility of mental disorder in the course of mitigation and request adjournment for reports. Juristically, the less responsible the defendant can be shown to be, the more likely the court should be to sentence leniently. Unless the application for psychiatric assessment has no grounds at all, courts are most unlikely to refuse. Awareness has been heightened by the Home Office Circular and other policy statements. Moreover, before passing a custodial sentence on someone who is or appears to be mentally disordered, the court is required to obtain a medical report (Criminal Justice Act 1991, s.4(1)).

Browne is right to insist that if solicitors raise the issue of mental disorder in mitigation then they may well be mistaken: 'The assumption that a psychiatric disposal is a lenient one is highly dangerous' (Browne, 1990, p.31). But the further point is that no more than a small proportion of defendants who are psychiatrically assessed are subsequently sentenced to any form of psychiatric disposal. The effect of the assessment on the eventual punishment of this majority is quite unknown.

In the year ended 31 March 1992, 4732 psychiatric reports were prepared on persons remanded in custody (NACRO, 1993b, p.38). It is not clear what proportion of *all* assessments this represents, but it seems safe to say that there are at least as many prepared on people on bail, making not fewer than 10,000 prepared annually. Fewer than one-fifth of these reports (and probably many fewer) result in a specifically psychiatric outcome.

These are the possible outcomes of a psychiatric assessment:

1. the defendant is diagnosed mentally disordered and meets the requirement for admission to hospital under s.37; *or*
2. the defendant is found to have a degree of disturbance amounting to mental disorder but, for various reasons, is not suitable for admission; *or*
3. there is believed to be a degree of mental disturbance but this does not amount to disorder within the meaning of the Act; *or*
4. the defendant is found to be not disturbed.

In the first case, the court is likely to accept the doctors' assessment (Prins, 1986, p.56) unless there are strong over-riding considerations – usually the seriousness of the offence.

In the second case, a guardianship order or a psychiatric probation order are possibilities, but the defendant is vulnerable to a much broader range of penal dispositions. In the third case, a psychiatric probation order would again be a possibility, but all the court's powers may be invoked.

The concept of *treatability* is fundamental here. It is not lawful to make a hospital order for certain types of disorder unless they are treatable. Even when this is not a legal requirement (in cases of mental illness, for example), doctors may well seek to discourage courts from making an order by arguing that the defendant's condition is not amenable to treatment. But this concept is an elusive one, as Allen vividly shows:

> AUTHOR: What kind of disorder would you tend to regard as most treatable?
> DOCTOR: Oh that's a question we're so often asked!...I think it's the wrong question. Look. If you mean 'What disorders can I cure?', I'd probably have to say 'None'...If you mean 'What disorders can I give treatment to?' I could say 'All of them'. (It wouldn't necessarily do any *good*, but if you gave me the facilities I could have a go!) But if you mean 'Which disorders can I do some *good* by treating?', well I'd have to say, 'First show me the patient, second tell me what you mean by 'good', third tell me how much time and money and nurses and beds you're going to give me, fourth –and so on. It's a complete misunderstanding to say this disorder is treatable and that one isn't.' I'm constantly trying to get people to understand this (Allen, 1987, p.97).

Bean noted that '...opposition to...the use of hospital orders came from the psychiatric services whereby the right was claimed to treat those patients of its own choosing. That is mental hospital staff objected to patients being foisted upon them by the courts or by the prison service, many of whom would be regarded as untreatable or, if not, then sufficiently disruptive to upset the hospital routine.' (Bean, 1986, p.192) Allen's study shows that the way in which hospital staff manage their opposition is by using diagnoses as *resources,* which they may or may not deploy for a number of reasons, by no means all of which are clinical. Allen shows how the converse of this exclusion is the potential *in*clusion of people who are not (clinically) disordered. She shows how diagnoses (perhaps especially in the vague area between personality disorder and psychopathy) can be framed to lead courts to decisions which have a very tenuous clinical basis. Similarly, the Inspectorate found in their sample of psychiatric probation orders that:

> In one area up to a quarter of the sample had no clearly labelled illness or diagnosis and in another area it was doubtful whether some of the cases could or should have been categorised as mentally disordered. (HM Inspectorate of Probation, 1993, p.3.9)

Given the parameters of the sentencing decision, the people who are made subject to s37 are not necessarily any 'more ill' (if any sense can be attached to that concept) or more in need of medical treatment than those who are dealt with in other ways. When the psychiatric system is under pressure, the temptation will be to opt for a more exclusive approach. (Indeed, in competition for scarce medical resources, why *should* a doctor give priority to an offender?)

It is argued, then, that people who are found to be disordered, but deemed not to be suitable for a psychiatric disposal, and those whose disturbance does not amount to disorder (groups (ii) and (iii) above) may not be significantly different – morally, juristically, clinically – from those in the first group. What continues to be unclear is the difference that the psychiatric assessment makes to the sentencing decisions for these two groups. It is not at all clear that the ascription of disorder mitigates their position in any way. On the contrary, they stand before the court with a suspicion of disorder, unpredictable and uncontrolled offenders, yet denied the status of (undeserving) patient.

CENSURE AND STEREOTYPE

It is important to be aware of the powerfully evocative nature of the language in which mentally disordered offenders are characterised and the impact this is likely to have on the decisions that people are called upon to take, at every stage of the criminal justice process.

The sociology of censure, developed by Colin Sumner and colleagues, begins with the recognition that categories of deviance are contemporary forms of social *censure*. The use of the more familiar expression 'label' risks overlooking that deviance is labelled in a particular way: specifically, the labels we apply to deviant conduct are strongly charged with negative and condemnatory nuance. Like much other evaluative discourse, censures of deviance not only express judgements, they are used to elicit or evoke particular attitudes (compare Urmson, 1968). Sumner insists that 'Whatever the authority of their legal definition, or the pseudo-scientific validity of their use in social work or welfare agencies, these notions are still moral judgements.' (Sumner, 1990, p.16) Moreover, 'Although often presented in legal, technical or universal forms, as mere descriptions, they are organised slanders in what is essentially a political or moral conflict.' Their general function is to signify, denounce and regulate, not to explain.

Part of the argument of this paper is that censures can interact and amplify. Instead of receiving the legal entitlements of both groups, a mentally disordered offender is doubly censured and the combination introduces nuances of its own. A mentally disordered offender is an unpredictable, deluded and uncontrolled offender *and* an untrustworthy and undeserving patient.

David Garland considers the complexity of our emotional response to crime and punishment. He insists that:

> The punishment of offenders is capable of evoking a whole range of feelings from sympathy and compassion to anger and indignation. (Garland, 1990, p.64, chap. 10 *passim* and p.239)

He speculates that the origins of this complexity and ambivalence may be traced to early childhood and the psychic tensions that occur in the process of being socialised. It may be this that accounts for the intensity of feeling about crime and punishment and the peculiarly irrational character of so much debate.

Feelings about mental disorder are no less resonant. Scheff shows that the stereotyped imagery of mental disorder is learned in early childhood and that these images:

> ...are not discarded but continue to exist alongside the medical conceptions, because the stereotypes receive almost continual support from the mass media and in ordinary social discourse (Scheff, 1984, p.55).

One of the most potent of these stereotypes is that mentally ill people are unpredictably violent and this is an image that is reinforced through several media. Stereotypes of unpredictable, bizarre, frenetic and random behaviour are embodied in our language. Scheff argues that these stereotypes may be peculiarly resistant to change because 'they are functional for the current social order and tend to be integrated into the psychological make up of all members of the society' (Scheff, 1984, p.62). He emphasises that 'the concept of mental disorder serves as a fundamental contrast conception in our society, functioning to preserve the current mores'.

Yet – and this too is by no means uncharacteristic of a stereotype (Gilman, 1985) – mental disorder, like crime and punishment, evokes ambivalent responses: feelings of sympathy and compassion, as well as of threat and condescension.

The compound censure of 'mentally disordered offender' – the overlap between two charged and resonant images – is likely to be powerfully evocative. The more obviously negative feelings it evokes – perhaps above all of threat and danger – have been considered so far. Yet *ambivalence* still characterises the censure. Mentally disordered offenders may be less culpable, less deserving of punishment, in need of help: pathos, as well as fear, may be aroused. The way in which courts make use of psychiatric measures may be an expression of this ambivalence. We have seen that psychiatric measures are used instead of imprisonment for very serious offences, perhaps through compassion or pity; but they are also used in respect of quite minor offences, sometimes through fear, sometimes through a concern to safeguard the individual's welfare. Perhaps the one response that the censure cannot countenance is non-intervention. For welfare or punishment, mentally disordered offenders must be dealt with: diversion *from* is not enough.

DISCRETION AND DECISION

In his study of discretion in the criminal justice process, Davis suggested that:

> When we isolate what we regard as the exercise of discretion, we find three principal ingredients – facts, values, and influences. But an officer who is exercising discretion seldom separates these three elements; most discretionary decisions are intuitive, and responses to influences often tend to crowd out thinking about values (Davis, 1969, p.5).

When decisions about mentally disordered offenders are to be taken, 'facts' are typically elusive. Few of the personnel within the process would believe themselves competent to make judgements about disorder. The competent authorities, it has been argued, may use diagnosis tactically to bring about the preferred outcome. There may be several 'influences' at play, but many of them act against the declared policy. Unfamiliarity with processes, failures of systems and shortage of resources all militate against implementation. 'Values', beliefs about how mentally disordered offenders should be treated, are characteristically nebulous and inconclusive. The language in which these issues are discussed is rich in nuance and evocation, often meagre in informative and descriptive content.

Some of this would be true of many decisions within the criminal justice process. Hogarth's classic study demonstrates that sentencing decisions cannot be understood as a dispassionate application of statute or principle (Hogarth, 1971). Parker and colleagues found that moral assessment weighed heavily in the sentencing decisions of juvenile courts, while Fitzmaurice and Pease have challenged the conceit that the judiciary is somehow immune from the cognitive frailty which afflicts the rest of us (Parker *et al.* 1989, chapt.5; see also Brown, 1991; Fitzmaurice and Pease, 1986).

The 'human process' elements of decisions – and not only sentencing decisions – about mentally disordered offenders goes beyond this. Idiosyncrasy in sentencing is normally constrained by statute, by case law, by 'tariff', by court culture (Tarling, 1979). None of this applies to offenders with a mental disorder. The parameters set by statute, case law and regulation are completely inadequate. Even apparently prescriptive documents like the

Home Office Circular raise awareness (and anxiety?) rather than guide discretion. Tariff is explicitly repudiated for this group: desert is taken to be an inapplicable predicate and mentally disordered offenders to be a paradigm of the need to take careful account of the distinctive combination of circumstances in each individual case. Even a court culture is hard to establish – not least because, as a proportion of all defendants appearing in courts, this group remains very small.

Discretion must be confined, structured and checked if injustice is to be opposed (Davis, 1969, p.26). Discretion in dealing with mentally disordered offenders is minimally confined and checked. None of the structuring which increasingly is being felt to be important in sentencing decisions (Fitzmaurice and Pease, 1986; Ashworth, 1992) is available to courts dealing with defendants described in this way. Sentencers are thrown back on their own judgements and intuitions in this strongly censured domain and left to play out society's ambivalence.

THE FUNCTION AND EFFECTS OF THE CENSURE

The initial task that Sumner sets in the study of any particular censure is to explore:

> What does the censure mean? When was it first used? And against whom? Who was behind it and who enforced it? What ideological concepts give it such a meaning? What was the political and structural context of its application? (Sumner, 1990, p.31).

A study of the censure of 'mentally disordered offender', its ancestors (for instance, 'criminal lunatic') and its cognates could be most instructive.

In its contemporary application, it could be said that the censure is central to the debate about mental disorder and its social significance. Psychiatry and other responses to mental disorder have always had a controlling function, but this is becoming more flagrant – and, it could added, much less likely to be couched in the language of benevolence. The government is to introduce a register of mentally ill people considered to be a risk to themselves or others and legislation is planned to introduce a new category of 'supervised discharge' (*Independent* 1993b). The Royal College of Psychiatrists has called for the introduction of community supervision orders to make sure that people would not be able to refuse treatment (NACRO, 1993c). What many see as a failure to provide service – people being turned away from hospital, prematurely discharged, inadequately supported in the community – is being reconstructed as a problem of the recalcitrance, irrationality and dangerousness of mentally disordered people (*Guardian*, 1993; *Independent*, 1993a). At the same time, as has been seen, the criminal justice system is being used as a point of access to psychiatric treatment. If an earlier era witnessed the medicalisation of crime, this could be said to be a time of the *criminalisation of mental disorder*.

Much of this is already familiar to Black communities. Errol Francis has shown that the position of Black people under compulsory psychiatric treatment is not just a consequence of over-diagnosis, over-prescription and cultural misunderstanding. There is also a failure to recognise need before crisis occurs, and a preference for intrusive legal sanction rather than support or care (Northern Curriculum Development Project, 1991; Browne, 1990). When crisis does occur, it may well take the form of a criminal offence (usually minor). The person is now believed to be a mentally disordered offender and treatment, if given at all, given compulsorily. In the process, the person has been effectively *criminalised*. Racism must be part of the understanding of what is taking place, but anti-racism *by itself* is not a sufficient response. Where a process is oppressive, then, in a racist society, its effect will be racist; but the remedy must be to oppose the process itself.

SOME CONCLUSIONS AND IMPLICATIONS

The Legal Framework

The discrimination which has been argued to characterise the criminal justice system in its dealings with mentally disordered offenders is not a contingent defect, but a direct consequence of the inadequacies of the legal framework itself. Fitzgerald has shown that:

> ...discrimination is likely
> - where there is an absence of clear guidelines about the criteria on which decisions should be taken;
> - where decisions depend on subjective judgements rather than (or in addition to) objective criteria;

- where the criteria used are not strictly relevant to the decisions to which they relate and have a disproportionately adverse impact on certain groups;
- where there is considerable scope for the exercise of individual discretion;
- where there is no requirement to record (and even less to monitor) the reasons for decisions...

(Fitzgerald, 1993b, p.11).

At sentence, *but at other strategic points in the process too*, all of these deficiencies can be detected. The principles which are intended to structure the court's decision for all other defendants – specifically the principle that the punishment must be proportionate to the wrong done – need not apply to mentally disordered offenders and will not apply when Part III of the Mental Health Act is invoked. Even if a diagnosis is granted the status of objectivity (and it has been argued that this assessment is circumscribed by many other than clinical factors), the judgement about whether the defendant is to be dealt with as a mentally disordered person or as an offender is a matter for the sentencer's subjective judgement. Since the nature of the decision to be taken is unclear, it is hard to know what the relevant criteria might be and impossible to be confident that the decision is untainted by extraneous considerations. The 'disproportionately adverse impact on certain groups' has by now been demonstrated by several studies (notably Cope, 1989; Browne, 1990). There is, finally, full scope for individual discretion and no requirement to record or monitor the reasons for decision.

The first requirement, then, is for statute and case law to begin to provide a proper framework within which courts must take their decisions. Section 37 of the Mental Health Act, it has been suggested, is deeply flawed. Section 37 denies defendants the rights of offenders and the rights of patients. It also legitimates the idea of 'occasionalism' and gives an authority to occasionalist thinking at other points of decision. So long as occasionalism is countenanced, the effect, especially in a time of diminishing resources, will be to make the criminal justice system a (perhaps *the*) point of access to psychiatric 'care' and so to criminalise mental disorder. This distorts not only mental health care provision, but (since the policy of diversion *to* will fail) has dreadful consequences for the penal system too. Decision takers will have to be willing to divert *from* and not use the criminal justice system to try to provide resources that society denies others.

This does not at all mean that courts are to disregard mental disorder on those occasions when mentally disordered people appear before them. On the contrary, existing criminal justice legislation enables a court to take full account of any reduction of responsibility resulting from disorder or to lessen any penalty if its effect on the defendant's health would be deleterious (Criminal Justice Act 1991, s.28 gives this general power of mitigation). It is this legislation, not mental health law, that should have application in a criminal court. Section 37, which represents an inappropriate relationship between the courts and offenders, ought to be repealed.

Attitudes to Mental Disorder

The law institutionalises and lends authority to seriously prejudicial attitudes towards mentally disordered people. Notably, the denial of responsibility to mentally disordered offenders and the consequent perceived irrelevance of justice not only deny them protection against excesses of punishment, but give legitimacy to a perception of mental disorder that dehumanises mentally disordered people. No 'community care' strategy, however resourced, could thrive against the prejudices that this sustains. For this reason, even when mentally disordered people benefit from individual decisions, the institutionalised discrimination they experience is sustained.

So far as possible the censure of 'mentally disordered offenders' and its cognates should be avoided. It is not supposed that substantial problems can be solved by linguistic *fiat*, but this particular censure has aggravated the difficulties. The language in which these issues are discussed should tend to increase people's dignity and rights, including rights of access to resources. It has been argued that this censure has helped to create a special class of people who are denied the rights of offenders *and* of mentally disordered people, instead of ensuring them the rights of both.

Probation Practice

Some of these conclusions do not sit comfortably with existing policy and practice. For instance, most national policy papers emphasise the importance of a prompt identification of mentally disordered people (Home Office, 1990c) and this is reiterated in the statements of those agencies that have established their own local policies. It has been argued, however, that it is by no means always in the interests of a defendant (or in the interests of anyone else) to be regarded as 'a mentally disordered offender'. Self-evidently what matters is what *results* from any such identification. If the effect is to make diversion from prosecution more difficult or to reduce the likelihood of bail being granted or to debar someone from service or to expose them to disproportionate and oppressive sentencing, then some defendants may well prefer not to be so identified.

This thesis must not be mistaken for an encouragement to pretend that 'mentally disordered offenders' do not exist or that they do not have special vulnerabilities and needs. Some specific practical proposals may be made:

1. There must be greater clarity of the purpose of diversion. When the alleged offence is a serious one, the CPS will not divert (CPS, 1992). When it is less serious, diversion should be advocated for its own sake and should not be contingent (as it is not for other defendants) on the availability of other resources to which people may be diverted.
2. The Probation Service must seek to challenge the idea of 'occasionalism'. CPS and Magistrates must be asked to consider that the criminal justice system cannot and should not be a gateway to health care which would otherwise not be available.
3. In preparing reports for the court, probation officers should be sensitive to the implications of invoking psychiatric interpretations of conduct and aware of their reasons for doing so. White, male officers may be more likely to do this when writing reports on defendants who are not white or male. Reports should help the courts to disentangle the conceptually and morally distinct issues of a defendant's culpability and associated liability for sentence from their medical and other needs.
4. Probation officers must be aware that a suggestion of mental disorder, which may be made by the defence in mitigation, may have a very different impact on the court. There may be pressure on officers to collude with a psychiatric interpretation.
5. Services should be made available and not denied:

   ...most mentally disturbed offenders have needs which can be met by services which are equally relevant to mentally disturbed people who are not offenders. Only a small proportion will have committed offences that are serious enough ... for them to need any service specifically aimed at them (NACRO, 1993a, p.19).

By the same token, almost all of this group could and should receive the services of probation *where appropriate*. Some hostels are diffident about accepting mentally disordered offenders, but it is not at all clear that, to the (doubtful) extent they can be considered as a group, they pose problems that are more demanding than do very many other hostel residents. The objection that the Probation Service does not have the resources to assist mentally disordered people is not to the point. In this sense, the Service does not have the resources to assist most of its clients, but can as well advocate, negotiate and enable provision by other agencies for mentally disordered people as for anyone else.

6. A corollary is that the creation of special facilities is mostly to be avoided. To create a hostel (say) for 'mentally disordered offenders' would stigmatise residents, contribute to the denial of access to ordinary facilities and further institutionalise the oppressive censure.
7. Probation Service policies relating to mentally disordered offenders should be sufficiently explicit to avoid the discriminatory potential that Fitzgerald identifies (Fitzgerald, 1993b, p.11).
8. Neither probation officers nor anyone else should imagine themselves to be so emancipated from their culture as to be uninfluenced by stereotypical images of mental disorder – especially images of unpredictability, irrationality and dangerousness. Throughout this paper, I have tried to show that the strongly censured and resonant discourse in which these issues are discussed evokes feelings that often lead to oppressive decisions, sometimes to leniency, but rarely and only by accident to justice.

Acknowledgements

I am grateful to Professor Herschel Prins for his encouragement in the writing of this paper. I should also like to thank my colleague, Patrick Murphy, for his comments on an early draft. Neither should be taken to agree with the arguments put forward. Errors of fact and of judgement are all my own work. I wish to record here my gratitude to one of my first teachers in social work, John Pendelton, who helped me to understand the importance of combining humanity and scholarship.

Notes

1. By 'mentally disordered' I shall mean those categories of person diagnosed by the competent authorities as suffering from a mental disorder within the meaning of Section 1 mental Health Act 1983: mental illness, impairment, severe impairment, psychopathy. (By s.1 a person may not be dealt with under the Act 'as suffering from mental disorder...by reason only of promiscuity or other immoral conduct, sexual deviancy or dependence on alcohol or drugs'.)
2. Part III is that part of the Mental Health Act 1983 which deals with the powers of courts and the Secretary of State in respect of mentally disordered people who are accused or have been convicted of a criminal offence. There will also be some discussion of the relevant sections of the Criminal Justice Act 1991. The Criminal Procedure (Insanity and Unfitness to Plead) Act 1991 will not be discussed. In particular, a discussion of the notion of unfitness to plead is beyond the scope of this paper.
3. Although it is to be noted that Gunn includes people who are dependent on alcohol or drugs who are not 'disordered' within the meaning of the Act.
4. This includes arson.
5. About 25% of all magistrates courts' defendants are remanded at some stage in the proceedings and no more than about 10% of this group are remanded in custody (*Criminal Statistics England and Wales 1991*, Cmd 2134, Table 8.5 and pp. 171, 176). This is not a straightforward comparison: people are remanded for many different reasons and Browne's sample is scarcely typical. Even so, it is not distinguished particularly by the seriousness of its offending with only about a fifth of his sample convicted of an offence of violence or robbery.

Section III

Justice and the Organisation

Fourteen
Black professionals in search of race equality: The proactive role of black professionals

Basil Hylton

The aim of this paper is to portray an understanding of racism that in turn sheds light on relevant aspects of behaviour or policies which, if inadequately or superficially addressed, can too often undermine good intentions and authentic anti-discriminatory efforts. A crucial objective of the author is to present some of the struggles of black professionals to belong and to make their contribution – struggles made more arduous by continued exploitation and negation of the black experience.

In his opening comments at the Kapila Lecture 1993, the Lord Chief Justice, Lord Taylor of Gosforth, remarked that 'racial awareness in the Criminal Justice System is a very *topical issue*'. In fact 'racial awareness training' was introduced to sections of the Criminal Justice System (namely to the Police and the Probation Service) over twelve years previously. Clearly, progress towards race equality within the Criminal Justice System has been pursued so slowly and reluctantly that its relevance to ensuring that justice is done *and seen to be done* is also effectively delayed.

Most Black people would say that for them the race issue is not a mere 'topical issue' – implying, as it does, unending discussions with tangential outcomes. The all-pervasive and impinging realities of racism on black people inform our self-perceptions and aspirations, including the desire to contribute to a fairer and more humane society. They also affect feelings of confidence in the Criminal Justice System and of belonging to this society. For black people, these realities and feelings are inextricably linked with both the need to experience fairness, and the aspiration to assist in the maintenance of order and law.

RISKY AND COSTLY CONTRIBUTIONS

The racist experiences of black professionals in public sector service organisations vary between the indignities suffered by them because of their colour to the limited opportunities provided for them to function and progress in these organisations.

In depicting some themes from those experiences, one might include the frequent collusion with racism. The ways in which it adversely affects the black people have been repeatedly chronicled by researchers, reports and complaints of racial discrimination. One might also point to the exploitation of easily accessible black people by white persons attempting to resolve personal guilt without a clear view of institutional responsibilities which could be more appropriately tackled. This apparent ignorance masks a kind of 'neo-slavery' in which black professionals make extensive contributions to the cause of anti-racist work but do so at their own risk and personal cost.

Three instances worth citing in support of these themes are:

Collusion

I was asked at my very first Probation job interview: 'How do you think the people of South Gloucestershire will respond to you, Mr. Hylton?' Having understood the implied, '...you, as a black man, Mr. Hylton', I felt obliged to explain that during my training all the clients but two I dealt with were white! It was both demoralising and depressing to accept that my appointment might have hinged on white clients' willingness to accepting my colour. The irony was that on a number of occasions I was denied initial access to white clients' homes. 'We don't allow *any* black person in our home', a mother in Marshfield once insisted.

Institutional Racism

Some years ago, I visited a headmaster in Bath to discuss two (white) children appearing in court. He subsequently used up a disproportionate amount of my time apparently seeking a solution to his concern about the deleterious effect that two or three of his few black pupils were having on other pupils. This school had no black staff in it and black posters were limited to those of 'suffering Biafran children'.

Exploiting at a Cost

I was a member of the Bishops' Catholic Commission for Racial Justice that was responsible for a controversial report on 'Racism in Britain', which led to the Home Office instructing prisons to stop forcibly cutting the hair of Rastafarians. In addition to being a former member of UKIAS (The United Kingdom Immigration Advisory Service), I proposed the first NAPO motion calling for anti-racist action by that union in 1977. Such contributions, mostly done in my own time, have helped in sensitising the Service to the reality of racism.

Though these instances are now rather dated, similar contributions by black professionals have continued unabated. However, the degree to which such largely 'unique' contributions to the professions are being rightly owned and built on by public sector service organisations remains doubtful. For example, while efforts are being made to increase proportionately 'black faces' in many of these organisations, there is still an uncertainty about the value of and reasons for their recruitment, and an ambivalence about the *proactive role* they should or can play.

PROGRESSIVE POLICIES AND PRACTICE

One Probation Service in the Midlands perhaps came closest to spelling out the real reasons it employs black staff. In doing so, it offers the rationale of the Race Relations Act regarding the 'proportion of the workforce or population' requirements (RRA 1976, s.37 and s.38). Thus, apart from the justice of those legal requirements, the act was used as a platform on which to promote that Service's rationale that further states:

> The Service needs the unique contribution of black staff if it is to be anti-racist and therefore effective in its task.
>
> It is uneconomic and inefficient to restrict the contribution of black people.
>
> A failure to employ black people contributes to the general disadvantage in employment experienced by black people and adds to the level of social injustice that the Service seeks to counter.
>
> The policy of anti-racism would be best done by all staff regularly working as part of a multi-racial work force.

Like most policies, it reads well and even outlines arrangements for its implementation. In practice, however, the real problem regarding implementation is ignored. In short, profound policy statements such as these must be viewed and managed strategically; and that strategy must include staff (including managers) with sound knowledge and genuine commitment to achieving desirable race equality goals. So, for example, recruitment, training, supervision and appraisal systems should be required to show significant engagements in their practice as opposed to policy documents.

ORGANISING FOR EFFECTIVENESS

The fact of white organisations needing more black people in them is itself a *premium* placed on the heads of black people. This is because exclusively white institutions in a multi-racial society are less likely to provide an anti-discriminatory service to the black community. That premium therefore reflects the organisation's *need* and not its patronage to black recruits. Its task is to be able to deliver a service which is demonstrably fair to the community as a whole, and which, as a result, creates and maintains confidence in the system and ultimately in our democratic way of life.

Maintaining the confidence of black professionals is an important task. Correspondingly, the ease with which that confidence can be demolished by managements that do not understand the 'black perspective', nor make any real effort to do so, is particularly striking. Not that black people are unique in having this need. However, in predominantly white organisations white professionals numerically have more allies, more places to 'hide away' and greater choices than black workers. Increasingly black support groups or associations have been formed as a measure to bridge that gap.

However, the initial unease of white public sector service organisations (such as the Probation Service and some local authority departments) about black support groups within their ranks was only slightly different from the Labour Party's response to the setting up of the Black Section a few years later. That initial unease, however, has been overtaken by the general tacit acceptance of black support groups as a reasonably safe and occasionally helpful mechanism.

Some comments on that transitional period might assist in

clarifying some of the challenges and accumulated difficulties that confront the struggle to implement race equality.

THE NEED TO JOIN AND BE SEEN

Dr. Kenneth Pryce (1974), in his study entitled *West Indian Lifestyles in Bristol*, commented on the position and role of black social workers between 1969-74. In it he linked the members of the then Bristol Black Social Workers Association (BBSWA) with the 'Mainliners' whom he described as largely the older, self-appointed, 'out of touch' black leaders in Bristol.

Ken Pryce, himself a West Indian, hardly said anything positive about 'black social workers'. He stressed their 'lack of militancy' and the opinion that they were 'imported from outside the community by local government and other statutory bodies to whom they were answerable'. However, I believe he failed to represent the struggles of black social workers in Bristol, because at the time he did not recognise BBSWA as part of the struggle of the black community. Perhaps the initial title of his study (*A Study of a Black Toiling Class In An English City*) offers a clue to that omission.

Yet, there are, on the other hand, several valid criticisms levelled by Ken Pryce that aptly described the situation in which black probation officers and social workers have since found themselves. Individually and on their own 'frontlines', black social workers felt that they were seeking to overcome the issue of racism within their organisations by 'representing the issue' to their organisations, not to the black community. However, in the very move to establish collective support and to make links with the community, BBSWA was implicitly recognising both the inadequacy of *white* organisations tackling race equality, and black staff not explicitly forging links with the black community.

It is a fact that unless internal collective demands of black people are made of white organisations, the preferred invisibility of black people and their communities will be reinforced. After all, to be 'integrated' (in the racist sense of the word) is to become *invisible* through a process of suppressing genuine, morally and professionally justifiable feelings and demands in the workplace. In that sense, to *join* is to disappear.

AFFIRMING BLACK PRESENCE IN THE 1980S

In the West Midlands the decision in 1980 by black probation officers and social workers to meet outside working hours to lend support to one another was initially done with some trepidation. Later when it became more generally known that a Black Social Workers and Probation Officers Group (called BSWAPO) was meeting, objections against it were fairly hostile. Additionally even a small number of black probation officers sought to distance themselves from the group on the basis that it was not sanctioned by the Service management.

BSWAPO, like BBSWA before it, might have been accused of 'playing it safe' by meeting outside working hours. 'How could the Service be expected to address adequately the issue of race if its black staff were meeting in 'secret'?', one officer once rhetorically asked.

In reality BSWAPO was an umbrella group which supported Probation members in developing strategies for influencing the Service's work on race issues. Having made its influence felt, it successfully formed the nucleus from which developed the Association of Black Probation Officers.

THE ASSOCIATION OF BLACK PROBATION OFFICERS

ABPO is a group of black professionals who believe that the Probation Service operates within a multi-racial society. They feel that the Service should therefore provide an appropriate service to all its clients. It further believes that racism is about *colour* not culture, and that it is important to know the difference. ABPO therefore seeks to project a black perspective on professional issues and on service delivery.

In 1983 ABPO grew out of the BSWAPO group, having identified a few other black probation officers in different parts of the country. They were all similarly experiencing a lack of support from their respective organisations and felt that there was a necessary role for an association of fellow black colleagues. Following some meetings in 1983, ABPO's inaugural meeting took place on 24th February 1984 in Birmingham.

ABPO agreed to pursue two basic aims:

a) The maintenance of a support network for members of the organisation; and

b) The promotion of appropriate service delivery to the black community.

Regarding the first aim, the association insisted that its members working in pre-dominantly white institutions, sustained real feelings of isolation, which neither the Probation Service management nor the probation officers' union, NAPO, was adequately dealing with. ABPO's belief was that realistically support could come only from black workers themselves acting together.

Constitutionally ABPO's aims are:

1. To encourage and maintain a support group of members to promote a black perspective on professional issues;
2. To promote and help the appropriate training and education of Probation Officers and all other Probation staff regarding racial issues;
3. To act in an advisory capacity to black students entering the profession;
4. To ensure the monitoring of the quality of services given to black clients and to report any malpractice to appropriate bodies;
5. To initiate and campaign, where necessary, for changes in the Probation Service to adjust the balance of disadvantage suffered by both workers and client groups;
6. To ensure that the Probation Service acknowledges the implications of living and working in a multi-racial /multi-cultural society and thereby ensure that service delivery is appropriate to that society's needs; and
7. To liaise with other groups and individuals who share their aims.

Membership of ABPO is open to all African, African-Caribbean and Asian Probation staff and to black students undertaking social work training prior to entering the Probation Service. At its AGM in 1989 ABPO membership totalled 192 including 94 black Probation Officers. This seemed incredible following the 1988 Home Office Survey that revealed that of the 6000 probation officers in the country, there were only 127 black officers: those figures included seven black Senior Probation Officers and one Assistant Chief Probation Officer. In 1994 over 250 members attended its three-day Conference and Annual General Meeting.

The Association, divided into three regions – the Midlands, the

North and the South – is managed by an elected Executive. These regions are largely autonomous, with contact being maintained through the Executive Committee and through a system of elected Convenors for each region. Regional meetings are held on a regular monthly or bi-monthly basis with the venues varying to allow support to isolated members. Bi-monthly meetings of the Executive are generally well attended with a full agenda of local and national concerns as well as requests for assistance and support from other bodies.

Funding is a combination of:

- trust grants – for specific areas of work or activity (e.g. general secretary and newsletter);
- Union grant – to meet travelling expenses of Executive Committee members whose areas were not yet happy at supporting their attendance at these meetings;
- membership subscriptions;
- regional fund raising events.

In 1984 ABPO won full support and 'recognition' from ACOP (the Association of Chief Officers of Probation). It had *strongly recommended* to chief probation officers that support in 'time off' (sic), travelling and subsistence allowances be accorded to ABPO members concerning their work through ABPO.

It ought to be noted that in many areas some Services have formed 'their own' black officers/staff support groups. Often this was done with the support of some black officers. In some places it has been done in a manner inimical to the support, development and influence of ABPO as a way of ensuring control of the development and activities of black staff. In one or two cases chief officers have been parties to the attempt to split or to sustain a split between black officers – namely between Asian and African-Caribbean staff. In each case the neo-colonialist attitude has been apparent, disguised in talk of 'firm and controlling management', feigning being 'wise' to the needs and position of black people.

White people 'wise' to the needs of black people but without an understanding of the 'black perspective' and of *their* need to challenge the spurious 'white perspective', are rightfully maligned as 'white liberals'. They often inadvertently subscribe to the subtle racist changes that effectively perpetuate racism, and divide black people in the well-intentioned attempt to mediate between them. Note how that lesson was well taught in East Africa, leading, for example, to the current parallel pre-occupation regarding whether 'Asians' (itself a generic term) are really 'black'.

RACISM AND RACE CATEGORIES

As previously said, ABPO holds that racism is about colour, not culture. Institutionalised prejudice and hence the basic discriminatory practices against black people in this country are not perpetuated because of 'cultural differences'. However, this is not to deny the valid view that any refusal to cater for significant cultural differences (e.g. language and religious practices) could well be overtly racist.

The real question here is whether people who are deemed NOT OF THE CATEGORY, 'WHITE', should be rejected and made to feel rejected as 'club members' of that category. 'Yes', says the racist, 'though there might be the occasional scope for bestowing 'white' honorary membership to some lesser people'.

'We reject that CLUB and its racist connotations, and we proactively seek to distance ourselves from its bestowed privileges', say the anti-racists. This actual and/or political disassociation can be done by people of whatever skin colour. Neither is it a matter of being 'politically correct'. Rather, it is a matter of bringing one's behaviour in line with one's conviction – an apparent incapability of the pragmatist. As Bernard Lonergan (1965) argued, it is far easier to bring one's conviction in line with one's behaviour. Unfortunately, the price of that easier path leads to the dulling of one's conscience and the convenience of opposing uncomfortable options.

Fortunately, the rule of that racist category game is changing world-wide perhaps for three more basic reasons. First, black people are rejecting membership to that 'club' and they know that the way to reject it is not to reject the term 'black'. Secondly, they accept that politically the term, 'black', needs to be *exorcised* of its notions of 'bad', 'inferiority', and 'miscegenation'. The 'black-is-beautiful' movement strongly projected that aim, and those who understand its importance are less likely to be embarrassed by the term. Finally, they are aware that, paradoxically, black people seek the acceptance and use of the term 'black' to be inclusive to *people genuinely seeking racial justice* as opposed to being related to a *colour category*.

The true black vision is thereby that of a family of human

beings not based on sexist notions or on spurious concepts based on pseudo-scientific explanations of how human beings originated.

Black people have an excellent history of extending goodwill and tolerance in living and working with people deemed 'white', and have sought to extend that tolerance. Therefore, the authentic 'black perspective', which by definition is already multi-racial and inclusive of people who are different, has the conceptual 'germ' for giving rise and meaning to an all-inclusive 'People of Colour'. And, if this belief will take another three generations to gain ascendency, it seems a very good reason for expounding now.

SOME ACHIEVEMENTS

Bearing in mind that ABPO works essentially for the enhancement of the Service's work (and is not a union), some of its achievements for the Service could be briefly listed as follows:

1. Greater participation of black officers in the management and practice issues of the Service.
2. Greater participation and influence of race/equality policy issues within the union (NAPO).
3. Greater awareness by sections of the black community of the role, practice and areas of work and interests of the Probation Service.
4. A clear recognition of allied professionals regarding the practice and potential of the Probation Service as an agent of change and benefit to the black community.
5. Greater confidence and conviction given by the Probation Service in recognising and exploring the need to tackle racism in the Criminal Justice System.
6. An increased number of black people entering the Probation Service and participating in the Union, NAPO; this includes supporting the work of social work training establishments;
7. Latterly the appointments of qualified and capable black officers into senior management positions within the ranks of the Service.
8. A small contribution to the experience and knowledge of the former Chair of the CRE, Michael Day, an ex-Chief Probation Officer of the West Midlands, who had supported and successfully managed many conflicts and criticisms generated by, among other race-related occurrences, the development of ABPO.

These are modest claims compared to the degree of effort and energy that most black Probation staff have made within the ranks of the Service regarding anti-racist practice. Yet, ABPO is unlikely to receive accolades for these achievements. A Home Office study in 1990 on 'Race Issues In The Probation Service', for instance, gave no credit to the role and contribution of ABPO. Yet this omission was viewed, in retrospect, as ABPO's failure to publicise itself and its work.

A PROACTIVE ROLE FOR BLACK PROFESSIONALS

The NACRO report (1991b) *The Black Communities and the Probation Service* recommends the development of links with black community groups by the Service. 'Partnership' was implied. However, there is always the likelihood of well-intentioned policy aimed at fairness and equality for black people 'out there' whilst those staff inside the Service remain marginalised, mis-used and even abused.

The desired partnership between the Probation Service and the black community must commence with the partnership between black professionals and their own organisations. The latter partnership is not an end itself but a means to an end – that 'end' being the delivery of appropriate service and enhancing the confidence of the black community against the strident attacks of racial discrimination and oppression. Justice means nothing if it does not include the manifestation of racial justice, *done and seen to be done.*

A case in point is the development of the Handsworth Cultural Centre in the West Midlands. An initial inspiration and aspiration of black staff (supported by Inner City Partnership funding), the Handsworth Cultural Centre became a meaningful symbol to the local black community in partnership with the West Midlands Probation Service. Over a period of 15 years it became a public statement that the social, psychological and cultural oppression of a significant section of the black community could and would be challenged by and through a Probation Service willing to use a relevant if unorthodox method of art and culture to lend support to the black community. National prominence has been given both to the centre and to a few individuals and groups that started there (for example Kakouma Dance Group). Justice was seen to be pursued.

However, recent unilateral Service decisions, informed solely by economic considerations sought to change the use of the Centre without any prior consultation with either the black community or black staff. The resultant petition by the black community and the disgruntlement shown by black staff is to be recognised as a response to the attack on the confidence of the black community. A signed petition called on black staff within the Service to take *action*. This could be read as a positive demand in the attempt to sustain the partnership and the community's confidence both in its black members who are in the Service and in the ultimate expectations of the Service as a public organisation.

It has been argued that the contributions by black professionals of public sector service organisations can and do play a necessary and unique role in their organisations. In doing so, they very often enable desirable institutional and potential social changes, particularly in pursuit of equal and appropriate service delivery to the community. Over the last twenty-five years, the experience of black professionals in the Probation Service has shown that the collective support and shared responsibility by black professionals are vital to the task of public sector service organisations (including the Police) to pursue the matter of race equality competently, confidently and realistically. However, they do so at a cost to themselves.

Enabling good community relations must be seen alongside the ultimate goal of public sector service organisations in their servicing role. Therefore, the 'black perspective', as represented by the experience described, needs to be grasped and acted upon by public sector service organisations and their managements. Racism might be an embarrassment or even a source of guilt to most white people, but its all-pervasive existence continues to be an oppressive and discriminatory force in the lives of most people not deemed 'white'.

A CORPORATE STRATEGY

Most public sector service organisations over the last few years will have been encouraged to produce 'mission statements'. Components of a viable strategy to pursue the goals of racial justice and thereby good race relations should be reflected in their 'mission' and thereby include the following factors:

1. Black people are not indiscriminatingly used as experts regarding race; but neither should they be treated as if they

were invisible. Management is always likely to act at the level of their (in)competence; and their sense of commitment can often be limited to securing next year's budget. Their knowledge and competence should be frequently tested.

2. Consequently senior managers should be appraised for their competence in relating to and representing the aspirations of the black community. The limited gains achieved after years of painstaking work and sacrifices cannot continue to be undermined by ill-informed power-wielding managers.
3. Black professionals should be encouraged to show as much practical and responsible commitments to the black community as to their respective organisations.
4. Decisions that effectively and mostly undermine the confidence of black professionals should be identified, examined and if necessary rescinded. This is not an argument for not doing likewise to white professionals. The point is that adverse effects of even well intentioned decisions ought to be anticipated and avoided as part of the premium placed on the heads of black professionals. Collectively black professionals are uniquely placed to help in this process!
5. White professionals, particularly those who work in variable multi-racial areas, should be required to be formally or informally involved with sections of the black community. Indeed, the logical consequence of a real partnership between white organisations and the black community is that it should be clearly seen in the activities of its professional staff.

In relation to working with black professional staff, practice rather than policy needs to be the primary focus. There is a serious underestimation of the intrinsic racial power dynamics to most black-white relationships in this country – be it marital, neighbourhood or supervisory. 'I am not racist because I...' should not be silenced but be pondered on. A statement of belief or even of good intention might be said in *all* honesty; however, it might not correspond to reality.

The solution and resolution, therefore, lies in exploring that dynamic (or expression of honest intention), not in burying or denying it. Pointers to this approach do include practical elements of the following:

1. Making the expectations and premium placed on black staff coming into the Service more explicit to individuals: e.g.,

concerning mutual fears and expectations in supervisory relationships.

2. Highlighting the unavoidable reality in predominantly white organisations that colleagues at all levels will be in a process of attempting to work through ideas and feelings about race. They will, on occasions, invariably attempt to draw on and use the experiences and views of their black colleagues (with full recognition of the unacceptability of overt or covert racist behaviour). This process of learning, however, must be ostensibly reciprocal so that black colleagues' own learning opportunities are catered for as a (training) priority.
3. Expecting white supervisors (through training if necessary) to be disposed to develop their anti-racist practice. They should attempt to promote an atmosphere of mutual learning by drawing on the experiences and skills brought by the black staff. They should do so by ensuring the development of new skills and knowledge, including those developed through valuable links with the black community.
4. Asserting that new black professionals will need to become aware of the prevailing perceptions and concerted efforts within their Service, aimed at promoting anti-racist practice. They will need to be invited to contribute to it according to their skills and interests. If the new black professional has to relate to a black supervisor or line manager, she/he might need to be assured that white line managers too are fully aware and accepting of progressive agency policies regarding anti-racism.

These suggestions are but a few to approaching a process of continued engagement between black and white staff. The aim of this approach is to begin to nullify the predominant 'white/black' and thereby exploitative racist power element in these relationships, which are in turn framed with the structures of the organisation.

CONCLUSION

In short, the views and experiences represented in this paper show, firstly, that black professionals can succeed (though at a price); and, secondly, that the real 'enemy', chameleon by nature and patently apparent in language, is racism. The waste of energies, resources and lives resulting from this evil are sources of injustices, potential violence and community instability. As Jessie Jackson once said, 'those who fail to demand justice yesterday, cannot credibly call for peace today.' Furthermore, those who tax payers pay to serve should do so with respect and without subjecting members of the community to unequal treatment. After all, the confidence of the black community in the fairness of the law is vitally important in ensuring the stability of our wider community.

Fifteen
Equality in the Probation Service

Norman Flynn

Equality of opportunity and equality of treatment are important values for any criminal justice system which aims to uphold citizens' rights. Practices which do not produce fairness and equity of treatment do not contribute towards a justice system but create an arbitrary or discriminatory allocation of punishment and help.

There are two aspects of equality. The first is the right to be treated similarly for a similar crime and not have a different sentence or treatment because of race, age or gender. The second is to have equal access to employment and career prospects, regardless of these characteristics. Of course, success in the second would have a big impact on achieving the first. It is clear that in both respects the service is not producing equality.

EQUALITIES POLICIES

In the first Three-Year Plan for the Probation Service (Home Office, 1992e), 'achieving equality of opportunity throughout the service and all its activities' was listed as one of the eleven main goals of the service:

> All probation services must have a stated equal opportunities policy and ensure that it is effectively implemented, monitored and reviewed. National standards also require probation practice which prevents discrimination on any improper grounds ('anti-discriminatory practice')...Section 95 of the Criminal Justice Act requires the Secretary of State to publish information each year to help the authorities and agencies of the criminal justice system (including the probation

> service) examine the effects of their practices and procedures in order to ensure that discrimination, whether intended or unintended, does not occur.

The first year's objectives under the plan included:

> To ensure that area services are aware of, and comply with, the provisions of equal opportunities legislation. To achieve 100% coverage of race and ethnic monitoring of staff and caseload. To ensure that areas identify, and address, imbalances in service delivery. To ensure that areas identify, and address, imbalances in their staffing profile.

The National Standards (Home Office, 1992b), first published in 1992, defined anti-discriminatory practice:

> Effective action to prevent discrimination (anti-discriminatory practice) requires significantly more than a willingness to accept all offenders equally or to invest an equal amount of time and effort in different cases. The origin, nature and extent of differences in circumstances and need must be properly understood and actively addressed by all concerned – for example, by staff training, by monitoring and review and by making extra effort to understand and work most effectively with an offender from a different cultural background.

With reference to Community Service Orders, the Standards state that:

> The probation service should make particular efforts to find suitable work for people with disabilities, for women offenders and single parents, and for offenders from minority ethnic, racial or other groups (chap. 5 para. 17).

The revised national standards, for example for Pre-Sentence Reports,[1] are less strongly in favour of anti-discriminatory practice:

> PSRs must be free of discrimination on grounds of race, sex, age, disability and any other improper grounds. The PSR writer should take all necessary steps to understand and work effectively with an offender from a different cultural background. Where language differences impair effective communication between the report writer and

anyone who should be interviewed, an accredited interpreter should be used.

Whether services apply anti-discriminatory policy, or a looser, equality policy is partly a matter for local discretion and policy. Whichever approach is adopted, services need to understand the sources of discrimination, then to take effective action to counter it.

SOURCES OF DISCRIMINATORY PRACTICE

Race and Sentencing

Barbara Hudson (1993b) has felt able to assert:

> One of the undisputed facts about race and criminal justice is that black offenders are less likely than their white counterparts to be made the subject of probation orders (p.10).

Certainly the evidence for different treatment is strong. Roger Hood's (1992) study of race and sentencing in the Crown Court in the West Midlands found some variations in the sentences imposed on whites, 'blacks' and Asians. The greatest differences in sentences given to blacks and whites were in those cases classified as of medium seriousness: the difference between custodial sentences given to blacks and whites amounted to a 13% higher probability of custody for a black offender than a white one. All the differences were accounted for by differences in sentencing behaviour towards people over 21 years old. For the black and Asian over-21s there were also significantly longer sentences, after correction for seriousness of offence.

His overall estimate of the 'race effect' on the proportion of people from ethnic minorities serving custodial sentences was:

> ...about 80% of the difference between the proportion of black males in the general population and their proportion among those serving prison sentences, can be accounted for by the greater number of black offenders who appeared for sentence in the Crown Court and by the nature and circumstances of the crimes they were convicted of. The remaining 20 per cent could be attributed to their subsequent different treatment by the courts: one third of this (7%) to more being sentenced to custody than expected

> and two-thirds (13%) to more pleading not guilty and to the consequent longer sentences imposed (p.203).

Asians generally suffered less intrusive penalties than either blacks or whites.

With regard to sentences for black women, Hood found that while more black women than white received custodial sentences, this was explained by the nature of the offences. There were no significant differences in length of sentence explainable by race. Women, whether black or white, were less often sentenced to custody than men. Asian women were rarely seen in the Crown Courts. There were differences in the use of the probation service:

> Amongst young people, black offenders with a medium risk of receiving custody were more likely than whites to get a Community Service Order or to be sent to an Attendance Centre, and less likely to be placed on probation (p.204).

Probation officers recommended probation orders less frequently for blacks and Asians than for whites, and a higher proportion of blacks and Asians were sentenced without a Social Inquiry Report, even among those pleading guilty. In the case of one of the Dudley courts, those black offenders who had a social inquiry report were more likely to receive a custodial sentence, often a greater sentence than that recommended.

The main source of possible indirect discrimination was the different treatment of those who plead guilty from those who plead guilty, given that black people are less likely to plead not guilty than whites. The range of information to the courts about black offenders will be more restricted because Social Inquiry Reports are not written for people who plead not guilty.

In a review of 20 studies of potential racial bias in the probation service between 1976 and 1990 Denney (1992) found that in the nineteen studies which found bias, six offered no explanation for the differences in treatment ofblack offenders, four found evidence of racism or possible racism in some part of the system and three studies found inept practice, the domination of white values or ethnocentric practices. However, Denney was unsure about the validity of the methodology in some of these studies and adopted a different approach to his work.

By deconstructing the language used by probation officers in interviews and reports, Denney discovered that the 'vocabulary of motive' used by probation officers and offenders do not coincide. For example, experience of racism as an explanation of motive is not part of the conventional code of probation. Denney argues that probation officers have a choice of two 'codes': a 'corrective code' which is used when the offender is judged to have committed the offence voluntarily and an 'appreciative code' when the offender is judged to be the victim of external forces. He argues that the conventional language used in professional discourse discriminates against some offenders. His solution is to deconstruct the official discourse and change the 'linguistic rules of engagement' of probation officers. If it is the case that the language of both thought and reporting to courts by probation officers fails to connect with the experience and motivation of black offenders, then the service will be accidentally discriminatory against this group. Training in the use of alternative methods of discourse would be the only way to end the discrimination.

Barbara Hudson (1993b) is sceptical about anti-racist policies:

> By the late 1980s every agency and institution within what had been the welfare state and the criminal justice system had, or was in the process of developing, anti-racist statements, anti-racist policies, anti-racist strategies, anti-racist codes of practice and sanctions for breaches of same. The enthusiasm of the Home Office, the probation service, the Central Council for Education and Training in Social Work, and a multiplicity of other public sector organisations and agencies, for anti-racism was paralleled only by an almost universal vagueness about what it was (p.103).

Race and Work in Probation

However, NACRO (1993f) have summarised efforts to create anti-racist policies of recruitment and retention and found that almost all probation areas have an equal opportunities policy with reference to race. However, they found that positive efforts were required to recruit and retain black staff. Efforts such as working with black community groups, recruiting volunteers as a route into the service, training in race issues, monitoring are required to increase the number of black and ethnic minority officers.

They made four recommendations for the probation service:

- The probation service should establish a national forum and resource centre to enable areas to share good practice, and help establish a national strategy for recruitment and training.
- Entry routes to the service should be widened...
- Management practices should ensure that staff are supported in their work, and that disciplinary codes are enforced as needed. Equal opportunities training should be developed.
- Routes to senior positions should be examined to ensure they are free from discrimination and operate within equal opportunities policies...

Experience of equalities work in other sectors suggests that a written policy on equal treatment is simply not enough to ensure that it takes place. An effort has to be made to counter racism at all stages in the employment process: at the stage of creating a field of candidates for recruitment; the recruitment process; training and promotion; training for white staff. Without efforts in these areas, the service will continue to have under-representation of many parts of the community and be an unattractive employer to many potential recruits.

Racist Offenders

Recent discussions about making racial attacks an identifiable offence have not resulted in changes in the law, on the grounds that proof of racial motivation would be an additional burden in a process of justice which first has to prove that the offender committed the offence. However, Andy Gill and Trevor Marshall (1993) have reported on work which they have being doing to deal with racist offenders.

They argue that often racist offenders can be dealt with by the probation service without their racism being addressed for various reasons: white officers may be themselves racist or uninterested in offenders' racism; collusion or inability to deal with racism; black officers may be unable to deal with racism; the agency itself may not be supportive of anti-racist action; no materials or guidance are available to help.

At the stage of the preparation of the Pre Sentencing Report and the stage of supervision, they argue, should be brought through a process which intervenes in their racism, even if race was not an overt element of the offence. Their work has been in three stages: exercises in race awareness; challenging the myths that 'justify' racism; empowerment in positive attitudes and the possible development of anti-racism. They have integrated such work in their offending behaviour programmes, for white offenders.

Gender and Probation Services

Women are imprisoned with fewer convictions than men: 53% of women have two or fewer convictions when they first go to prison, as against 22% of men. Kennedy (1992) explains the difference in the treatment of women and men by the courts by deep-seated discriminatory practice. However, there has been no systematic study of the difference in treatment by the probation service of women and men.

However, NACRO (1993e) have looked at the way in which women are treated after they leave prison. They found that they have insufficient support and are unlikely to voluntarily seek help from the probation service. This is for four reasons. There are very few women in prison and therefore released from prison and so the probation service does not have as much experience in dealing with women as with men. Since women prisoners are often housed far from home they are remote from their local probation service. In any case, NACRO found that women prisoners regard the probation service as a part of the criminal justice system which put them in prison in the first place and that it was predominantly male-oriented.

The NACRO report recommended various changes in the way in which women are helped after release.

- Standards: in 1991 only 9 probation services had a written statement of standards for women's treatment after release, which recognises their special case. Every service should have such a statement.
- Special consideration should be given to probation services for short stay and remand prisoners.
- Services should be designed which are suitable for women.
- Women prisoners and ex-prisoners should be allocated a woman probation officer wherever possible.
- Because of the suspicion of the probation service, probation should work closely with voluntary organisations providing services for women.

Gender and Management

While there is rough equality between the sexes in appointment to main grade probation officer jobs, the proportion of women is less than equal at senior level (about 20% of seniors are women) and there are currently eight women Chief Probation Officers. Why should this be?

Michelle Hayes (1989) reported on a survey of women probation officers in 1989. She found that women were reluctant to apply for promotion because of the style of behaviour required in more senior positions. In particular she found that her respondents found that 'agency' was felt to require masculine behaviours which women were not comfortable with:

> ...agentic principles appear to have gained, and to be continuing to gain, substantial ground over communal strategies. The move towards mechanistic interventions and the growth of bureaucracy are two illustrations of this advance...My research suggests that there is a consensual antipathy amongst women towards more mechanistic activities, that relational elements are central to the work of women (p.15).

Because of this, she suggests, women are unlikely to seek promotion. The only solution is for women to seek support for a different way of managing:

> ...women who are considering applying for promotion should consider carefully what style of management they see themselves offering and seek support networks which will enable them to support their style...There is little evidence to suggest that reformist 'equal opportunities' strategies, on their own, will improve the representation of women within the organisation (p.17).

Sue Kay (1993) surveyed all the women probation officers with five years experience in a service in which there were only 12.5% women Senior Probation Officers. Of 31 women who completed her questionnaire, in response to a question about whether they were interested in promotion, the results were:

Very interested	2
Interested	6
Considering applying	1
Not interested	14
Definitely not for me	8

It was unlikely that 22 would apply for promotion.[2]

Her respondents expressed two main problems: how women and men were assessed for promotion; the problems experienced by women who were promoted. They thought there was more informal encouragement, and formal encouragement through the appraisal process, for men to apply for promotion than women. When women were promoted, many felt that they had to adopt male attitudes and styles:

> ...because of their small number they were seen to be spread across the divisions and isolated, having little effective say in divisional management and facing the personal dilemmas of having to suppress their creativity, being unable to challenge the dominant style of management and therefore being unable to create their own style. As a result they were rendered 'invisible' as a recognisable force and were only able to influence the position of other women informally (p.63).

Sue Kay's conclusion on the future of promotion prospects for women is that they will not be promoted unless the service changes its management style:

> Profound changes would need to take place within the Service to encourage these women to apply for promotion. The Service would be required to transform its organisation so that women's values were recognised as worthwhile in their own right and women were able to develop alternative management styles appropriate to them (p.65).

Janet Newman (1994) takes a similar view about the place of women managers in public services which are undergoing change. She argues that a specific management style is required in 'transformational' cultures:

> ..the most important problem lies in the model of leadership on which 'transformational' cultures are based. The emphasis is on the need for an inspirational and visionary leadership, which operates through affective (rather than cognitive) modes of interaction ... Leadership of this type is seen as mysterious and elusive, based on unique qualities of exceptional individuals. Leaders, we learn, are almost always born rather than made, and they are nearly always born male (p.197).

While cautious about defining a stereotypical women's style of management, she argues that only if there is an emphasis on communication, empowerment, consensus building and teamworking will there be a fit between the values which women carry in their jobs and the cultures in which they work.

These arguments point to the need for more than an effective anti-discriminatory set of policies and practices. What is required is a change in the way in which the service is managed, both to ensure more equal access to higher level jobs and to allow the service to benefit from the skills, values and qualities of women in managerial positions. More radically, it could be argued that the probation service would need to be 'regendered'.[3]

It could be argued that some of the recent changes in the Probation service represent a move from a 'professional' to a 'machine' bureaucracy.[4] A professional bureaucracy has independent professional practitioners, acting on the basis of their professional training and experience, managing themselves, judging and being judged by their peers. The main coordinating mechanism is the standardisation of skills.

In a machine bureaucracy, the main coordinating mechanism is the standardisation of work processes, policing by the people who design and monitor those processes. Work is controlled from the outside. As Mintzberg (1983) says, this form is 'unfashionable' (p.163). The standardisation of procedures (Home Office, 1992b) and the introduction of performance measurement in relation to tasks performed moves the service towards a machine bureaucracy, with implications for the way in which work is managed and supervised.

A similar movement may be represented by the need to enter 'partnership' arrangements, especially if these are made through a formal contracting process. Already there is some collaboration with the voluntary sector. The Home Office Circular on Partnership (1992c) increased the proportion of the budget to be used in this way and raises expectations about the level of voluntary and private sector collaboration. Managing through other organisations requires a different approach to managing direct provision: contracts have to be written and monitored; services have to be defined; appropriate relationships have to be established. The old form of grant aid does not work in a 'contract culture'. I have argued elsewhere (Flynn, 1994) that formal contracting with detailed specifications leads to hierarchical control and detailed supervision.

Linked to this initiative, but more tentative, is the main thrust of government policy, as set out in Competing for Quality (Cmd 1730, 1991) and the Citizen's Charter initiative towards 'market testing' (which means competitive tendering) or since July 1994 'benchmarking' (which means checking your costs against those which would prevail in an alternative supplier).

As far as we know there are not yet any specific initiatives to market test the main elements of the probation service. But the prison service and the prison education service are already subject to these disciplines. It would not be any more difficult to invent a set of rules about market testing the core probation service. The emphasis on costs and demonstrating performance which this would imply would also lead towards a more 'controlling' form of management.

CONCLUSIONS

There seems to be no doubt that the result of the practices of the probation service, in conjunction with and influenced by other parts of the criminal justice system and the government, is unequal treatment of women employees and offenders of different ethnic origins. While there are official policies to counter these tendencies, implementation has not been completely successful.

Explanations for this state of affairs range from racism and sexism on the part of individuals making decisions, to 'institutionalised' racism and sexism of the practices, to a linguistic and cultural failure to construct a discourse which would produce equality of understanding, treatment and employment.

If the more deep-seated, structural explanations are correct, then what is required to achieve equality is no less than a new set of linguistic constructs and rules and practices of behaviour. In any case it would seem that the policies, guidelines and practice protocols have yet to produce truly equal treatment.

This is an urgent task, not only in the probation service. If there is to be a just system of justice, the institutions which make up the system, from police to courts to prison services, have themselves to act in a just way. If there is discrimination on race and gender grounds, not to exclude the more obvious class biases of appointments and behaviours of parts of the system, nobody will have faith in the process of law. Large parts of the population will be alienated by a system which they see as at best unfair and at worst oppressive. Such alienation will in turn make the whole process of combating crime ineffective: there is more at stake in this question than morality.

Notes

1. Draft revised pre-sentence report national standard as at 1 March 1994.
2. Of course, we have no comparative figures about how many male probation officers also do not consider applying for promotion or the reasons for it. We have all met main grade officers who do not agree with hierarchical management arrangements and 'masculine' approaches to management. However, there are clearly enough men for whom this is not a problem for the upper ranks to be mainly populated by men.
3. One view of gender and organisation is that classical management produces a patriarchal organisation (see Witz and Savage, 1992).
4. Definitions from Mintzberg (1983).

Sixteen
Justice and civil work in the Probation Service: The case for the consumer

Steve Goode

There is continued debate about the place of civil work within the overall framework of the Probation Service. The use of language is important; use of the word 'civil' has been replaced with the term 'Family Court Welfare', which is more in line with the spirit of the Children Act (Home Office, 1993b). This hides or obscures the real tensions inherent in the present organisational framework; should criminals and individual parents and their children, who are experiencing the emotional turmoil of separation and divorce, be dealt with by the same agency?

Increasingly the Probation Service is being influenced by a growth of consumerism, which seeks feedback from the customers of the Service as to the quality and effectiveness of the service provided. Principles of good practice must include providing a service which is validated by recipients and, to that extent, parents and their children involved in divorce proceedings have a right to expect a quality service from the Probation Service.

Another relevant consideration for an analysis of civil work in the Probation Service is Weber's four qualifying criteria for legitimacy of any state intervention. These are tradition, effectual attitudes usually emotional, national belief in the absolute value of the intervention and that the intervention is recognised to be legal (Weber, 1947). Then there is the question of justice. The definition provided by Hume (1939) is also very pertinent, in that justice is portrayed as a device for preserving social order, by settling disputes between individuals who are making incompatible claims on property. Justice in this context is concerned with the distribution of benefits and burdens and thus injustice may be regarded as a characteristic of situations where one person or group wrongly receives less or more than other persons or groups. But in addition, there is inescapably the notion of social justice, where justice is linked to the promotion of the interests of the oppressed, the weak and the exploited (Campbell, 1988), is closely associated with considerations of poverty and the provision for the less fortunate members of society.

Let us unscramble the message for the benefit of the consumer of the family court work welfare service. Is the service attempting to protect the interests of the exploited? What traditions underpin such a service? Are customers attracted to such a service and feel affection for the professionals employed in this branch of the Probation Service? How much does a potential customer know about such a service and how much would lobby groups/interest groups seek to protect such a service? What is the legal framework for such a service and has such radical change as the underlying philosophy of the Children Act 1989 really made any difference to the service provided? What role does the Family Court Welfare Service have in settling disputes between partners and how do officers of such a service go about the complex task of distributing the benefits and burdens of future parenthood, once a marriage has broken down?

Family Court Welfare Officers operate in the context of rapidly changing social mores and new patterns of social relationships. It is self-evident that principles of justice need to be applied within such a framework but should such a service seek to embrace such change or implicitly or explicitly seek to preserve a particular form of social order? There is no more emotional issue than protecting an 'innocent' child, either from the horrors of crime, or from the devastation of a destructive and protracted marital breakdown. In a recent well-publicised case, a man received 18 months for contempt of court for kidnapping his child, having alleged that access broke down, after his former wife had left the country. The 14 year old boy was dubbed as being at risk of severe psychological harm from this particular tug of war and, on being reunited with his mother, looked uncertain and apprehensive and indicated a very different preference for his future. (*Sunday Times*, 9 January 1994). This particular high profile case was administered by the Official Solicitor but in a less dramatic form, such cases are the life blood of the Family Court Welfare Service. Such struggles are perennial and encapsulate the requirement for a sensitive and mature service which assists couples to value the strength of their commitment to their children but recognise the fallacy of trying to prove their individual worth to themselves or their children by fighting endless battles or skirmishes about the living arrangements of their offspring. Justice is therefore served, as Hume anticipated, by the operation of an efficient and sensitive service for settling disputes between parties who are making incompatible claims about their children.

Such a process would, it could be argued, be required whatever patterns of social relationships were becoming the norm or were significantly prevalent within contemporary society. But is there any link between the service provided to the customer and a particular set of values espoused by law makers? The current Government's 'back to basics' campaign seeks a return to so-called traditional forms of social relationships. The nuclear family is seen to epitomise stability, a sense of personal responsibility and an avoidance of costly dependency on the state. Such a family provides protection against the supposed damaging effects of different forms of social relationships, such as single parenthood, which is erroneously and mischievously linked to the threat of delinquency. Whilst the evidence is at best inconclusive (Goode, 1992), it is a commonly accepted mythology that single parents per se equate with disturbance in their children. Alternatively this campaign may be explained in economic terms as the state is required to meet the burgeoning costs of social security payments for single parents. Consequently, the re-emphasis of family ties in the late 1970s, 80s and early 90s, could be seen as a response to increased public expenditure.

Jenkins (1994) eloquently argues that there are problems in such an approach and not just because of the peccadillos of senior Ministers:

> I believe politicians merely look foolish when they tell private citizens how to order this aspect of their lives. Social historians such as Peter Laslett and Ferdinand Mount have charted the continuity of marital relations since the dawn of time, amid constant attempts by both Church and State to regulate it. Divorce may be made easier, or harder. Bastardy may be condoned or stigmatised. Raising children in a nuclear family seems to be a fairly constant feature of human intercourse, but so

> too does the regular breakdown of such families. The sanction of the law or religious damnation makes little impact on this intimate and difficult relationship.

There are considerable dilemmas for officers who are operating in this moral quagmire but does this really affect their decision making? Lemert (1986) argues that Probation Officers and Social Workers will frequently make choices which reflect neither their values, nor their hierarchy but rather that which is directly possible. Consequently, Family Court Welfare Officers are likely to be pragmatic and not display a very specific value position.

Modern divorce law has increased the availability of divorce to all social classes. Administrative conveniences have been devised to cut down court time. However, it cannot be said that such developments have been matched by changes in relation to perceptions of the position of children in divorce proceedings. There remain powerful stereotypes of the defencelessness of children in the midst of their parents' divorce. Practitioners are therefore unlikely to be 'individualists' who view rising divorce rates with equanimity and point to the positive benefits divorce may bring to the individual and hence to society. Further, they are more likely to be 'traditionalists' who see increased divorce as thwarting the emotional development of adults and children and the difficult process of self-discovery through a long term relationship (Thornes and Collard, 1976). Nevertheless, for a woman, divorce may mean a start of a new emotional and intellectual freedom where, if emotional traumas can be contained and the demands of dependent children are not too restricting, increased financial, employment and educational opportunities may pertain. However, it is clear that although liberalising influences have increased the availability of divorce, the Court's principle function is to ensure the future well-being of children. This may not always accord with the concept of minimum state intervention in a parent's resolution of their own problems, with a high emphasis on reaching amicable compromises, without resource to excessive and harmful litigation.

So what of justice and the Family Court Welfare Service? In protecting children by safeguarding their welfare in family proceedings, the Service is not engaging in a value free activity. It is part of the structure of child protectionism which seeks to defend the interests of a future work force. To some recipients this may feel oppressive and some critics of techniques used to involve parents in reaching decisions over their children's future, have contended that they too easily mirror the power imbalances, already evident in some relationships between women and men. It is difficult to see the Family Court Welfare Service actively promoting the interests of the oppressed or the exploited, although it does continually protect the interests of individual children in disputes between parents, which in the short term and long term may be very damaging to their emotional and possibly their physical development. Such activity takes place within the context of a moral debate about the place of the family in society.

Justice may be seen to be enacted if principles of legitimacy as set out, can be established. Although the Family Court Welfare Service is well established, being founded in 1958, and therefore has established legitimacy by means of 'tradition', it is more difficult to establish 'effectual' attitudes towards such a Service. This is because the Family Court Welfare Service is very much part of the court process, which hides the Service from public attention except at times of individual contacts by parents and their children. Indeed, it could be argued that the work of the Probation Service as a whole similarly does not always command the public attention that is required to demonstrate that constructive ways of working with offenders can make a real impact on crime, and for too long 'civil work' has been left in a shadowy corner. Why is that the case?

The criminal emphasis of the Probation Service does not sit comfortably with a Family Court Welfare Service and individual Chief Probation Officers may have not always recognised the potential benefits of a high profile for a Family Court Welfare Service, which can offset the damaging consequences for the Probation Service of being perceived to be too closely linked to the interests of offenders, as opposed to those of victims. However, there is no more powerful an image of a victim than a child involved in painful divorce proceedings. Nevertheless, the low profile of the Family Court Welfare Service is well established. This is partly due to important issues of confidentiality, its very close association with the courts rather than the public, a well established tension between the criminal preoccupations of the Home Office and proper consideration of the resource implications and strategy required for effective civil work. In addition, the Family Court Welfare Service often appears to be a 'service within a Service'. There are indeed real dilemmas in deciding what should be the core business of the Probation Service and whether civil work should be part of the future make up of the Probation Service.

The Probation Service Statement of Purpose and Three Plan 1994-97 includes the aim of safeguarding the welfare of children in family proceedings. Each Probation Service must now have a civil work strategy which is consistent with the framework set by the national strategy document. More attention is to be given to monitoring civil work caseloads and to producing national standards, in line with other aspects of service delivery. All of these developments would suggest an enhancement of the role of the Family Court Welfare Service within the Probation Service, with an approximate share of the budget of between one eighth and one tenth.

However, the future is less clear if some observers are to be believed. For instance, Judge Jean Graham-Hall (1993) observed:

> What is the justification for leaving the Civil Court Welfare Service within the Probation Service which is overwhelmingly concerned with the criminal justice system. The question is not being addressed satisfactorily, if at all. The most powerful answer put forward in an aura of silence is 'if it ain't bust don't mend it'.

Judge Hall favours an expanded civil work welfare service within the Lord Chancellor's department, more able to deal with future demands of increased family jurisdiction. This may secure funding and provide a more coherent organisational framework for a court based service, but would this development be in the spirit of divorce law reform and in the interests of the consumer?

Most divorcing couples with children do not have any dealings with Family Court Welfare Officers, as divorce is often a paper exercise. Some officers are available in Children's Hearings and are now more readily available for informed advice or guidance when court proceedings involve in-court conciliation or mediation. Nevertheless, court advice, however skilled, may be too late to avoid acrimonious disputes between parents over the arrangements for their children. Recourse to legislation usually suggests that positions are entrenched and in itself the court operates as primarily adversarial. A service based in the community, rather than in the court, which is accessible to couples at an early stage might be welcomed by consumers and therefore establish more effectively effectual attitudes towards the 'legitimacy of' a Family Service.

Justice may be promoted not only in those respects but also by making a valuable resource of skilled staff much more available to individuals who are both poor and exploited, who would wish to avoid the cost and formality of court proceedings. To this extent, principles of social justice would be furthered.

The present Lord Chancellor, Lord MacKay is to be applauded in maintaining the principles of the Law Commission in his own Green Paper, which has proposed some practical changes designed to make divorce proceedings less adversarial and less likely to end up in courts. The proposal that the concept of fault should be taken out of all divorces (but with the stipulation of a minimum delay of one year before a divorce could be granted), is accompanied by a proposal for the provision of a mediation service, available to provide counselling if breakdown might be prevented and helping with settling matters of access to children and division of property, if it cannot.

The concept of no fault divorce is not new. Mrs White MP had tried to introduce a Matrimonial Causes Bill in 1951 with the aim of introducing a new ground for divorce, other than matrimonial offence, based on the doctrine of the breakdown of a marriage. She withdrew the Bill in favour of a Royal Commission (1951-55), the same Royal Commission which recommended the establishment of a Divorce Court Welfare Service to be run by the Probation Service, which was enacted in 1958.

Lord MacKay has had to run a gauntlet of opposition from other government Ministers, who have raised the spectre of increasing numbers of single parents, arguing for an extension of a one year cooling off period to two, and that an element of fault in divorce proceedings should be retained (*The Independent*, January 1994). He may have been aware that similar concerns were around at the time of the establishment of the Divorce Court Welfare Service in the late 1950s. McGregor (1957) in describing the social context at the time of the Royal Commission (1951-55), pointed to the break up of the mid-Victorian family code. This was welcomed by some, who saw a transition to a more democratic family unit in which the rights of individuals and personal choice were emphasised at the expense of institutional claims. Equally, however, there were others who saw such changes as leading to the destruction of family life and the corruption of morality, and who interpreted the rise in divorce proceedings, after the Second World War, as indicative of increasing moral decay. Thus, the concern of the state to effectively regulate personal relationships is a recurring theme. However, no matter what the political imperatives at play, such attempts to achieve consistency in aspects of social policy are impossible to achieve and arguably positively unhelpful:

> A study of social policy will yield a confused position because of the diverse and often conflicting values in any society, particularly in a period of social change (Eyden, 1969, p.2).

Lord MacKay's proposals for the network of local mediation/conciliation services offer a significant challenge to the future structure of the Family Court Welfare Service and, indeed, to the Probation Service as a whole. The Law Commission's present proposals emphasise the importance of the use of conciliation and mediation during the one year cooling off period. Even though the later court proceedings will have the power to direct a party to meet a conciliator or mediator to discuss the nature and potential benefits of conciliation or mediation, the most dramatic change is the proposal for community based facilities to provide monitoring and support for divorcing couples and their families during the period of reflection and consideration. The present provision for independent conciliation/mediation is patchy and reflects the initiative of local groups and to some extent the sponsorship of larger organisations, such as the Probation Service.

Commentators have observed that far more work is required on how the available resources might most profitably be used (Schuz, 1993). One source of revenue is more systematic funding by the 55 area Probation Services who, by 1996-97, are required to spend 5% of their budget on partnership programmes with the voluntary/independent sector (Home Office, 1990b). The worth of such investment might be to offset more costly court based facilities such as providing welfare reports in cases where couples are entrenched in disputes over their children. Although a back stop would still be required, of a court based provision, in cases where child protection issues are paramount, the provision of community based facilities which are openly accessible would uphold principles of social justice by providing quality advice to couples from a whole range of social groups.

Such is the funding formula for the Probation Service that this provision is not likely to generate income for the Probation Service, as the level of Family Court reports is not at present an indicator for core funding for individual Probation Services. Senior managers and Probation Boards will have to be creative about income generation to meet such a community provision and will need to influence the Home Office over the workload aspect of the cash limits formula.

The balance of court based services and community based services will need further attention. The Probation Service will need to be clear about how many court based officers they should employ and how much resources should be reallocated to community based provision, either provided on a partnership basis by the voluntary or independent sector, or by a reorganised and devolved 'Family Service' managed by the Probation Service directly. It seems essential that specific outcomes are specified for such new provision, before individual Probation Services decide whether they are purchasers or providers.

The mere transfer of a Family Court Welfare provision from the Home Office to the Lord Chancellor's department would be unlikely to guarantee the establishment of such a nationwide conciliation/mediation service, delivered locally. The Probation Service should seize the opportunity to put forward its own case. It is locally structured and can provide a quality provision for parents and their children, quite separate from services for offenders. The Service is well placed to ensure the principles of social justice are enshrined in any developments. Strategic considerations must be addressed, taking a lead from the most recent Home Office Strategy Document which recognises the requirement to give further attention to strategy. Referring to the Home Office proposals for partnerships with the voluntary and independent sectors, the document states:

> These will allow the funding of activities in support of dispute resolution such as access centres, and of divorce experience courses, as well as independent conciliation and mediation organisations, in conjunction with other funding by the independent sector. *These medium term issues, whilst they need not affect the immediate planning process, may mean that the strategy outlined in this paper has to be revisited sooner than could otherwise have been the case* (Home Office, 1993b, p.3).

The Family Court Welfare Service does intervene in one of the most sensitive areas of personal life, the breakdown of relationships with its associated potential of personal trauma and social and financial disintegration. It is necessary to examine the Service's role within the framework of the state's intervention in the family for which Eekelaar (1984) provides three justifications:

1. To provide mechanisms and rules for adjusting the relationship between family members when family units break down.
2. To provide protection for individuals from possible harm suffered within the family.
3. To support the maintenance of family relationships.

The most recent legislative framework for the Family Court Welfare Service is the Children Act 1989. This legislation provides legal legitimacy for such a Service and a future for its role. The Children Act 1989 is framed within principles of minimum state intervention, in particular the avoidance of unnecessary court orders, and the minimisation of delay to obviate distress to children. The Act continues the tradition that the child's welfare shall be the paramount consideration. It is in so far as it meets those principles that the real legitimacy of such a service should be judged. Although our historical traditions have been more interventionist and our service delivery may not have always considered the timescales on children, we have a strong case to make, especially if we show our commitment to improving practice. The Welfare Checklist provided in the Children Act an excellent focus for this approach:

Welfare Checklist

a) Ascertain and present the views of the child, depending on age and understanding.
b) Consider the future physical, education and emotional needs of children.
c) Consider the likely affect of change in circumstances.
d) Present the relevant circumstances as regards age, sex and background.
e) Consider the harm suffered by children and the risk of any future harm.
f) Consider the capability of parent(s) (or other persons) to meet the needs of children.

g) Consider the applicability of the range of court powers available.

(Children Act 1989)

The application of principles of justice to the practice of civil work in the Probation Service indicates areas of difficulty and some important strengths and opportunities. The role of the divorce court must be to limit any future damage to the parties involved in proceedings, both parents and children. Nevertheless, no court system could remove all of the feelings of injustice that some spouses will feel about the transition from being married to being divorced, particularly when they did not seek such a change in status. On the other hand, Family Court Welfare Officers do provide an invaluable 'arm', alongside a number of other organisations, such as Relate or independent conciliation/ mediation services, to those parties who require time to be spent with them so they can visualise their role as future parents and put aside their own very personal feelings of hurt, betrayal, fear and failure. The resolution of such highly charged personal disputes is at the heart of the operation of justice. Likewise, principles of justice demand that children should be diverted from court processes and the establishment of comprehensive community based 'family advice' centres, either purchased or provided by the Probation Service would mark a worthwhile step in this direction. Court expertise, provided by the Probation Service would have to be retained for more complex child protection issues. This is in line with the traditions of juvenile justice, which seek to limit court labelling and improve non-stigmatising community provision. In these ways, in the constantly changing moral debate about the stability of the family and the desirability or otherwise of particular forms of social relationships, opportunities to develop more relevant provision should be grasped.

The present court based service makes 'effectual' attitudes towards such a service difficult to achieve and it cannot easily relate to the interests of the poor and the exploited. Its role is largely hidden, despite progress with interpreters and consultants from ethnic groups. Another impediment may relate to the long established tension between the criminal and civil work within the Probation Service and the historical lack of strategic direction given to the subject by both the Home Office and individual Chief Probation Officers.

> How should the public be given the message about the importance of the stability of marriage in our society...the key is to...educate people to cope better with disappointment and frustration by focusing on the positive aspects of their relationships rather than the negative aspects (Schuz, 1993).

A reorganised Family Service has a key role to play in such a dialogue, whatever one thinks about it, and this may do more to uphold social order than many other aspects of the Criminal Justice System!

Seventeen
Partnership, punishment and justice

Mike Nellis

INVENTING THE INDEPENDENT SECTOR

The Probation Service was itself borne of voluntary enterprise in the 19th century and throughout its most recent post-war history it has developed and maintained links with both national and local voluntary organisations, with churches and charities and with smaller commercial organisations in the accommodation and employment fields (Fulwood, 1992). Rule 54(1) of the 1949 Probation Rules, for example, required that every probation officer 'shall encourage every person who is under his (sic) supervision...to use the appropriate statutory and voluntary agencies which might contribute to his welfare, and to take advantage of the social, recreational and educational facilities which are suited to his age, ability and temperament'. The extent to which the rule was followed may well have varied (Bennett, 1991; Jack, 1993) but the *ideals* of integrating an offender into a local community, of stimulating the development of community networks and of harnessing voluntary effort, has been restated several times since then, especially for young offenders, for example in the White Paper *Children in Trouble* (1968). Each version has reflected the mores of the era in which it was written, but until the advent of debates on 'punishment in the community' (Allan, 1990) and on corporate management (Statham and Whitehead, 1992) in the late 1980s, none had either threatened the identity of the Probation Service nor the character of the voluntary sector in quite the way that is happening now.

It was clear from the early Green and White Papers (*Punishment, Custody and the Community*, 1988; *Crime, Justice and Protecting the Public*, 1990a; *Supervision and Punishment in the Community: A Framework for Action*, 1990b) and the Audit Commission (1989) report which launched these debates, that the government had it in mind for the Probation Service to make even more use of service-providing voluntary organisations, unpaid volunteers, local community associations and private companies than they had done in the past. Largely to heighten the contrast with allegedly unenterprising and moribund state bureaucracies, the Home Office coined a new collective term for these bodies, 'the independent sector' and, although competitive tendering and purchase-of-service was apparently to be the main form of relationship between the sector and the Service, the arrangement overall was to be designated 'partnership'.

The precise rationale for this proposed restructuring (i.e. its specific advantages for work with offenders) was initially unclear, but it was consistent with a broad emphasis in Conservative government policy to (ostensibly) role back the frontiers of the state and to create a 'mixed economy' in various fields of social policy (Brenton, 1985; Knapp, 1989). Such developments were generally justified in terms of improved managerial efficiency, increased value for money and the self-evident virtues of firstly, enterprise outside the state and secondly (in the case of unpaid volunteers) 'active citizenship'. Local authorities, particularly Social Services Departments, were among the first to have a vigorous purchase-of-service approach imposed on them (*Caring for People*, 1989) and in *Partnership in Dealing with Offenders in the Community* (1990) – modelled, according to Kay (1991) on the Department of Health paper – the detail of what this might involve for the Probation Service was mapped out.

This document, (known as 'the Peppermint Paper' because of its colour), sought to stimulate debate on the administrative and practical aspects of partnership but still remained vague as to why it would be an improvement on the predominantly statutory status quo. Seven areas in which partnership might have a part to play were suggested; crime prevention in the broadest sense, services to those cautioned or charged, bail accommodation and support, supervision programmes for young adult offenders, work with prisoners before and after release, supporting victims of crime, and family court welfare work. The paper outlined several different scenarios, some (from a probation perspective) more acceptable than others. Parts of it read as if the Probation Service would clearly be the dominant partner, with increased regulatory powers over the independent sector. Others seemed to be proposing no more than a supplementary role for the independent sector, leaving the core functions of the Probation Service intact. The most threatening parts gave the impression that what was being proposed was the substitution and 'asset-stripping' of at least some of the core functions themselves (Nellis, 1990).

Ryan and Ward (1991, p.62) saw in this latter strategy a means of either 'replacing schemes which do not comply with government policy...implementing measures unacceptable to the Probation Service' or simply 'hiving off low priority areas of work'. They felt in particular that the government was 'concerned to ensure compliance with its wish to introduce more punitive alternatives to custody in the face of opposition from NAPO' and underplayed the potentially regulatory elements of the proposals. These anxieties were certainly justified, but they neglected the fact that not all Probation Services, or all probation officers, regarded NAPO's hostility to tougher community penalties as politically progressive; some believed that they could be used to reduce custody and provide more intensive forms of support for offenders than hitherto and did not need the inducement (or threat) of independent sector competition to be persuaded of their value. Ryan and Ward also neglected the fact that there were hardly any voluntary organisations who were willing to act more punitively than the Probation service and no established commercial organisations (at that time) who were seriously interested in doing so.

Public discussion of the Peppermint Paper took place against the backcloth of debate on the Green and White papers generally, not least that aspect of them which spoke of learning the lessons of juvenile justice with young adult offenders. The 'successful revolution' (Jones, 1989) in juvenile justice which took place during the 1980s (significant reductions in the use of custody for 15-16 year olds and increased diversion from prosecution) was built to a very large extent on a partnership between voluntary organisations and local authority Social Service Departments (Nellis, 1989; NACRO, 1991; Smith et al., 1993), rather than Probation. This achievement however, although a source of pride to some, was not necessarily typical of all partnerships, and as the regulatory intentions behind the government strategy became clearer, a rather more sombre mood began to affect the parties to it.

In formal statements, both ACOP (1990a) and especially NAPO (1990b) reacted defensively, seeing in partnership just one of several unwelcome changes that were being imposed on the Probation Service, and expressing satisfaction with the levels of partnership *already achieved.*[1] Both emphasised a supplementary rather than a substitutional role for the voluntary sector, with ACOP allowing it rather more scope for innovation in new areas of work, such as bail support, where a probation presence had yet to be fully established. On the ground, formal statements notwithstanding, some NAPO branches were deeply hostile to particular voluntary projects (Greater Manchester NAPO, 1988) and were unable to see any merit in what was being proposed. Some managers, on the other hand (e.g. Harman, 1990), saw in the caring and campaigning traditions of the voluntary sector a potential ally against the worst excesses of 'punishment in the community' and in a joint statement from the leaders of ACOP and NACRO, partnership was encouraged so long as 'the strategic potential of the voluntary sector', its capacity to identify new needs and to criticise both government and local agency policy if circumstances warranted it, was not jeopardised (Stern and Weston, 1990).

Elsewhere in the voluntary sector, as both large and small organisations grasped the extent to which they were being turned into instruments of government policy, more searching questions were being asked. Few organisations were convinced that a genuine partnership was on offer, given the Peppermint Paper's favourable view of competitive tendering, which ran the risk of wasting scarce resources and setting different organisations against each other in the search for contracts. The Director of the Rainer Foundation, in particular, took exception to the way in which the term 'independent sector' blurred important differences between voluntary and commercial bodies, in respect of their values and traditions, their legal and financial constraints and their governance structures. He encouraged resistance to government attempts to make the larger, professionalised voluntary organisations act more like private ones, and proposed a more authentic vision of partnership, based on joint planning and reciprocity, rather than mere contracting (Kay ,1991).

Steeper ironies still were to arise in respect of the so-called independent sector. Even as the newly enacted CJA 1991 – the first legislative outcome of 'punishment in the community' – was giving powers for Probation Committees to grant-aid voluntary bodies, it was clear that, in the country as a whole, the voluntary sector was finding itself in an increasingly difficult situation, as financially hard-pressed local authorities reduced or cut their level of support, and as the balance of charitable giving tilted decisively in favour of the larger, national, professionally organised bodies, and away from the smaller, more local volunteer bodies (Charities Aid Foundation, 1992). It was suggested, furthermore, by the stance the government took to two established voluntary bodies in the criminal justice field with whose work they found fault – Apex Trust and the Intermediate Treatment Fund[2] – than independence was not, in reality, the quality they most wanted to see in voluntary organisations, a supposition which received further support from the Home Office's eventual response to the Peppermint Paper.

PARTNERSHIP AND PUNISHMENT

The response appeared somewhat later than expected, in July 1992, and it is this 'decision document' (otherwise known as 'the Lavender Paper' because of its colour) which still, overall, frames policy development in this area, although more detail has been filled in since it first appeared. It sought, firstly, to clarify terminology, insisting, despite criticism, that the term 'independent sector' was a useful umbrella term for the agencies it wished to involve and support in work with offenders, and that the term 'partnership' could legitimately include both 'work done under competitive contract for a probation area, as well as jointly planned projects' (Home Office, 1992c, p.2).

Unlike the Peppermint Paper, the decision document at least attempted to explain why partnership with the independent sector would assist in the implementation of 'punishment in the community'. It stressed, firstly, that the shift towards more community penalties, and towards the more structured supervision of newly released prisoners, requires that 'there are wider opportunities for offenders to be dealt with in the community' (Home Office, 1992c, para. 5). Secondly, the creation and coordination of a network of agencies in the community was deemed to have advantages for all concerned parties. For the Probation Service a more 'efficient, effective and economical' (Home Office, 1992c) use of resources was on offer. For the (now law-abiding) offender there was a better chance of 're-establishment' in the community (Home Office, 1992c). For any given community, partnership presented better opportunities for 'protection against crime, taking responsibility for dealing with crime and ensuring wide acceptance of, and provision made for offenders' (Home Office, 1992c). For the independent sector itself there would be 'a greater range of opportunities to make their unique contributions and to use their skill, imagination and commitment in the service of the community' (Home Office, 1992c).

The document acknowledged more clearly than its predecessor that the general thrust of this policy was not new, that 'many useful schemes exist already and provide links in the community to meet offenders needs in a variety of linked and integrated ways' (Home Office, 1992c, para. 9), but it reframed the plethora of existing practices and rationales in terms of the over-riding aims of 'reducing and preventing crime' (Home Office, 1992c, para. 7), marking the beginning of a process by which it would be easier to measure the subsequent performance of independent sector organisations. It went on:

> The Government wishes to establish *a more formal relationship* between such organisations and local probation services to ensure the availability of as wide a range of options for dealing with offenders as possible. This will enable each probation officer to select and manage the most effective options to meet the objectives of supervision in each case (Home Office, 1992c, emphasis added).

The compatibility of independence (which surely connotes creativity, freedom and autonomy?) with 'greater formality' in terms of funding and monitoring was not explored, but the emphasis on the latter fitted well with the directiveness of the decision document as a whole. Language such as 'the Government has decided that the probation service should take the lead in developing local partnership arrangements and should make financial provision for resourcing this work' (emphasis added) not only asserted the authority of government over the Probation Service, but also pushed local Services towards a more managerial stance with voluntary organisations and community associations than they may have wished to have.

The document envisaged that each local strategy group would draw on guidance from a 'National Partnership Forum' (NPF), chaired by the Home Office, and comprising relevant Probation

Service and independent sector interests (up to a membership of 15). This forum, which was first to develop guidance[3] on the planning process and later to monitor devolution and delivery of service began meeting in late 1992 and required Probation Services to set their planning in the context of the Three Year Plan (Home Office 1992f), which had not been published when the decision document first appeared. Its guidance on the composition of local strategy groups indicated that partnerships might be significantly wider than with the independent sector alone, and that other public bodies and statutory agencies could be included, the proviso being that:

> ...it will be more important that the local strategy group is effective than that it represents the whole range of interests in the community. For this reason it will also be important to consult outside the formal strategy groups to ensure specialist groups are taken into account ... Since it is important that Probation Committees are involved in the planning process, Committees may wish to consider representation on the strategy groups. Membership should not simply reflect existing service providers. Local sentencers should be invited to join (Home Office, 1993d, paras.9-10).

The role given to the NPF (and the Inspectorate, who were to be formally accountable for the development of partnership) complicated somewhat the government's claim that it is relinquishing its 'current, close involvement in the administration of a wide range of grants to voluntary organisations for supervision projects' (Home Office, 1992c, para.11). Given the extent to which Probation Services were still to be monitored from the centre, this was not a straightforward process of devolution (as para 15 implied) or of creating a purely local decentralised system of control over grant-aid. The Home Office insisted that all local plans meet national criteria and support the (centrally-determined) objectives of the criminal justice system, while the NPF itself has admitted that to begin with the new Probation Rules (governing grant-aid from Probation Committees) may need to be drawn quite tightly. It remains to be seen what kind of voice local independent sectors will have in fora which may be dominated by other statutory criminal justice agencies, each of whom have increasingly to follow tightly regulated agendas set by central government.

Basic funding arrangements were set in place early. The expenditure of each Probation Service was cash-limited by the Criminal Justice Act 1991. The power to grant-aid local independent sector organisations was bestowed on Probation Committees by the same legislation, although how much of their budget was to be set aside for this purpose – 'around 5%' (Home Office, 1992c, para 2.) – was fixed by the decision document. This figure, much greater than what the majority of Service's currently spend, may be increased by the Home Office in years to come, generating fears that the independent sector may yet encroach on the Service's core functions. Accommodation projects (bail and probation hostels), for which there was a well established system of central funding, were to be temporarily exempted from local funding arrangements, then brought into line with them at a later unspecified date. The Home Office also retained the power to core-fund certain national organisations working with offenders (idem; para 31) and also to fund 'innovatory projects for which (local) probation areas are invited to compete' (Home Office, 1992c, para. 11).

Within the framework set by the CJA 1991 and the Three Year Plan the significance of partnership planning seemed at first to be quite clear, but in the course of 1993 the climate in which the NPF, and indeed the Probation Service itself, worked became rather more uncertain. Even while Michael Jack (1993, p.5), then Minister of state at the Home Office was telling ACOP's 10th Annual Conference, in May 1993, that the Probation Service was a 'bridge to other services' and that partnership was still a priority, political and judicial unease with the sentencing restrictions in the newly implemented legislation began to grow. This, coupled with media concern about the juxtaposition of an initially falling prison population with rising crime figures, outcries against car crime and bail bandits, and alarm at the state of the nation's youth enabled Conservative politicians to manufacture a 'new' law and order crisis and facilitated the appointment of harder-line ministers at the Home Office. Their subsequent 27-point plan to reduce crime, (at the core of which was a philosophy of 'prison works' (to incapacitate, if nothing else), showed scant regard for their predecessor's intention to move the Probation Service 'centre stage', and had nothing to say about the merits or otherwise of independent sector partnerships. In the Criminal Justice and Public Order Bill 1993, which incorporated many of these points, the principle of consultation with relevant bodies that the partnership policy had at least sought to promote was noticeably less in evidence.

Such debate on partnership as occurred in this period confirmed the existence of long-suspected biases in the type of independent sector organisations that would be welcome in the government's new criminal justice strategy. Private prisons were to be expanded, and electronic monitoring resurrected, but Bryn Melyn, an innovative private children's home in Wales, which included the politically unpalatable luxury of foreign travel in its treatment plans for disturbed and delinquent adolescents, became the focus of hostile criticism by ministers and media alike (McCrystal, 1994), despite apparent satisfaction with the results among the local authorities who contracted with it. In deriding an independent sector organisation which had strayed rather spectacularly from the punitive ideal, central government departments cast further doubt on the rhetoric of enterprise, innovation and flexibility with which partnership policy had traditionally been justified.

COMMUNITY DEVELOPMENT OR COMMUNITY ACTION?

Suggestions that the new harder-line approach within the Home Office presages the curtailment of multi-agency strategies, and, by implication, of partnership (Taylor, 1993) may be premature. Although the climate in which the Probation Service and the independent sector operate is undoubtedly being tilted in a more repressive direction, it is unlikely that all the established political and administrative advantages of multi-agency structures will be sacrificed in respect of crime control, when they are still so prevalent in other fields of social policy. Deakin's (1989, p.10) observation that 'multiplicity of new bodies now putting in an appearance' – housing action trusts, city technology colleges and urban development corporations – were 'rapidly developing an interest in the voluntary sector as a means of padding their soft edges' remains valid, and the momentum behind the 'quangocracy'[4] (as the many new bodies have been collectively named), will not be easy to deflect. It is still, therefore, worth asking what opportunities such partnerships could yield for the Probation Service.

The seven areas in which the Home Office has suggested partnership would be appropriate (and these may not be exhaustive, given the range of ideas to which diverse membership of local strategy groups may give rise) do not have a great deal in common with each other, but are loosely unified in the decision document by the rhetoric of 'community involvement'. This notion is worth exploring. According to the decision document, 'community involvement can range extremely widely from possible providers of practical assistance (Social Services, prospective employers or fundraisers, voluntary organisations, adult education projects), to community organisations and associations with no overt role in working with offenders' (Home Office, 1992c, para. 21).

These latter bodies are usually understood as *the informal* sector rather than the voluntary sector. They include tenants associations, play schemes, youth groups, welfare rights projects, crediot unions, food co-ops, victims groups, transport schemes, crash pads and arts projects, any one of which may have something to contribute to the integration, support and control of a particular offender in a given neighbourhood. Although many women's groups and Black groups are located in this sector, partnership *policy* has not so far favoured such associations, and, as some critics have observed (Butcher, 1992, p.154), the government is seeking to mobilise communities to take constructive action against crime at a point in time when 'there are fewer openings for community groups and organisations to play a participatory role in local community-led government'. There is however a tentatively emerging view that while community associations may be no real substitute for involvement in local government (which should be reinvigorated by other means) they can, especially if supported by larger voluntary organisations, contribute considerably to an improved quality of life and morale on estates blighted by the depredations of un- and underemployed and aggressive young men. Thus:

> In the Nineties many estates in Britain were being galvanised not by political parties but by traditional charities which were modernising their social base and their professional practice by breaking away from their role as rescuers of the perishing. Several were filling the space left by the political vacuum (Campbell, 1993, p.251).

The seeds of such progressive practice as partnership permits probably lie here. There has been belated recognition on the part of some Probation Services that they have neglected community work for too long on deprived, high-crime and riot-prone estates (e.g. Northumbria Probation Service, 1992), despite the body of knowledge generated from special projects during the 1980s (Scott et al., 1985; Henderson, 1986; Broad, 1988, 1991). Neither the Peppermint Paper nor the decision document referred to this literature, which acknowledges the top-down model of community development, enshrined in the official partnership approach, but also gives equal weight to community initiatives from below. In the first instance such initiatives often provoke conflict and seek power rather than partnership, and it is unclear how well this will be handled within the new framework. Nor do the official documents on the independent sector fully acknowledge the overlap with crime prevention policy, or point out that they are, in effect, envisaging a leadership role for the Probation Service in this field that other commentators had denied to it.[5]

CONCLUSION

The overt formality of 'the Decision Document' points inexorably towards the incorporation of the voluntary sector into multi-agency structures of crime control, led initially by the Probation Service, but not only by them, as other state-funded bodies are looking to involve the sector too. Levels of resistance and support for the process of incorporation will vary across the sector, but many voluntary organisations are in too poor a financial shape to resist for long, if they wish to survive. Any attempt to remain aloof from the new structures is likely to result in another, more competitive and more 'enterprising' organisation responding to the opportunity instead, including those in the private sector.[6]

The development of partnerships can be set in the context of recent theoretical work on the growth of corporatism as a strategy of social control. This strategy is distinct from both 'just deserts' strategies and 'rehabilitative' strategies although it frequently borrows ideological and practical elements from both of them (Peters, 1986; Pratt, 1989; Rutherford, 1993). Pratt (1989, p.245) has defined corporatism as a tendency 'to be found in advanced welfare societies whereby the capacity for conflict and disruption is reduced by means of the centralisation of policy, increased government intervention and the cooperation of various professional and interest groups into a collective whole with homogeneous aims and objectives'. Contrary to the commonly accepted view that in recent times the historic shift in criminal justice policy has been from 'welfare' to 'justice', Pratt suggests that it is corporatist structures – i.e. 'the centralisation of authority and coordination of policy, growing involvement of non-juridical bodies, including the voluntary sector' (Pratt, 1989, p.245) – that best explain the evolving shape of 'punishment in the community'.

The growth of such structures forces us to re-examine what is meant by rolling back the frontiers of the state. The state may well have been shrinking in size under the Conservative government, as this or that agency or function has been 'contracted-out' or cut, but it has not been shrinking in regulatory influence; quite the contrary, as the power of the 'quangocracy' testifies. The growth of this bureaucracy is not, despite appearances, incompatible with the rhetorical promotion of an enterprise culture, although it is, as Marquand admits, 'a paradox' which official discourse has routinely sought to mystify:

> The cultural revolution implied by the project of creating an enterprise culture can be carried out only by a strong, and above all, intrusive state, which intervenes incessantly in 'low politics'. Only the state can change the mixture of incentives and disincentives that traps fallen late twentieth century men and women in the dependency of bloated public provision and attenuated private enterprise; only the state can humble or disarm the vast range of intermediate institutions that embody and transmit corrupting, anti-entrepreneurial values. If an enterprise culture is to come into existence, universities must be remodelled, the freedom of action of local authorities must be much more tightly curtailed, the self-governing professions must be 'marketised' and the trade unions must lose power (Marquand, 1993, p.70).

And, it might be added (as a worst-case scenario), Probation Committees must themselves be drawn into the 'quangocracy', the Probation Service deprofessionalised and the capacity of the voluntary sector to innovate and campaign seriously undermined. Peters (1986, p.32) anticipated much of this, and saw also that corporatism represented a shift in the purpose of criminal justice policy, away from a concern with 'justice' as such. The new approach, he says:

> ...is characterised by a withdrawal from the idea that the problem of crime can be eliminated, or even that it can be brought under control. Emphasis has shifted from maintenance of the criminal code and the other criminal statutes to more general control of volumes of criminal activity. Criminal policy is no longer preoccupied with concrete offenders, nor with the problem of doing justice, but with the management of aggregate phenomena of social activity, with criteria for selective law enforcement, with quantitative regulation in the organisational processing of offenders.

The watchwords of the new approach are policy, planning and management, and in the relentless pursuit of efficiency and effectiveness, the moral dimensions of practice and organisation – issues of what is just, right and good – can easily be sacrificed to expediency (Christie, 1993).

Moral and political, as opposed to managerial, arguments for greater Probation Service involvement in local communities do exist (Northumbria Probation Service, 1992), and a case could be made for regarding 'restorative justice' and 'community safety' (as well as 'anti-custodialism') as core probation values (Nellis, forthcoming). Guided thus, partnership may well create new opportunities for constructive practice in crime-prone localities, but much depends on the creativity with which local Services implement the decision document. In terms of their traditions and principles the Services may well be more sensitive to the array of local voluntary sector interests than the Home Office itself was (though not all national voluntary organisations believe this) but if Service discretion is greatly restricted by central government (as the tone of the decision document suggests it will) fewer local benefits are likely to accrue.

The top-down approach is too rigid a framework to be genuinely responsive to all the voluntary and informal sector organisations which are being 'invited' to participate, given than many of them will come to local strategy groups not only as potential or actual service-providers, but also as campaigners with highly politicised agendas. If the Probation Service chooses, or submits to Home Office pressure, to respond in a predominantly managerial and contractual way, it may simply re-make the larger, more professionalised voluntary organisations in a statutory or commercial image, and it may exclude the smaller community associations altogether. Multiple funding of the larger voluntaries by several different statutory organisations (sometimes seen as a way of guaranteeing the former's 'independence') may neither protect them from this transformation nor help them preserve their organisational integrity – it simply increases the number of contractors who are subjecting them to commercial pressures. Thus, until the real practical meaning of 'independence' has been established within the new framework, more general anxieties about the colonisation of the voluntary sector by the state will inevitably continue to surface.

In order to work constructively and in genuine (mutual if not fully equal) partnership with local communities, probation's managerial ethos must be diminished, and then augmented by a sensibility which is more responsive to demands for justice (for both victims, offenders and neighbourhoods) than it has become in the recent past (Nellis, forthcoming). An emphasis on formality and an obsession with cost, quantification and performance is rarely conducive to the forging of credible and trusting relationships on deprived and crime-prone estates, even by voluntary agencies acting as proxies of the Probation Service. In view of the relentlessly increasing support for corporate management in the Service (Statham and Whitehead, 1992), and the growing belief that it is at best a benevolent and at worst a neutral force (Nellis, 1995), such a reorientation may seem an unlikely development. However, the tight financial, administrative and temporal structures in which probation planners increasingly conduct internal service business may simply work less well in a 'partnership' context, by making it difficult to undertake the time-consuming, sometimes unpredictable, rarely measureable and often intangible work with the voluntary bodies and community associations whose involvement is essential to mutually-owned success.

'Success' in government terms may, however, mean something different from an improved quality of life in local areas with high crime rates or reduced re-offending among a given cohort of offenders. Despite the rhetoric of crime *reduction* that has pervaded the 'punishment in the community' debate and now the 'prison works' debate, the corporatist model which is slowly being set in place is primarily about the *containment* of crime within an economically excluded and spatially segregated underclass, (where victims are less visible and less vociferous), rather than its reduction (Christie, 1993). Although this subtle distinction between reduction and containment is not deliberately obscured in media debate it is rarely highlighted – a vague expectation of reduction therefore remains, endlessly fuelled by forlorn claims, from both political ideologies and the tabloid press, that if only prison and community penalties can be made tough enough then the crime figures will inevitably begin to fall.

But when the current approach to crime reduction fails – and any nation-wide attempt at reduction which does not take account of poverty, unemployment and inequality is unlikely to succeed (at least in a big way) – the terms 'independent' and 'partnership' may prove to have as yet unforseen advantages for the government. Contained within them are potential explanations for such failure. It may be possible, in five or so years time to blame voluntary organisations, or more generally 'the community' for not having 'taken responsibility' (Home Office, 1992, para. 5) in an ostensibly joint venture of crime reduction – 'after all', it might be said by the Home Office, 'these groups were our equals in the enterprise, they were after all independent of us, we (the government) can't shoulder all the blame'. But the image of independence and equal partnership that has been fostered by the government is, more than ever at the present time, at odds with reality. Even as it creates structures which increase the dependence of the professionalised voluntary sector and threaten the future of small community associations in the informal sector, the government is already using language which could provide it with a useful alibi, and a ready-made set of scapegoats, for rising crime in the late 1990s.

Notes

1. The ACOP Partnerships Groups (1993) surveyed existing partnership expenditure in 51 of the 55 probation areas in early 1993. It estimated that 1.39% of the Service's 80% grant-aided budget was already spent on partnership work. 76.8% of the partnerships were with voluntary organisations, representing 88% of expenditure. 20.1% of partnerships were with other statutory organisations, representing 10.9% of expenditure. 'Arrangements with commercial organisations tend to be fairly small, mostly making input to probation centres/or crime prevention schemes where they occur'. Staff secondment (37.8%), rather than grants (27.2%), was the dominant form of probation support for partnerships. Accommodation was the most

commonly purchased service, comprising 30.3% of partnership expenditure.

2. Apex Trust had a proven record of finding employment for ex-offenders, but continuation of Home Office funding was made dependent on its willingness to agree to certain management and staff changes. The DoH decision to terminate its grant to the Intermediate Treatment Fund, given its support for voluntar organisations at the preventive end of juvenile justice, was even more surprising, although it was also subsequently reprieved, and transformed into a new organisation, the Divert Trust, one of whose roles was to act as a consultant in the setting up of local partnerships.
3. The NPF guidance (Home Office, 1993d) covered the planning process itself (i.e. the relationship of 'partnership' arrangements to the Three Year Plan); the consultation process (with a broad range of statutory and independent organisations); the content of the plans (objectives, performance indicators and quality standards); funding arrangements (preference for programme funding over core funding, limitations on the size of grant that can be paid to any one body) and the principles of effective partnership (mutual understanding, flexibility, shared goals and regular dialogue).
4. Despite its stated opposition to them, the Thatcher government transferred ever greater powers from local authorities to 'quangos' – quasi-autonomous non-governmental organisations – throughout the 1980s, thereby introducing a major 'democratic deficit' into local administration. The unaccountable, and often secret decision-making of these bodies, of which there are both local and national examples, was further aggravated by central governments packing of their management committees with known political supporters. Stewart (1992) has called them a 'new magistracy', likening them to the lay elites of JPs who governed counties in the early and mid-19th century. There is a certain irony in Probation Committees, dominated by magistrates, becoming part of the local 'quangocracy' in the 1990s, and it is worrying that so little attention has been paid to the issue of democratic accountability in the partnership debate.
5. The proposal by the Home Office Standing Conference on Crime Prevention (1991) to give a leadership and coordination role to local authorities in multi-agency crime prevention was politically unacceptable to ministers, although they suggested no formal

alternative. The Standing Conference sought to draw voluntary and commercial organisations into crime reduction partnerships on much the same terms as the decision document (Home Office, 1992c) had done; in many respects the same organisations were being targeted. In this same period the Probation Service was rightly becoming more involved in crime prevention and community safety, and while there is no evidence of deliberate intention on the Home Office's part, the decision document does give it something akin to the leadership role which the Standing Conference had denied to it.

6. The most worrying possibility in this respect is the interest shown by Group 4 and Securicor (two private security companies operating in Britain, the former already involved in prison management and prisoner escort services) in setting up 'secure training units' for 12-15 year old juvenile offenders (*Guardian*, 15 May 1993). These were proposed by the Home Secretary in early 1993, against the grain of established opinion in the childcare/youth justice field, as a response to media and public concern about juvenile crime. A coalition of voluntary organisations, to whom the Home Secretary might have looked for this provision, publicly indicated their unwillingness to become involved with what they saw as a retrograde development.

Section IV

Conclusion

Eighteen
Finding the balance

David Ward

When we began to invite contributions to this book in 1992, we looked upon a Probation Service that appeared to be at a turning point, needing to review and recast its identity in a rapidly changing criminal justice system. However, little did we realise how rapid would be the changes in the period of the book's gestation. The talk at that time was of the service playing a role 'centre stage' in the criminal justice system. The 1991 Criminal Justice Act, although viewed with suspicion and hostility in some quarters in the Service (NAPO, 1991) was now accepted as fait accompli, less than ideal but offering positive opportunities for a fairer deal for offenders, victims and their communities. The Service was expected to be a key player in the new arrangements, making a focused, disciplined and creative contribution, equipped by the most extensive Service wide training programme yet seen. Whatever the reservations, there was a buzz of excitement and keen anticipation. While there were concerns, particularly about the apparent loss of some of the Service's core reference points - the nature of the probation order as an alternative to a sentence, the importance of the client's 'voluntary' consent - the Service appeared to be assuming a position where it would be playing a central and expanding role.

The idea for this book was to contribute to the construction of the definition of this new and evolving role. Justice, however defined, represented the 'end' for which all of these changes had been made; 'justice' both as an 'end' and in a very practical sense as a 'means' lies at the core of what the Probation Service sees its mission to be. Our contributors were, therefore, asked to disentangle and examine critically contemporary practice within all aspects of the Service as it reveals and interprets a commitment to enhancing justice.

To our increasing fascination the complexities of this enterprise quickly became apparent as contributors discussed with us their ideas and submitted early drafts of their chapters. They revealed not only the intricacies and varying interpretations of the notion itself, as understood and aspired to by our writers, but also the overarching impact of a justice system going through unprecedented change which is producing uncertainty in the present and a far from clear future. Certainly we had not anticipated the profound changes that have taken place over these two years. Far from assuming a place centre stage in the criminal justice system, the Service has come to be subject to savage attacks, questioning the very basis of its professional purpose and competence. Rather than expansion, it has found itself subject to real cuts in its resource base, and potentially a reduction and/or a dispersal into the 'market' of its responsibilities and activities. Beyond these, it has come even to be questioned whether training for new entrants should remain within the ambit of social work education or in Universities.

In such circumstances, the issues raised by our contributors are of even greater import. There is a real danger that, reeling under these assaults, the Service becomes even more vulnerable unless it has a sense of where it stands and where it might go.

A commitment to justice is a commitment to 'one of the greatest goals society has set itself' (Douzinas and Warrington, 1994, p.21). For too long, it may be argued, the Service has understated the importance of its role and its work to claims that this society is just civilized and humane. It has beavered away at the edges of the justice system's main institutions, content, mistakenly as we now can see, that its value was taken for granted and its position secure. The Service must now spell out, in both its rhetoric and its practice where it stands. But this is not a call for slogans. We know that the culture of the 'sound bite' diminishes justice by reducing complex problems to crude and simplistic solutions. Rather, if we can accept that 'what we call justice is our judgement...*in the flickering light of our favoured beliefs*' (Gibson, 1995, p.18 my emphasis), we must expose the reality that working for justice means managing a contested and uncertain notion and, in the world of human transactions, a site where expectations and interests collide. The Service must demonstrate its accumulated experience and skills, so clearly visible in the foregoing chapters, of achieving reconciliation, of balancing needs and interests, of assessing and managing conflict and risk, of cajoling persons and institutions to change. Its knowledge of and messages about the real rather than wished for nature of the world around, must not be underplayed. It goes without saying that none of this can be achieved without a highly trained, knowledgeable, reflective and creative workforce of valued and motivated practitioners.

Accordingly, we did not seek to impose a core definition of justice but asked and have encouraged our contributors to bring forward an express their own meanings out of the aspects of probation practice and policy they chose to explore. We considered that such imposition would be false and would fail to reflect contemporary practice. Moreover, we felt that to have sought to establish such a definition would itself, in its message, have replicated the creeping authoritarianism which we, and many of our contributors detect and deplore.

As we have said, at the core of the notion lies an inherent tension. Douzinas and Warrington (1994, p.21) explain this as being between justice as uniformity and certainty, the application of rules, democratically legislated, in a consistent and uniform manner, and justice as uncertainty, answering, as a moral duty, 'the request of the suffering other', which is always unpredictable and, to some extent, unknowable. Contrary to much popular rhetoric, therefore, to remain open, uncertain, unfinished is not a sign of weakness and evasiveness, but a necessary reflection of a commitment to justice as an end and as a process which is balanced and humane.

A commitment to the humanity of justice runs throughout all our contributions - we would expect nothing less from a Service based collection. There are plentiful indications that, when faced with the stark evidence and, in some cases, personal experience of injustice and oppression, a commitment to humanity, expressed in forms of social justice, remains strong. Indeed, this commitment has official sanction to some degree. The Three Year Plan's statement that the Service is committed to working at all times to bring out the best in people, and associated pronouncements, indicate a contribution which the Service explicitly is expected to make to the justice system. Such an expectation is laid on no other part of the system.

Nevertheless it is necessary to acknowledge the importance of consistency and due process in ensuring that justice is done. As several contributors point out, humanity, reflected in discretion, can lead to demonstrable injustice. If the system is to be manifestly fair then due process is an essential feature. The question is, therefore, one of balance, of not drifting to the extremes.

There are, however, serious threats to this centre ground. Certainly we should be alarmed at some of the more lurid speechmaking, at tabloid prognostications on crime and criminals and at attacks on the integrating of members of the Service (*Daily Mail*, 29 December 1994). However, another threat which several contributors detect lies in a withdrawal towards the pragmatic approach in which justice comes to be expressed as '...more a process than an ideal, more a Weberian bureaucratic application than an aspiration towards one of the greatest goals society has set itself' (Douzinas and Warrington, 1994, p.21). One aspect of this is the culture of 'effectiveness, efficiency and economy', market testing and cash limits. In this culture, the Service's distinctive contribution is being diminished by time and cost calculations, in which 'averages' slide imperceptibly into ever shorter and lower norms, to becoming a machine for the mass production of PSRs and the processing of offenders through community sentences. History shows that vengeance and humiliation are well fitted to mass production processes; mercy, humanity and fairness require a lighter and more subtle touch.

JUSTICE IN THE BALANCE

What can be deduced from the issues raised and the practices described by our contributors about the position of the Probation Service on justice and its contribution to the process and the ideal? Many start from the position that justice, as a self evident good, involves equity and fairness; it is humanitarian in its commitment to human dignity and a valuing of individual people as ends in their own right; it is inclusive and concerned with reintegration rather than excluding and stigmatising offenders. In fact, the discourse of exclusion, argues Lacey, is unreal because we are all involved and implicated. One man in three has a criminal conviction by the age of 35; we are the people who prefer not to ask questions about the 'bargains' we pick up through second hand shops, car boot sales and pubs. Therefore, it would be supremely foolish not 'to answer the request of the suffering other' (Douzinas and Warrington, 1994. p.21) because, to draw from the advertisement for the National Lottery, 'It Could be You!' Such principles however, do not imply a one sided nor sentimental pre-occupation with an idealised offender. Rather, they reflect a commitment to the inclusion, the re integration, and the rights and dignity of all those involved in crime, not just offenders, but victims also. It involves a balanced commitment to the offender, combined with a genuine concern for the rights of the victim and the protection of the public.

It is this humanity and balance at the heart of justice which is central to the thinking of John Pendleton in his keynote paper. He raises many of the issues which emerge again and again in subsequent contributions. For John Pendleton justice requires 'spirit', meaning human commitment and motivation. As such it is ultimately a personal matter and cannot be imposed from outside. Overformalisation, he argues, reflected in a preoccupation with administration and processing, on calculating seriousness and 'just deserts', will stifle the life out of justice as a meaningful end, and as a process. It leaves out the victim and the community, by which he means the public as real people, not a rhetorical device serving political expediency. It divorces offenders from what they have done and relieves the community from considering both the implications and the causes of offending. Taking inspiration from the 8th Century Prophets, Pendleton argues the 'righting of wrongs' as a framework for human conduct in a civilised society.

For Pendleton, the 'righting of wrongs' has two elements which are inextricably interlinked and cannot stand alone. One is 'upholding the rights of the underdog' which requires attention to 'structures', specifically economic and political arrangements which he saw as contributing to the disadvantage of the poor and oppressed. Justice, he says, is about the creation of a quality of life in which those who offend face the consequences of their actions and take responsibility. In saying this he is clear that this does not mean that wrong actions condemned in the rich should be condoned in the poor. Far from it this is merely one side of a dynamic equation within which, if there is anything like a balance, in all justice, it is fair and equitable to demand reparation from the wrongdoer. However, reparation, he argues, should itself be person centred, a process of repair and reconciliation which only becomes possible when the wrongdoer and victim recognise the humanity and the problems of each other.

Very similar thinking underpins other contributors allusions to 'atonement' (Reeves and Wright) and 'reintegrative shaming' (Raynor). All have in common a rejection of utilitarian notions in which the treatment of offenders and victims is subsumed within instrumental purposes for the 'public interest' and 'common good'. Instead they represent a restatement of a 'personalist' (McWilliams, 1987) value base expressing the humanity of both offender and victim as subjects, not objects, in social processes, people to be valued in their own right, who have the potential to grow in understanding and to change (Spencer ,1994). However, Pendleton discerns, in both its inequity and its depersonalisations, that our justice system and the society it represents, does not facilitate such productive processes.

Were such arrangements of 'righting wrongs' to exist, as Lacey's discussion of atonement suggests, instead of a downward spiral of crime, fear of crime and victimisation, repression and more crime, we might look forward to a society in which offenders could take responsibility for their actions in the face of the proper anger and outrage of the victim. 'The procedure for punishment would be transformed into a dialogue.' (Christie, 1982, quoted by Lacey), in which 'instead of the unsatisfied aspirations rebelling against the poverty of the present, the fulfilled aspirations reveal the poverty of the past'. (Morris, 1931, as quoted by Lacey).

John Pendleton's paper provides a fine introduction to the key issues. Although written prior to the major changes of the early 1990s, it is uncannily prophetic in its signalling of the questions and concerns of contemporary debate. Perhaps also it shows to us how enduring and deepseated are those matters, reflective maybe of fundamental and unresolvable questions about the human condition. Greater appreciation of this might bring humility, patience and openness into the current rancour, itself driven by political expediency and ambition disingenuously proffering one line solutions to complex problems. We should take note of Lacey's insight from Rawls (1973) that 'no democratic society can commit itself to the pursuit of a single ideal since there can be no consensus about the nature of that ideal...it is a characteristic of totalitarian regimes that they do have such a commitment...'.

Many of our contributors highlight how far our society is failing in terms of meeting the necessary preconditions for meaningful justice. The equity and fairness on the basis of which the wrongdoer can be called to responsibility, demands 'social justice.' Cox and Pritchard show how far Britain is falling short as measured against the UN Declaration of Human Rights. Their assessment has now been reinforced by the United Nations' own investigation into the UK's performance in its treatment of children. Cox and Pritchard show that on almost all counts - the right to work, to housing and medical care, to security in the event of unemployment, sickness, or other lack of livelihood - that the U.K. not only falls short, but is regressing.

In addition, as Flynn, Hylton, Francis-Spence and Worrall highlight, there is the structural disadvantage, the racism and sexism, experienced by women and Black people, both as recipients of the justice system and as probation employees, which reflects oppressive processes in wider society. Canton and Cowburn and Modi bring out parallel experiences in the lives of mentally disordered and gay people. Together, these authors highlight how deeply racism, sexism, homophobia and stereotypes of mental illness are embedded in society, creating a discourse which stigmatises, exploits and excludes. In such ways are the dignity and sense of humanity upon which justice depends undermined.

For Cox and Pritchard the effective abandonment of a commitment to social justice, whether or not combined with these wider oppressions, has serious and frightening implications. They show from the results of their research how people in poverty, 'those who have not had equal access to fulfil their citizenship' feature disproportionately in care, as unemployed, in debt, with housing difficulties, with higher suicide rates, with drug and alcohol abuse and other manifestations of 'deforming poverty.' Again, a descending spiral is at work. In an increasingly competitive socio-economic environment, they observe, these people are less likely to be able to compete. The outcome is an utterly alienated and excluded underclass members of which, as vividly portrayed by Campbell (1993, quoted by Lacey), have no stake in present arrangements and can wreak havoc. Cox and Pritchard argue the case for alternative economic policies to include these people. Even a pension for people with 'psycho social deficits they argue, 'might be financially beneficial to all', whatever rationale there might be on practical grounds not just those based on grounds of humanity, equity and justice.

Reinforcing these conclusions, David Faulkner contrasts the real opportunities for greater justice provided by the 1991 Criminal Justice Act, with the retreat from justice aspirations he sees taking place since the 1992 General Election. Of course, as a significant architect of the 1991 legislation, Faulkner has an interest, but his critique of recent developments is devastating. He sees progressive developments undermined by the ' prison works' philosophy, the setting up of secure training centres for juveniles, restrictions on bail, and the creation of new 'public order' offences. All this reflects in his opinion an instrumental view of justice, a coarsening of standards and, if unintentionally, contributes to a more repressive approach generally. In this, the focus is on arrests, convictions and escapes rather than more subtle and less unquantifiable matters like prevention and changes in patterns of offending. All this, he argues, contributes to greater injustice reflected in oppressive styles of policing and arbitrary administration of justice. Echoing Cox and

Pritchard, he asserts that in its divisiveness it is risking the creation of an excluded and criminalised 'underclass.' Mike Nellis characterises such an approach in crime control as 'corporatism'. Corporatism specifically eschews justice considerations. Policy is no longer concerned with individual offenders, with the problem of doing justice, but with more general control of criminal activity. In practice this means, in Nellis's view, 'the containment of crime within an economically excluded and spatially segregated underclass where victims are less visible and vociferous.' Within such a framework, he says, what is right and just is sacrificed to expediency and the watchwords are policy, planning, management, efficiency and effectiveness, terms which resonate strongly with the developing culture of the Probation Service in the 1990s.

Reeves and Wright argue that justice for victims, equally, involves the question of balance. On one side is support and compensation for which the State should take responsibility. On the other is reparation (in terms defined earlier) by the offender which may, through the services of mediation, be direct and face to face in certain circumstances. Just and humane treatment for victims means a process in which they are treated decently and respectfully as people in their own right, with a legitimate interest, and not devalued, exploited and mistreated, as mere bit players in the theatre of justice. It is true that 'civilized societies withdraw from the victim the enforcement of criminal laws' (Lesser, 1995, p.18). However, the momentum towards mechanistic processes and exclusive forms of justice, which our contributors so clearly signal, has damaged the interests of the victim no less than the prospects for the offender, and has limited the contribution the Service can make.

From the evidence provided, the obstacles to Pendleton's essential notion of a balance appear severe, both in the face of entrenched, and apparently worsening, social and economic inequity and, if Nellis is right, even a flight from justice as an ideal. In one paper however it is possible to detect a more optimistic scenario. Steve Goode, in evaluating the work of the Family Court Welfare Service, finds indications of the essential interlinking of personal and social justice in work in this setting. Perhaps, if justice within the criminal system is compromised to the level that so many of our contributors argue, then Goode's case for the retention of Family Court Welfare, and for the Probation Service to demonstrate an unequivocal commitment to its place in the agency, is all that more important.

PRACTISING FOR JUSTICE

Many of our contributors identify specific factors at play in the practices of the Probation Service which mirror the pressures on 'working for justice' highlighted so far. Some of these are mere reflections of the wider framework and system within which the Service operates; some, our contributors argue, are within the power of the Service to alleviate or change. Faulkner, for instance, takes issue with some of the manifestations of the 'new managerial culture'. While positively there has been a concern for greater openness, accessibility and accountability, there is a clear downside. He identifies a pre-occupation with output measures and performance indicators which bring in their wake lower levels of discretion and imply less trust in professionals. This, he argues, leads to a narrowing of vision, drives out initiative and distorts priorities. The effect is to flatten true levels of performance and quality, leading to conformism, a reluctance to question received ideas, and 'ultimately to secrecy and defensiveness.' The consequence is a 'filofax mentality in which time and resources are efficiently managed but the purpose of the enterprise is lost from sight'. Nellis provides, in his analysis of 'partnerships' a clear case in point. He argues that while the State may have appeared to have 'shrunk as functions of public sector organisations have come to be contracted out', it has not shrunk in 'regulatory' influence. Voluntary sector organisations are being incorporated into wider spanning structures of crime control and are being regulated by the Probation Service on the government's behalf by the mechanisms Faulkner describes. Harnessing the innovation and creativity of the voluntary sector is nice sloganising, but in practice it is being stifled by a combination of what Flynn calls 'machine bureaucracy' - standardisation, policing, control from outside, an emphasis on costs and performance indicators and, ultimately market testing - and an increasing dependence for funding on providing services to public sector 'purchasers', a role which the Probation Service has now assumed.

In particular, Flynn describes how the discourse of the 'new managerialism' acts to block justice in the form of equality of opportunity in relation to the career prospects of Black people and women in the Service. Besides recent changes of style reflecting a move from a professional to a 'machine bureaucracy' with the consequences described above, the new managerialism, as he sees it, represents a profound injustice to women entrants. This will not change, he argues, unless the Service alters its managerial style and 'regenders' to an emphasis on 'communication, empowerment, consensus building and teamworking'.

Injustice, as reflected in the inequities encountered by Black workers in the Probation Service, which itself mirrors the injustice experienced by Black people generally, is taken up by Marcia Francis-Spence and Basil Hylton in two powerfully argued chapters. For these authors, 'justice means nothing if it does not include the manifestation of racial justice, *done and seen to be done*'. It involves valuing the Black perspective which is a 'perspective which reflects, is informed by and is defined by Black people's experience.' Justice is impeded by differential application of the law, by the lack of representation of Black people in the decision making of the Criminal Justice system which denies them the right of being judged by their peers, and by Black People's experience of being welcomed initially but then subsequently exploited devalued and excluded. These are, Francis- Spence argues, the experiences of Black people in Britain, and there is an uncanny mirror image in the fortunes of Black workers in the Service. Tackling injustice, she argues, requires that the Service clarifies exactly why it is employing Black staff. Numbers mean nothing when turnover is so high. Certainly, states Hylton, the Service needs Black staff to provide an anti-discriminatory service to the Black community but Black workers must not be used thoughtlessly as experts on Black offenders and race issues. To do so may mean imposing responsibilities workers are not equipped to deal with, but for which they will be held accountable. Equally, they must not be pressurised into areas they are not interested in.

For Hylton, Black officers have been expected for too long to take undue responsibility for anti racist work at their own personal cost, a form of exploitation or 'neo slavery' which reflects racist stereotyping and a failure to treat people as individuals. Francis-Spence and Hylton demand that the Service stops speaking *at* or *for* Black people, but *with* them, that white people take responsibility for anti racism, that white managers be trained to value And work with diversity, and that Black workers' own development be catered for in its own right as a priority. These are some of the pre conditions for the Service to retain its Black staff. Only then will they achieve promotion by merit and attain positions where they can powerfully and legitimately influence change. Only when excluded groups are, and can be seen to be, included in this way, can justice be advanced.

When it comes to direct practice, two of our contributions, revisit assumptions and methods, which have become increasingly taken for granted in the work of the Service. The chapter by Anne Worrall and that by Malcolm Cowburn and Panna Modi issue some serious challenges.

Worrall looks at the disadvantages for women, particularly Black women, of uncritical implementation of 'equality' approaches in Probation practice, in which 'gate keeping' has assumed a central place. In Worrall's view, a crude approach to equality 'may have simply resulted in women being sent 'in their droves to dirty, violent and overcrowded prisons for longer periods of time' ' (Worrall, quoting Smart, 1990). As Pitts (1994) has put it:

> The central problem of the 'politics of oppressions'...has been that it has trivialised real oppression by representing complex social problems as bureaucratic anomalies...(and)...simply edits out social reality if it is not amenable to its administrative solutions (p.4).

Echoing Faulkner and other contributors, Worrall argues that 'blinkered adherence to consistency and equality discourages the creative thinking and intellectual dexterity' which is needed to tackle the 'conundrums' and contradictions which are part and parcel of genuine efforts to challenge discriminatory practice both within the Service and in other parts of the system.

Malcolm Cowburn and Panna Modi proclaim a similar message in their evaluation of current approaches to dealing with sex offenders, which appear to have assumed a measure of authority and universality, which they barely merit if measured against justice values. The dominance of conventional values which are, they argue, racist and homophobic leads to an inaccurate and unfair spotlight on Gays and Black men as the problem in sex offending. They see in the prevalent practice of confrontation with sex offenders reinforcement of this oppression and urge a re evaluation. Practice must aim to build positive identities not to crush them. Their concern, as eloquently expressed by Anne Worrall, is for the Service to regain some of its critical capacity in a forward looking, open and creative mode, rather than its own processes replicating the authoritarianism and regulation of the wider system. Worrall asks whether it is now time the Service said 'we just do what we think is right.' For her, given the low level of women's offending, the Service can afford to experiment and take risks, from which 'lessons might just be learned about provision for all offenders.'

Another area where Worrall's 'conundrums' are at play is the notion of 'just deserts.' Faulkner takes for granted that its establishment, together with basing sentencing on measuring the 'seriousness' of the offence, in the 1991 Criminal Justice Act was a step forward in achieving greater justice. However, as noted earlier, John Pendleton, although pre dating the debates around the Act, thought otherwise and other contributors, Peter Raynor and Brian Williams, present trenchant critiques of 'just deserts' in current use. Raynor argues that 'just deserts' and 'back to justice' have been associated with massive increases in imprisonment. They can differentially disadvantage the poor and least powerful by failing to account for, even denying, economic and social influences including race, gender and like factors on crime and responses to it. Just deserts and seriousness in crude form do not consider 'morally relevant differences in circumstances of people who commit crimes' and as such contain 'no wider social vision.' Seriousness as a basic sentencing principle, says Raynor, is particularly open to political perceptions of public mood and electoral advantage. Williams sums this up, echoing somewhat Nellis's comments, by stating that in 'just deserts' a system of justice is converted into a mechanistic system of crime control. Such mindless 'justice' is a step down the road to totalitarianism.

Williams identifies how 'just deserts' has 'seeped' into prison regimes and urges probation officers to counter this, to work for justice, in their work with prisoners by maximising the opportunities for achieving greater openness and fairness through their involvement in contracts and sentence plans. They should monitor the rights of prisoners' access to reports, challenge discriminatory comments and actions and use Section 95 of the 1991 Act as a platform for building campaigns, in particular, forging active links with voluntary organisations which might be able to act more independently.

Peter Raynor points out that much of the impetus for 'back to justice' lay in the pessimistic view that in personal direct work with offenders 'nothing works.' He points to doubts about the conclusions of the research on which this view was based and goes on to present empirical evidence that 'some things do work.' His argument is not simply utilitarian, however. He acknowledges the real dangers to justice of 'overintervention' if sentencing is used for therapeutic ends and is, therefore, inequitable between offenders, and if it introduces discretion and uncertainty about the degree of restraint and imposition. However, he argues that some degree of looking forward is morally and pragmatically justifiable, and demonstrates how the dangers can be controlled. To help people identify more options in the face of difficult situations can, he says, be seen as empowering and can assist in restoring an offender to full membership of the community.

Rob Canton, in his scathing critique of the way mentally disordered offenders are dealt with highlights the dangers of 'discretionary justice.' Noting how the 'back to justice' movement has passed by this group of offenders, he sees discretion, and the injustices it creates, being rooted in, deeply embedded cultural attitudes and prejudices towards mentally disordered people. It would be overly simplistic to see in Canton's closely argued paper a case for 'just deserts'. Rather, he connects with many of our other contributors in highlighting how oppression and discrimination are maintained and supported by crude populist rhetoric on the part of government and policies to match. Striking a chord with Francis-Spence, Hylton and Worrall, Canton urges the Service to strive for greater clarity of purpose and to help the courts 'disentangle' the conceptually and morally complex issues involved.

Raynor's 'effectiveness' rests largely within what has become known as the cognitive behavioural approach to practice. Several of our contributors give reasons for not leaping into uncritical acceptance of this method in terms of 'justice' considerations. Cowburn and Modi's critique of practice with sex offenders is pertinent to any consideration of cognitive behavioural work and Lacey highlights the importance of 'non possessive warmth, genuineness and empathy', characteristics which are often passed over in this method of practice. However, it is Roy Bailey who most strongly asserts, and justifies, the importance of the quality of the relationship between officer and offender as 'critical in determining whether things change for good or ill'. In Bailey's view, concern for this 'helping' has become unfashionable in the new managerial culture of the Service, the preoccupation of which with costs and turnover has contributed to a 'fragmentation of practice into disconnected specialisms'. In an emphasis on courses and programmes Bailey detects a danger that the offender becomes an object to be processed, rather than an individual with her/his own biography. There is evidence of this in some prison run programmes and it is an underlying concern in Cowburn and Modi's critique. From his analysis of offender officer transactions, Bailey makes some suggestions of characteristics linked with 'effectiveness'. They take us very much back to John Pendleton's duality, stressing a combination of personal openness, respect and trust, and practical support and assistance. Both are required to deal with, as Cox and

Pritchard put it, some of the 'social deficits' which contribute to the 'spoiled identity' which so many offenders carry.

So, how should we conclude? The signs of a gathering momentum towards greater **in**justice are clear. The service must stand up to these. Certainly, due process, with consistent and predictable procedures and outcomes, is vital in ensuring that justice is done and seen to be done. However, a criminal justice system geared towards crime management through containment and punishment, and a Probation Service reduced to servicing community corrections will not work. This is evident not simply from the statistics of increasing crime, fear of crime, and imprisonment. As our contributors show, the case rests also on moral and ethical grounds, on logic, on knowledge and experience, on practical grounds and on 'common sense'. An alternative approach is visible and, almost prophetically, John Pendleton has provided the framework upon which it can be built.

He calls for attention to the 'spirit' of justice, to the 'righting of wrongs' and to a form which is human in scale and humane in operation. Proper condemnation of wrong doing and reparation by the wrongdoer must be balanced by genuine commitment to remedying the disadvantages of the poor and oppressed. In this 'spirit' lies the interlinking of justice as due process, and justice as concern for social and economic circumstances which might otherwise remain unseen (Gouldner, 1975, as quoted by Lacey) and for the needs of 'the suffering other' (Douzinas and Warrington, 1994, p.21) both victim and offender. On this, we speculate, might rest our chances of escape from a downward spiral to the disintegration of community and society as we know them, where those who can afford it retreat into enclaves of safety cut off from those who are perceived as dangerous.

Clearly, we must act, but John Pendleton would have cautioned against attempting simplistic solutions which, by their nature, merely replicate the conditions for doing injustice. He would have charged us to bring our behaviour into line with convictions, but he would have demanded also the humility not to imagine that we can so emancipate ourselves from the world in which we live as not to perpetuate and reproduce it. Therein lies the challenge of working for justice.

References

Abel, G. and Rouleau, J-L (1990) 'The nature and extent of sexual assault' in Marshall, W.L., Laws, D.R., and Barbaree, H.E. (eds.) *Handbook of Sexual Assault.* New York: Plenum.

Abel, G. Becker, J.V., Mittelman, M., Cunningham-Rathner, J., Rouleau, J.L. and Murphy, W.D. (1987) 'Self-reported sex crimes of non- incarcerated paraphiliacs', *Journal of Interpersonal Violence*, 2(1), pp.3-25.

Abernethy, R. and Hammond, N. (1992) *Drug Couriers: A Role for the Probation Service*. London: Middlesex Area Probation Service.

Ahmad, B. (1992) *Black Perspectives in Social Work.* Birmingham: Venture Press.

Ahmed, S. (1988) 'Defining and assessing black families' in *Planning for Children*. London: Family Rights Group.

Ahmed, S., Cheetham, J. and Small, J. (eds.) (1991) *Social Work with Black Children and Their Families.* Buckingham: Open University Press.

Alibhai, Y. (1988) 'Criminal injustice: how the legal system, treats Blacks', *New Statesman and Society*, 8 July.

Allen, H. (1987) *Justice Unbalanced: Gender, Psychiatry and Judicial Decisions.* Milton Keynes: Open University Press.

American Friends Service Committee (1971) *Struggle for Justice: A Report on Crime and Punishment in America.* New York: Hill and Wang.

Amir, M. (1971) *Patterns of Forcible Rape*. Chicago: University of Chicago Press.

Anderson, B. (1979) *The Eighth Century Prophets*. London: Society for the Promotion of Christian Knowledge.

Anderson, B. (1984) *The Living Word of the Old Testament*. London: Longman.

Andrews, D.A. et al. (1990) 'Does correctional treatment work? A clinically relevant and psychologically informed meta-analysis', *Criminology,* 28(3), pp.369-404.

Anne The Princess Royal (1994) 'Address' to NACRO/ Crime Concern Conference *Crime and the Family Conference*. London: Families Policy Studies Centre.

Ashworth, A. (1987) 'The 'public interest' element in prosecutions', *Criminal Law Review,* pp.595-607.

Ashworth A. (1992) *Sentencing and Penal Policy.* London: Weidenfeld and Nicolson.

Association of Chief Officers of Probation (1990a) *Position Statement on HIV, AIDS, Confidentiality and the Probation Service*. Wakefield: ACOP.

Association of Chief Officers of Probation (1990b) *Position Statement on Relations with the Voluntary, Independent and Private Sectors*. Wakefield: ACOP.

Association of Chief Officers of Probation (1993) *Work with Women Offenders: Developing a Strategic Policy*. Unpublished.

Association of Chief Officers of Probation Partnerships Group (1993) *Survey of Existing Partnership Expenditure from Probation Services 80% Grant Aided Budgets.* Wakefield: ACOP.

Audit Commission (1989) *The Probation Service: Value for Money*. London: HMSO.

Bailey, R. and Ward, D. (1992) *Probation Supervision: Attitudes to Formalised Helping*. Nottingham: Centre for Social Action, University of Nottingham.

Baldwin, J. and Bottomley, A.K. (eds.) (1978) *Criminal Justice: Selected Readings.* Oxford: Martin Robertson.

Barker, M. and Morgan, R. (1993) *Sex Offenders: A Framework For The Evaluation Of Community-Based Treatment. A Report for the Home Office*. Bristol: University of Bristol Faculty of Law.

Bean, P.T. (1986) *Mental Disorder and Legal Control.* Cambridge: Cambridge University Press.

Beccaria, C. (1764) *Dei Delitti e Delle Pene*. Translated (1963) as *Of Crimes and Punishments*. Indiana: Bobbs-Merrill.

Beck, A.T., Steer, R., Beck, J.S. and Newman, C.F. (1993) 'Hopelessness, depression and suicidal behaviour', *Suicide and Life Threatening Behaviour,* 23(2), pp.139-45.

Benn, S.I. and Peters, R.S. (1959) *Social Principles and the Democratic State*. London: George Allen Unwin.

Bennett, D. (1991) *Probation and Voluntary Agencies: A Study of the Factors Which Encourage Effective Partnership*. London: Centre for Voluntary Organisations/London School of Economics.

Bentham, J. (1789) *Introduction to the Principles of Morals and Legislation*. Reprinted 1967. Oxford: Oxford University Press (with *A Fragment on Government*).

Bentham, J. (1823) *Introduction to the Principles of Morals and Legislation* in edition by Harne, W. (ed.) (1948), chap. XIII, section, 1.2.

Berger, P.L. (1971) *A Rumour of Angels*. Harmondsworth: Penguin.

Berry, B. and Matthews, R. (1989) 'Electronic monitoring and house arrest: making the right connections' in Matthews, R. (ed.) *Privatizing Criminal Justice*. London: Sage.

Blackburn, R. (1993) *The Psychology of Criminal Conduct: Theory, Research and Practice*. Chichester: Wiley.

Boswell, G., Davies, M. and Wright, A. (1993) *Contemporary Probation Practice*. Aldershot: Avebury.

Bottoms, A.E. (1977) 'Reflections on the Renaissance of dangerousness', *Howard Journal,* 16(2), pp.70-96.

Bottoms, A.E. and McWilliams, W. (1979) 'A non-treatment paradigm for probation practice', *British Journal of Social Work,* 9(1), pp.159-202.

Box, S. (1987) *Recession, Crime and Punishment.* Basingstoke: Macmillan.

Braham, P., Rattansi, A. and Skellington, R. (eds.) (1992) *Racism and Anti-Racism: Inequalities, Opportunities and Policies*. London: Sage.

Braithwaite, J. (1989) *Crime, Shame and Reintegration*. Cambridge: Cambridge University Press.

Braithwaite, J. and Pettit, P. (1990) *Not Just Deserts*. Oxford: Oxford University Press.

Brenton, M. (1985) *The Voluntary Sector in British Social Services*. London: Longman.

Broad, B. (1988) *Enquiries into Community Probation Work*. Cranfield: DSP Publications.

Broad, B. (1991) *Punishment Under Pressure: The Probation Services in the Inner City*. London, Jessica Kingsley Publishers.

Brody, S.R. (1976) *The Effectiveness of Sentencing*. London: HMSO.

Brooks, J. (1993) 'High Court judge warns of race discrimination in justice system', *Guardian*, 19 November, p.10.

Brown, L. (1993) 'An anti-discriminatory approach to child protection', *SCOSAC Newsletter*, pp.4-7.

Brown, S. (1991) *Magistrates at Work*. Milton Keynes: Open University Press.

Browne, D. (1990) *Black People, Mental Health and the Courts*. London: NACRO.

Brownmiller, S. (1975) *Against our Will: Men, Women and Rape*. London: Secker and Warburg.

Bryant, M., Coker, J., Estlea, B., Himmel, S. and Knapp, T. (1978) 'Sentenced to social work', *Probation Journal*, 25(4), pp.110-14.

Buchanan, J., Collett, S. and McMullan, P. (1991) 'Challenging practice or challenging women? Female offending and illicit drug use', *Probation Journal*, 38(2), pp.56-62.

Butcher, H. (1992) 'Community work: current realities, contemporary trends' in Carter, P., Jeffs, T. and Smith, M. (eds.) *Changing Social Work and Welfare*. Milton Keynes: Open University Press.

Campbell, B. (1993) *Goliath: Britain's Dangerous Places*. London: Methuen.

Campbell, T. (1988) *Justice*. London: MacMillan Education.

Carlen, P. (1990) *Alternatives to Women's Imprisonment*. Milton Keynes: Open University Press.

Carlen, P. (1992) 'Criminal women and criminal justice: the limits to, and potential of, feminist and left realist perspectives' in Matthews, R. and Young, J. (eds.) *Issues in Realist Criminology*. London: Sage.

Cavadino, M. and Dignan, J. (1992) *The Penal System: An Introduction*. London: Sage.

Central Council for Education and Training in Social Work (1991a) *One Small Step Towards Racial Justice: Anti-Racism in Diploma in Social Work Programmes*. London: CCETSW.

Central Council for Education and Training in Social Work (1991b) *Requirements and Regulations for the Diploma in Social Work. Paper 30*. London: CCETSW,

Central Council for Education and Training in Social Work Northern Curriculum Development Project (1991) *Setting the Context for Change: Anti-Racist Social Work Education*. London: CCETSW.

Charities Aid Foundation (1992) *Charity Trends 1992*, Tonbridge, Kent: Charities Aid Foundation.

Cheney, D. (1993) *Into the Dark Tunnel: Foreign Prisoners in the British Prison System*. London: Prison Reform Trust.

Christie, N. (1977) 'Conflicts as property', *British Journal of Criminology*, 17(1), pp.1-15.

Christie, N. (1982) *Limits to Pain*. Oxford: Martin Robertson

Christie, N. (1993) *Crime Control as Industry*. London: Routledge.

Clarke, J., Cochrane, A. and McLaughlin, E. (eds.) (1994) *Managing Social Policy*. London: Sage.

Clear, T.R., Flynn, S. and Shapiro, C. (1987) 'Intensive supervision in probation: a comparison of three projects' in McCarthy, B.R. (ed.) *Intermediate Punishment*. Monsey: Criminal Justice Press.

Cmd 424 (1988) *Punishment, Custody and the Community*. London: HMSO.

Cmd 532 (1988) *The Parole System in England and Wales: Report of the Review Committee*. London: HMSO.

Cmd 849 (1989) *Caring for People – Community Care in the Next Decade and Beyond*. London: HMSO.

Cmd 965 (1991) *Crime, Justice and Protecting the Public: The Government's Proposals for Legislation*. London: HMSO.

Cmd 966 (1990) *Supervision and Punishment in the Community: A Framework for Action*. London: HMSO.

Cmd 1456 (1991) *Prison Disturbances April 1990: Report of an Inquiry by the Rt. Hon. Lord Justice Woolf (Parts I and II) and His Honour Judge Stephen Tumim (Part II)*. London: HMSO.

Cmd 1599 (1991) *The Citizen's Charter*. London: HMSO.

Cmd 1730 (1991) *Competing for Quality*. London: HMSO.

Cmd 2088 (1992) *Review of Health and Social Services for Mentally Disordered Offenders and Others Requiring Similar Services*. The Reed Report. London: HMSO.

Cmd 3601 (1968) *Children In Trouble*. London: HMSO.

Cmd 6244 *Report of the Committee on Mentally Abnormal Offenders*. London: HMSO.

Cmd 9678 *Royal Commission on Marriage and Divorce 1951-55*. London: HMSO.

Coid, J. (1988) 'Mentally abnormal prisoners on remand: rejected or accepted by the NHS?', *British Medical Journal*, 296, 25 June, 1779-82.

Comer, J. and Pouissant, A. (1975) *Black Child Care*. Pocket Books.

Committee on the Penalty for Homicide (1993) *Report*. London: Prison Reform Trust.

Conte, J., Wolf, S. and Smith, T. (1989) 'What sex offenders tell us about prevention strategies', *Child Abuse and Neglect*, 13, pp.293-301.

Conte, J.R. (1991) 'The nature of sexual offences against children' in Hollin, C.R. and Howells, K. (eds.) *Clinical Approaches to Sex Offenders and Their Victims*. Chichester: John Wiley and Sons.

Cook, D. and Hudson, B. (eds.) (1993) *Racism and Criminology*. London: Sage.

Cook, T. et al. (eds.) (1992) *Meta-Analysis for Explanation: A Case-Book*. New York: Russell Sage.

Cope, R. (1989) 'The compulsory detention of Afro-Caribbeans under the Mental Health Act', *New Community*, 15(3), pp.343-56.

Cowburn, M. (1991) *Sex Offenders in Prison: A Study of Structured Interventions to Change Offending Behaviour*. Nottingham: The University of Nottingham. Unpublished MPhil Thesis.

Cowburn, M., Wilson, C. and Loewenstein, P. (1992) *Changing Men: A Practice Guide to Working with Adult Male Sex Offenders*. Nottingham: Nottinghamshire Probation Service.

Cress-Welsing, F. (1991) *The ISIS Papers: The Keys to the Colours*. Chicago: Third World Press.

Criminal Justice Consultative Council (1993) *Mentally Disordered Offenders* London: CJCC.

Crown Prosecution Service (1992) *Code for Crown Prosecutors*. London: CPS.

Crown Prosecution Service (1993) *Statement on the Treatment of Victims and Witnesses*. London: Crown Prosecution Service.

Cupitt, D. (1979) *Jesus and the Gospel of God*. London: Butterworth.

Dahrendorf, R. (1987) The Underclass and the Future of Britain quoted by Stern, V. 'Director's Review', *NACRO Annual Report 1992-3*. London: NACRO

Daily Mail (1994) 'Howard calls up probation troops', 29 December, pp.6-7.

Davis, A. (1981) *Women, Race and Class*. London: Women's Press.

Davis, K.C. (1969) *Discretionary Justice: A Preliminary Inquiry*. Baton Rouge: Louisiana State University Press.

Day, P. R. (1981) *Social work and Social Control*. London: Tavistock.

De Haan, W. (1990) *The Politics of Redress: Crime, Punishment and Penal Abolition*. London: Unwin Hyman.

Deakin, N. (1989) 'Voluntarism in the 1990s', *NCVO News*, 8 October, pp.11-13.

Denney, D. (1992) *Racism and Anti-Racism in Probation*. London: Routledge.

Department of Health (1989) *Caring For People*. London: HMSO.

Department of Health and Home Office (1992) 'Review of health and social services for mentally disordered offenders and others requiring similar services', *Services for People from Black and Ethnic Minority Groups: Issues of Race and Culture. A Discussion Paper*. London: Department of Health / Home Office.

Divine, D. (1991) 'The value of anti-racism in social work education and training' in Central Council for Education and Training in Social Work Northern Curriculum Development Project *Setting the Context for Change:*

Anti-Racist Social Work Education. London: CCETSW.

Dolan, K., Donoghoe, M. and Stimson, G. (1990) 'Drug injecting and syringe sharing in custody and in the community: an exploratory survey of HIV risk behaviour', *Howard Journal of Criminal Justice*, 29(3), pp.177-86.

Dominelli, L. (1984) 'Differential justice: domestic labour, community service and female offenders', *Probation Journal,* 31(3), pp.100-103.

Dooley, E. (1990) 'Prison suicide in England and Wales', *British Journal of Psychiatry,* 156, pp.40-45.

Douzinas, C. and Warrington, R. (1994) 'Practising law with a provisional licence' , *The Times Higher Education Supplement,* 18 November, p.21.

Doyal, L. and Gough, I. (1991) *A Theory of Human Need*. Basingstoke: MacMillan.

Drakeford, M. (1993) 'The probation service, breach and the Criminal Justice Act 1991', *The Howard Journal of Criminal Justice*, 32(4), pp.291-303.

Driver, E. and Droisen, A. (eds.) (1989) *Child Sexual Abuse: Feminist Perspectives*. London and Basingstoke: MacMillan.

Droisen, A. (1989) 'Racism and anti-semitism' in Driver, E. and Droisen, A. (eds.) *Child Sexual Abuse: Feminist Perspectives.* London and Basingstoke: MacMillan.

Dunkley, C. (1992) *Group Work with Women in Probation Day Centres.* Department of Social Policy and Social Work, Manchester: University of Manchester.

Duster, T. (forthcoming) *Post-Industrialism and Youth Unemployment: African-Americans as Harbingers*. Washington D.C.: Joint Centre for Political and Economic Studies.

Eaton, M. (1986) *Justice for Women?* Milton Keynes: Open University Press.

Eaton, M. (1993) *Women After Prison*. Buckingham: Open University Press.

Eekelaar, J. (1984) *Family Law and Social Policy*. London: Weidenfeld and Nicholson.

Elias, R. (1986) 'Community control, criminal justice and victim services' in Fattah, E.A. (ed.) *From Crime Policy to Victim Policy: Reorienting the Justice System.* London: Macmillan.

Ellis, L. (1989) *Theories of Rape: Inquiries into the Causes of Sexual Aggression.* Washington D.C. 20005: Hemisphere Publishing Corporation.

Eyden, J.J.M. (1969) *Social Policy in Action*. London: Routledge and Kegan Paul.

Farrell, G. and Pease, K. (1993) *Once Bitten, Twice Bitten: Repeat Victimisation and Its Implications for Crime Prevention.* London: Home Office Police Department.

Fielder, M. (1992) 'Purchasing and providing services for offenders: lessons from America' in Statham, R. and Whitehead, P. (eds.) *Managing the Probation Service: Issues for the 1990s.* Harlow: Basingstoke.

Finkelhor, D. (1986) *Child Sexual Abuse: Sourcebook*. Newbury Park, London, and New Delhi: Sage.

Fitzgerald, M. (1993a) 'Racial discrimination in the criminal justice system',

Home Office Research Bulletin, 34, pp.43-47.
Fitzgerald, M. (1993b) *Ethnic Minorities and the Criminal Justice System.* Royal Commission on Criminal Justice Research Study No. 20. London: HMSO.
Fitzmaurice, C. and Pease, K. (1986) *The Psychology of Judicial Sentencing.* Manchester: University of Manchester Press.
Flynn, N. (1994) 'Control, commitment and contracts' in Clarke, J., Cochrane, A. and McLaughlin, E. (eds.) *Managing Social Policy.* London: Sage.
Folkard, M.S., Smith, D.E. and Smith, D.D. (1976) *IMPACT Vol.II.* London: HMSO.
Ford, R. (1993) *Gay Identity and Probation Practice.* Norwich: The University of East Anglia. Unpublished MA Dissertation.
Ford, R. and Robinson, N. (1993) 'Gay men: discrimination within the criminal law and sex offender programmes' in McCaughey, C. and Buckley, K. (ed.) *Sexuality, Youth Work and Probation Practice.* Sheffield: Pavic Publications, Sheffield Hallam University.
Fosdick, H. (1954) *On Being Fit to Live With.* London: Student Christian Movement Press.
Fry, M. (1951) *Arms of the Law.* London: Gollancz.
Fry, M. (1959) 'Justice for victims', *Journal of Public Law,* 8, pp.191-94.
Fryer, P. (1985) *Staying Power: The History of Black People in Britain.* London: Pluto Press.
Fulwood, C. (1992) 'Partnerships in probation: setting the scene' in Statham, R. and Whitehead, P. (eds.) *Managing The Probation Service: Issues for the 1990s.* Harlow: Basingstoke.
Furby, L., Weinrott, R.M. and Blackshaw, L. (1989) 'Sex offender recidivism: a review', *Psychological Bulletin,* 105(1), pp.3-30.
Garland, D. (1990) *Punishment and Modern Society.* Oxford: Oxford University Press.
Garland, D. and Young, P. (eds.) (1983) *The Power to Punish.* London: Heinemann.
Gay, M.J., Holtom, C. and Thomas, M.S. (1975) 'Helping the victims', *International Journal of Offender Therapy,* 19(3), pp.263-69.
Gelsthorpe, L. and Morris, A. (eds.) (1990) *Feminist Perspectives in Criminology.* Milton Keynes: Open University Press.
Genders, E. and Player, E. (1989) *Race Relations in Prisons.* Oxford: Clarendon.
Genn, H. (1988) 'Multiple victimisation' in Maguire, M. and Pointing, J. (eds.) *Victims of Crime: A New Deal.* Milton Keynes: Open University Press.
Gibran, K. (1991) *The Prophet.* London: Pan Books.
Gibson S. (1995) Untitled contribution in 'Perspective: an inside job or a set up', *The Times Higher Education Supplement,* 10 February, pp.16-18.
Gill, A. and Marshall, T. (1993) 'Working with racist offenders', *Probation Journal,* July.
Gilman, S. (1985) *Difference and Pathology: Stereotypes of Sexuality, Race and Madness.* New York: Cornell University Press.

Gilroy, P. (1987) *There Ain't No Black in the Union Jack*. London: Hutchinson.
Glover, E. (1956) *Probation and Re-education*. London: Routledge and Kegan Paul.
Goffman, E. (1968) *Asylums*. Harmondsworth: Penguin.
Goldsmith, E. (1994) 'A strategy for ensuring the habitability of our planet', *Royal Society of Arts Journal*, 112(5446), pp.23-33.
Goode, S. (1992) *Children and Divorce: The Role of Statutory Supervision*. Aldershot: Avebury.
Gordon, P. (1992) 'Black people and the criminal law: rhetoric and reality', in Braham, P., Rattansi, A. and Skellington, R. (eds.) *Racism and Anti-Racism: Inequalities, Opportunities and Policies*. London: Sage.
Gouldner, A. (1975) The Sociologist as Partisan: Sociology and the Welfare State cited in Gouldner, A. *For Sociology : Renewal and Critique in Sociology Today*. Harmondsworth: Penguin Books.
Graham-Hall, Judge J. (1993) 'The future of civil court welfare', *Justice of the Peace*, 25 September, pp.613-14.
Greater Manchester NAPO (1988) 'Tackling offending: a reaction plan', 35(4), pp.137-39.
Grounds, A. (1992) 'Mental health problems' in Stockdale, E. and Casale, S. (eds.) (1992) *Criminal Justice Under Stress*. London: Blackstone Press.
Guardian (1993) 'Locking away our problems', 30 November.
Gunn, J., Maden, A. and Swinton, M. (1991) 'Treatment needs of prisoners with psychiatric disorders', *British Medical Journal*, 303 (6798), pp.338-41.
Hagel, A. and Newbuen, T. (1994) *Persistent Young Offenders*. London: Policy Studies Institute.
Hampshire Probation Service (1992) *Targeting Matrix: A Guide to Decision-Making for Practitioners and Sentencers*. Winchester: Hampshire Probation Service.
Harman, J. (1990) 'The quest for stronger probation management: threat or opportunity?' in Senior, P. and Woodhill, D. (eds.) *Criminal Justice in the 1990s: What Future(s) for the Probation Service*. Sheffield: Sheffield City Polytechnic PAVIC Publications.
Harris, R. (1985) 'Towards just welfare', *British Journal of Criminology*, 25(1), pp.31-45.
Harris, R. (1992) *Crime, Criminal Justice and the Probation Service*. London: Routledge.
Harris, R. and Webb, D. (1987) *Welfare, Power and Juvenile Justice: the Social Control of Delinquent Youth*. London: Tavistock.
Hayek, F.A. (1976) 'The mirage of social justice' in *Law, Legislation and Liberty*. Volume Two. London: Routledge.
Hayes, M. (1989) 'Promotion and management: what choice for women?', *Probation Journal*, March.
Hedderman, C. and Hough, M. (1994) 'Does the criminal justice system treat men and women differently? in Home Office (ed.) *Research Findings No. 10*. London: HMSO.
Henderson, P. (1986) 'Community work and the probation service', *Probation*

Journal, 33(2), pp.9-53.

Hentig, H. von (1948) *The Criminal and His Victim.* New Haven: Yale University Press.

Hirschi, T. (1969) *Causes of Delinquency*. Berkeley: University of California Press.

HM Inspectorate of Probation (1991) *Report on Women Offenders and Probation Service Provision.* London: Home Office.

HM Inspectorate of Probation (1993) *Probation Orders with Requirements for Psychiatric Treatment: Report of a Thematic Inspection.* London: Home Office.

Hogarth, J. (1971) *Sentencing as a Human Process.* Toronto: University of Toronto Press.

Holdaway, S. and Allaker (1990) *Race Issues in the Probation Service: A Review of Policy.* Sheffield: Sheffield University.

Hollin, C.R. and Howells, K. (1991) (eds.) *Clinical Approaches to Sex Offenders and Their Victims.* Chichester: John Wiley and Sons.

Holtom, C. and Raynor, P. (1988) 'Origins of Victim Support philosophy and practice' in Maguire, M. and Pointing, J. (eds.) *Victims of Crime: A New Deal*. Milton Keynes: Open University Press.

Home Office (1984) *Probation Service in England and Wales. Statement of National Objectives and Priorities*. London: HMSO.

Home Office (1988a) *Punishment, Custody and the Community*. Green Paper, Cmd 424. HMSO: London.

Home Office (1988b) *Tackling Offending: an Action Plan*, London: HMSO.

Home Office (1990a) *Crime, Justice and Protecting the Public*. Cm 965, London: HMSO.

Home Office (1990b) *Partnership in Dealing with Offenders in the Community*. London: HMSO.

Home Office (1990c) *Provision for Mentally Disordered Offenders.* Home Office Circular 66/90. London: Home Office.

Home Office (1992a) *Gender and the Criminal Justice System.* London: HMSO.

Home Office (1992b) *National Standards for the Supervision of Offenders in the Community*. London: HMSO.

Home Office (1992c) *Partnership in Dealing With Offenders in the Community: A Decision Document*. London: Home Office.

Home Office (1992d) *Race and the Criminal Justice System*. London: HMSO.

Home Office (1992e) The *Probation Service: Three Year Plan*. London: HMSO.

Home Office (1992f) *Three Year Plan for the Probation Service 1993-96*. London: Home Office.

Home Office (1993a) *Digest 2: Information on the Criminal Justice System in England and Wales. London*: Home Office.

Home Office (1993b) *Helping the Court to Serve the Needs of Children involved in Separation or Divorce: A Strategy Document for Probation Service Family Court Welfare*. London: HMSO.

Home Office (1993c) *HM Inspectorate of Probation Annual Report 1992-3.*

London: Home Office.
Home Office (1993d) 'Partnership in dealing with offenders in the community: submission of partnership plans 1994-1997', *Home Office Probation Circular*, 17. London: Home Office.
Home Office (1993e) *Probation Statistics: England and Wales 1992*. London: Home Office.
Home Office (1993f) *Statistics of Mentally Disordered Offenders 1991*. Home Office Statistical Bulletin 02/93. London: Home Office.
Home Office (1994a) 'Probation service three year plan 1995-98', *Probation Circular*, 102.
Home Office (1994b) 'The criminal histories of those cautioned in 1985, 1988 and 1991', *Statistical Bulletin*, 8.
Home Office (1994c) *Three Year Plan for the Probation Service 1994-97*. London: Home Office.
Home Office (1994d) *Three Year Plan for the Probation Service 1995-98*. London: Home Office.
Home Office Standing Conference on Crime Prevention (1991) *Safer Communities: The Local Delivery of Crime Prevention Through the Partnership Approach,* The Morgan Report. London: Home Office.
Hood, R. (1974) *Tolerance and the Tariff*. London: NACRO.
Hood, R. (1992) *Race and Sentencing*. Oxford: Clarendon.
Hooks, B. and West, C. (1991) *Breaking Bread: Insurgent Black Intellectual Life*. Boston USA: South End Press.
Hoover, K. and Plant, R. (1989) *Conservative Capitalism in Britain and the United States.* New York: Routledge.
House of Commons (1994) 'Written answers', *Hansard*, 24 February.
Howard, M. (1993) (Home Secretary), speech to Conservative Party conference, October.
Howard, M. (1994) 'Address' to NACRO/ Crime Concern Conference *Crime and the Family Conference.* London: Family Policy Study Centre.
Howells, K. and Hollin, C.R. (eds.) (1993) *Clinical Approaches to the Mentally Disordered Offender.* Chichester: Wiley.
Hudson, B. (1987) *Justice as Punishment*. London: Macmillan.
Hudson, B. (1993a) *Penal Policy and Social Justice*. London: Macmillan.
Hudson, B. (1993b) 'Racism and criminology: concepts and controversies' in Cook, D. and Hudson, B. (eds.) *Racism and Criminology*. London: Sage.
Hudson, B. and Roberts, C. (1993) *Training for Work with Mentally Disordered Offenders.* London: CCETSW.
Hume, D. (1939) *A Treatise on Human Nature*. London: John Noon.
Ibbs Report (1988) *Improving Management in Government: The Next Steps. A Report to the Prime Minister* . London: HMSO.
Independent (1993a) 'Crisis warning over mental hospitals', 11 December.
Independent (1993b) 'Mentally ill people to go on 'at risk' list', 28 December.
Jack, M. (1993) Speech to ACOP Annual Meeting, 10 May.
Jenkins, S. (1994) *The Times*, 8 January.
Jones, D. (1989) 'The Successful Revolution', *Community Care*, Inside

Supplement, 30 March.

Jones, M., Mordecai, M., Rutter, F. and Thomas, L. (1991) 'The Miskin Model of groupwork with women offenders', *Groupwork*, 4(3), pp.215-30.

Jordan, J. (1989) 'Problems of language in a democratic state' in *Moving Towards Home: Selected Political Essays*. London: Virago.

Justice (1962) *Compensation for Victims of Crimes of Violence*. London: Stevens.

Kay, R. (1991) 'Partnership and the peppermint paper', *Youth Social Work*, 3, pp.11-12.

Kay, S. (1993) 'Judgements of worth: women's attitudes towards promotion', *Probation Journal*, July.

Kelly, L., Regan, L. and Burton, S. (1991) *An Exploratory Study of the Prevalence of Sexual Abuse in a Sample of 16-21 Year Olds*. London: The Polytechnic of North London.

Kennedy, H. (1992) *Eve Was Framed*. London: Chatto and Windus.

Kennedy, M., Dhir, B. and Kelly, L. (1993) 'Recognising identity, Module I - Foundation and awareness', *The ABCD Pack: Abuse and Children Who Are Disabled*. Training and Resource Pack for Trainers in Child Protection and Disability. London: The National Deaf Children's Society, NSPCC, Way Ahead: Disability Consultancy, Chailey Heritage.

Kett, J., Collett, S., Barron, C., Hill, I. and Metherell, D. (1992) *Managing and Developing Anti-Racist Practice within Probation: A Resource Pack for Action*. Liverpool: Merseyside Probation Service.

Kimber, J. and Cooper, L. (1991) *Racial Harassment Project: Final Report*. London: Victim Support.

Knapp, M. (1989) 'Private and voluntary welfare' in McCarthy, M. (ed.) *The New Politics of Welfare: an Agenda for the 1990s*. Basingstoke: Macmillan.

Knopp, F.H. (1988) *Retraining Adult Sex Offenders*. New York: Safer Society Press.

Lacey, M., Pendleton, J. and Read, G. (1983) 'Supervision in the community: the righting of wrongs', *Justice of the Peace*, 120, February 19, pp.120-23.

LaFree, G.D. (1980) 'The effect of sexual stratification by race on official reactions to rape', *American Sociological Review*, 45, pp.824-54.

Launay, G. and Murray, P. (1989) 'Victim/offender groups' in Wright, M. and Galaway, B. (eds.) *Mediation and Criminal Justice: Victims, Offenders and Community*. London: Sage.

Lawson, R. and Wilson, J.W. (forthcoming) 'Poverty, social rights and the quality of citizenship', *European Journal of Social Policy* .

Lemert, E.M. (1976) 'The choice and change in juvenile justice', *British Journal of Law and Society*, 3, pp.59-75.

Lesser W. (1995) 'Court of appeal. The O.J. Simpson trial: judicial proceedings or popular entertainment', *The Times Higher Education Supplement*, 3 February, p.18.

Liebling, A. (1991) 'Where are the women in Woolf?', *Prison Report*, 15, pp.4-5.

Liebling, A. (1992) *Suicides in Prison*. London: Routledge.
Lipsey, M. (1992) 'Juvenile delinquency treatment: a meta-analytic enquiry into the variability of effects' in Cook, T. et al. (eds.) *Meta-Analysis for Explanation: A Case-Book*. New York: Russell Sage.
Lipton, D., Martinson, R. and Wilks, J. (1975) *The Effectiveness of Correctional Treatment*. New York: Praeger.
Littlewood, R. and Lipsedge, M. (1989) *Aliens and Alienists: Ethnic Minorities and Psychiatry*. Second Edition. London: Unwin Hyman.
Lonergan, B.J.F. (1965) *Insight: A Study of Human Understanding*. New York: Longmans.
Lowman, J. and MacLean, B. (1991) 'Prisons and protest in Canada', *Social Justice*, 18(3), pp.130-54.
Lucas, J., Raynor, P. and Vanstone, M. (1992) *Straight Thinking on Probation One Year On*. Second Report of the Evaluation Study. Bridgend: Mid Glamorgan Probation Service.
MacLean, D. (1993) (Home Office Minister), speech to Children's Society conference, 25 November 1993.
Madhubuti, H. (1978) *Enemies: The Clash of Races*. Chicago: Third World Press.
Maguire, M. and Corbett, C. (1987) *The Effects of Crime and the Work of Victim Support Schemes*. Aldershot: Gower.
Maguire, M. and Pointing, J. (eds.) (1988) *Victims of Crime: A New Deal*. Milton Keynes: Open University Press.
Marquand, D. (1993) 'The enterprise culture: new wine in old bottles?' in Heelas, P. and Morris, P. (eds.) *The Values of the Enterprise Culture: The Moral Debate*. London: Routledge.
Marshall, T. and Merry, S. (1990) *Crime and Accountability: Victim / Offender Mediation in Practice*. London: HMSO.
Marshall W.L., Laws, D.R. and Barbaree, H.E. (eds.) (1990) *Handbook of Sexual Assault*. New York: Plenum.
Marshall, W.L. and Barbaree, H.E. (1991) 'An optimistic evaluation of treatment outcome with sex offenders', *Violence Update*, 1(7), pp.8-11.
Martin, L.L. (1993) *Total Quality Management in the Human Services*. New York: Sage.
Martinson, R. (1979) 'New findings, new views: a note of caution regarding sentencing reform', *Hofstra Law Review*, 7, pp.243-58.
Matthews, R. and Young, J. (eds.) (1992) *Issues in Realist Criminology*. London: Sage.
Mawby, R.I. (1989) }The voluntary sectors role in a mixed economy of criminal justice' in Matthews, R. (ed.) *Privatising Criminal Justice*. London: Sage.
Maximé, J.E. (1991) 'Some psychological models of black self-concept' in Ahmed, S. Cheetham, J. and Small, J. (eds.) *Social Work with Black Children and Their Families*. Buckingham: Open University Press.
McBarnet, D. (1978) False Dichotomies in Criminal Justice Research in Baldwin, J. and Bottomley, A.K. (eds.) (1978) *Criminal Justice: Selected Readings*. Oxford: Martin Robertson.
McBarnet, D. (1983) *Conviction: Law, the State and the Construction of*

Justice. London: Macmillan.
McCaughey, C. (1993) 'Working with young lesbians' in McCaughey, C. and Buckley, K. *Sexuality, Youth Work and Probation Practice*. Sheffield: Pavic Publications, Sheffield Hallam University.
McCaughey, C. and Buckley, K. (1993) *Sexuality, Youth Work and Probation Practice*. Sheffield: Pavic Publications, Sheffield Hallam University.
McCrystal, .(1994) 'The Gospel of Bryn Melyn', *Independent on Sunday*, 2 January.
McDermott, K. (1990) 'We have no problem: the experience of racism in prison', *New Community*, 16(2), pp.213-28.
McGregor, O.R. (1957) *Divorce in England*. London: Heinemann.
McGuire, J. (1993) *What Works: The Evidence*. Paper to Conference on 'What works: the challenge for managers', Loughborough, October 1993.
McGuire, J. and Priestley, P. (1985) *Offending Behaviour*. London: Batsford.
McIvor, G. (1990), *Sanctions for Serious or Persistent Offenders*. Stirling: Social Work Research Centre.
McWilliams W. (1987) 'Probation, pragmatism and policy,' *Howard Journal*, 26, pp 97-12.
Mediation UK (1991) *Evidence to Royal Commission in Criminal Justice*. Bristol: Mediation UK.
Mendelsohn, B. (1947) 'New bio-psychosocial horizons: victimology', *American Law Review*, 13(4), pp.649-73.
Michie, J. and Smith, J.G. (eds.) (1994) *Unemployment in Europe*. Paris, Institute Political Population Research.
Mill, J.S. (1974 edition) *On Liberty* (1845). Harmondsworth: Penguin Books.
Minzberg, H. (1983) *Structure in Fives: Designing Effective Organisations*. New Jersey: Prentice Hall.
Mistry, T. (1989) 'Establishing a feminist model of groupwork in the probation service', *Groupwork*, 2, pp.145-58.
Mistry, T. and Brown, A. (1991) 'Black/white co-working in groups', *Groupwork*, 4(2), pp.101-118.
Mitchell, B. (1992) 'Preparing life sentence prisoners for release', *Howard Journal of Criminal Justice*, 31(3), pp.224-39.
Modi, P. and Pal, J. (1992) 'Beyond despair: child sexual abuse and the black community' in *Confronting the Pain of Child Sexual Abuse*. London: Family Service Unit.
Modood, T. (1994) *Race Equality: Colour, Culture and Justice*. London: IPPR.
Monger, M. (1965) *Casework in Probation*. London: Butterworth.
Monger, M., Pendleton, J. and Roberts, J. (1981) *Throughcare with Prisoners' Families*. Social Work Studies No. 3, Nottingham: University of Nottingham Department of Social Administration and Social Work.
Morris, A. and Giller, H. (eds.) (1983) *Providing Criminal Justice for Children*. London: Edward Arnold.
Morris, A. and Giller, H. (1987) *Understanding Juvenile Justice*. London: Croom Helm.
Morris, T. (1976) *Deviance and Control*. London: Hutchinson.
Morris, T. (1988) 'Punishment, custody and the community', *The Howard*

Journal of Criminal Justice, 6(4), November.
Morris, W. (1931) *News from Nature from William Morris: Prose Selections* in Ball, A. (ed.). Cambridge: Cambridge University Press.
Moxon, D. (1988) *Sentencing Practice in the Crown Court.* Home Office Research Study No. 103. London: HMSO.
Murphy, P. (forthcoming) 'Focusing on the invisible minority: Irish offenders and the British criminal justice system', *Probation Journal*.
Naik, D. (1991) 'An Examination of Social Work Education Within an Anti-Racist Framework' in Central Council for Education and Training in Social Work Northern Curriculum Development Project *Setting the Context for Change*, London: CCETSW.
Naik, D. (1992) 'The politics of anti-racist requirements and the role of the external assessor in relation to programmes and programme providers', *Issues in Social Work Education,* 12(2), pp.57-73.
National Association for the Care and Resettlement of Offenders (1986) *Black People and the Criminal Justice System*. London: NACRO.
National Association for the Care and Resettlement of Offenders (1990) *Seizing the Initiative*: NACRO's Final Report on the DHSS intermediate Treatment Initiative to Divert Juvenile Offenders from Care and Custody 1983-89. London: NACRO.
National Association for the Care and Resettlement of Offenders (1991a) *A Fresh Start for Women Prisoners: The Implications of the Woolf Report for Women*. London: NACRO.
National Association for the Care and Resettlement of Offenders (1991b) *Black Communities and the Probation Service: Working Together for Change*. London: NACRO.
National Association for the Care and Resettlement of Offenders (1992) 'Mentally disturbed offenders', *NACRO Briefing* 74. London: NACRO.
National Association for the Care and Resettlement of Offenders (1993a) *Community Care and Mentally Disturbed Offenders.* NACRO Mental Health Advisory Committee Policy Paper One. London: NACRO
National Association for the Care and Resettlement of Offenders (1993b) *Criminal Justice Digest,* 75, January. London: NACRO.
National Association for the Care and Resettlement of Offenders (1993c) *Criminal Justice Digest* , 76, April. London: NACRO.
National Association for the Care and Resettlement of Offenders (1993d) *Opening the Doors: The Resettlement of Prisoners in the Community.* London: NACRO.
National Association for the Care and Resettlement of Offenders (1993e) *Opening the Doors: Women Leaving Prison*. London: NACRO.
National Association for the Care and Resettlement of Offenders (1993f) *Race and Criminal Justice: Black People Working in the Criminal Justice System*. Race Issues Advisory Committee. London: NACRO.
National Association of Probation Officers (1987) *Access to Justice: Race, Class and Gender*. London: NAPO.
National Association of Probation Officers (1990a) *Anti-Racism Policy.*

London: NAPO.
National Association of Probation Officers (1990b) *Framework for Partnership between Voluntary Organisations and Probation Staff*. London: NAPO.
National Association of Probation Officers (1991) *Limiting the Damage*. London: NAPO.
National Association of Probation Officers, Professional Committee (1993) *NAPO Response to the Draft National Throughcare Document and Draft Throughcare Business and Three Year Development Plan*. London: NAPO, Mimeo.
National Association of Victims Support Schemes (1988) *The Victim in Court: Report of a Working Party*. London: NAVSS.
Neary, M. (1992), 'Some academic freedom', *Probation Journal*, 39, pp.200-202. Based on 'Robert Ross, Probation and the Problems of Rationality', Paper Distributed at the Salford University 'What Works?' Conference. Unpublished.
Neate, P. (1991) 'Bridging the cultural divide', *Community Care*, 21 November, pp.12-14.
Nellis, M. (1989) 'Juvenile justice and the voluntary sector' in Matthews, R. (ed.) *Privatising Criminal Justice*. London: Sage.
Nellis, M. (1990) 'Probation, the state and the independent sector' in Senior, P. and Woodhill, D. (eds.) *Criminal Justice in the 1990s: What Future(s) for the Probation Service*. Sheffield: PAVIC Publications.
Nellis, M. (1995) 'Probation values for the 1990s', Howard Journal, 34(1), pp.19-44.
Newman, J. (1994) 'Gender and the politics of change' in Clarke, J., Cochrane, A. and McLAughlin, *E. (eds.) Managing Social Policy*. London: Sage.
Niebuhr, R. (1949) 'Interpretation of Christian ethics' as quoted in Robinson, J.A.T (1980) 'The place of law in the field of sex' in Robinson, J.A.T *The Roots of a Radical*. London: Student Charter Movement Press.
Northumbria Probation Service (1992) *The Dog That Finally Barked: The Tyneside Disturbances of 1991 – A Probation Perspective*. Newcastle: Northumbria Probation Service.
Owusu-Bempah, J. (1990) 'Toeing the white line', *Community Care*, 1 November, pp.16-17.
Padel, U. (1993) 'Ask the family', *Prison Report*, Winter, pp.22-23.
Padel, U., Twidale, R. and Porter, J. (1992) *HIV Education in Prisons*. London: Health Education Authority/SCODA.
Parker, H. Sumner, M. and Jarvis, G. (1989) *Unmasking the Magistrates: 'The Custody or Not' Decision in Sentencing Young Offenders*. Milton Keynes: Open University Press.
Patten, J. (1988) *Punishment, The Probation Service and the Community*. ACOP Conference Paper, 15 September.
Pease, K., Billingham, S. and Earnshaw, I. (1977) *Community Service Assessed in 1976*. London: HMSO.
Pendleton, J. (1982) *Alternatives to Imprisonment: An Evaluation of RSDO Conference*. Keele: University of Keele.
Pendleton, J. (1985) *Reparation as a Judicial Measure of Punishment*. Paper

to the Conference European de la Probation, Karlsruhe, West Germany.
Pendleton, J. (1987) *More Justice, Less Law. New Perspectives on Crime and Justice.* Elkhart, US.: Mennonite Central Committee US Office of Criminal Justice. Reprinted as chapter one of the present volume
Peters. A.A.G. (1986) 'Main currents in criminal law' in van Dijk, J. et al. (eds.) *Criminal Law in Action*. Arnhem: Gouda Quint.
Petersilia, J. (1990) 'Conditions that permit intensive supervision programmes to survive', *Crime and Delinquency,* 36, pp.126-45.
Pithers, W.D., Kashima, K.M., Cumming, G.F. and Beal, L.S. (1988) 'Relapse prevention: a method of enhancing maintenance of change in sex offenders' in Salter, A.C. (ed.) *Treating Child Sexual Offenders and Victims: A Practical Guide*. Newbury Park, London, and New Delhi: Sage.
Pitts. J. (1994) 'Editorial', *Social Work in Europe*, 1(1), pp3-4.
Player, E. (1994) 'Women's prisons after Woolf' in Player, E. and Jenkins, M. (eds.) *Prisons after Woolf: Reform through Riot*. London: Routledge.
Player, E. and Jenkins, M. (eds.) (1994) *Prisons after Woolf: Reform Through Riot*. London: Routledge.
Porter, R. (1990) *Mind-Forg'd Manacles: A History of Madness in England from the Restoration to the Regency. Harmondsworth*: Penguin Books.
Pratt, J. (1989) 'Corporatism: the third model of juvenile justice', *British Journal of Criminology,* 29(3), pp.236-54.
President's Task Force on Victims of Crime (1982) *Final Report*. Washington, DC: US GP.
Prins, H. (1986) *Dangerous Behaviour, the Law and Mental Disorder* .London: Tavistock Publications.
Prins, H. (1992) 'The diversion of the mentally disordered: some problems for criminal justice, penology and health care', *Journal of Forensic Psychiatry*, 3(2), pp.431-443.
Prins, H. et al. (1993) *Report of the Committee of Inquiry into the Death in Broadmoor Hospital of Orville Blackwood and a Review of the Deaths of Two Other Afro-Caribbean Patients: 'Big, Black and Dangerous?'* London: Special Hospitals Service Authority.
Prison Report (1993) Editorial, 'Hard Times', *Prison Report,* 25, Winter, p.3.
Prison Service (1994) *National Framework for the Throughcare of Offenders in Custody to the Completion of Supervision in the Community*. London: Home Office.
Pritchard, C. (1992a) 'Children's homicide as an indicator of effective child protection: A comparative study of Western European statistics', *British Journal of Social Work,* 22(6), pp.663-84.
Pritchard, C. (1992b) *Partnership: Breaking Down the Barriers to Employment.* Bournemouth: Dorset Training Enterprise Council.
Pritchard, C. (1993) 'Re-analyzing children's homicide and undetermined death rate as an indication of improved child protection: a reply to Creighton', *British Journal of Social Work,* 23(6), pp.645-52.
Pritchard, C. (forthcoming) *The Ultimate Rejection: A Psycho-Social Study of*

Suicide. Buckingham: Open University Press.

Pritchard, C. and Clooney, D. (1994) *Single Homelessness: Fractured Lives and Fragmented Policies: A Report to the Department for the Environment.* Bournemouth: Bournemouth Churches Housing Association.

Pritchard, C. and Cox, M. (1990) 'Analysis of young adult clients in probation and social services caseloads: a focus on illegal drugs and risk of HIV infection', *Research, Policy, and Planning,* 8(2), pp.1-8.

Pritchard, C. and Taylor, R. (1978) *Social Work: Reform or Revolution.* London: Routledge and Kegan Paul.

Pritchard, C., Cox, M., Cotton, A., Godson, D. and Weeks, S. (1992) 'Mental illness, drug and alcohol misuse and HIV risk behaviour in 214 young adult probation clients: implications for policy and training', *Social Work and Social Science Review,* 3(3), pp.227-43.

Pritchard, C., Ford, P and Cox, M. (forthcoming) *Consumer Opinions of the Probation Service: Advice Assistance, Befriending and the Reduction of Crime.*

Pryce, K. (1974) *West Indian Life Styles in Bristol: A Study of a Black Toiling Class in an English City.* Bristol: University of Bristol, Department of Sociology. Later published as *Endless Pressure* (1979). Harmondsworth: Penguin.

Quinsey, V.L. (1984) 'Sexual aggression: studies of offenders against women' in Weistub, D. (ed.) *Law and Mental Health: International Perspectives.* Volume I. New York: Pergammon Press.

Raine, J.W. and Smith, R.E. (1991). *The Victim / Witness in Court Project: Report of the Research Programme.* London: Victim Support.

Ralli, R. (1994) 'Health care in prisons' in Player, E. and Jenkins, M. (eds.) *Prisons after Woolf: Reform Through Riot.* London: Routledge.

Rawls, J. (1993) *A Theory of Justice.* Oxford: Oxford University Press.

Raynor, P. (1988) *Probation as an Alternative to Custody.* Aldershot: Avebury.

Raynor, P. (1993) *Developing a Core Research and Evaluation Programme.* Paper to Conference on 'What Works: The Challenge for Managers', Loughborough, October 1993.

Raynor, P. (1993), *Social Work, Justice and Control.* Second Edition. London: Whiting and Birch.

Raynor, P. and Vanstone, M. (1994a) 'Probation practice and effectiveness and the non-treatment paradigm', *British Journal of Social Work,* 24(4), pp.387-404.

Raynor, P. and Vanstone, M. (1994b) *Straight Thinking On Probation: Third Interim Evaluation Report: Reconvictions Within 12 Months.* Bridgend: Mid Glamorgan Probation Service.

Raynor, P., Smith, D. and Vanstone, M. (1994) *Effective Probation Practice.* London: Macmillan.

Richardson, A. (ed.) (1951) *Theological Word Book of the Bible.* London: Student Christian Movement Press.

Richardson, G. (1994) 'From rights to expectations' in Player, E. and Jenkins,

M. (eds.) *Prisons after Woolf: Reform Through Riot*. London: Routledge.
Roberts, C.H. (1989) *Hereford and Worcester Probation Service Young Offender Project: First Evaluation Report*. Oxford: Department of Social and Administrative Studies.
Roberts, J. (1994) 'The relationship between the community and the prison' in Player, E. and Jenkins, M. (eds.) *Prisons after Woolf: Reform Through Riot*. London: Routledge.
Robinson, J.A.T. (1980) *The Roots of a Radical*. London: Student Christian Movement Press.
Ross, R.R. and Fabiano, E.A. (1985) *Time to Think*, Ottowa: Institute of Social Sciences and Arts.
Ross, R.R., Fabiano, E. and Elides, C.D. (1988) 'Reasoning and rehabilitation', *International Journal of Offender Therapy and Comparative Criminology*, 32, pp.29-35.
Rutherford, A. (1993) *Criminal Justice and the Pursuit of Decency*. Oxford: Oxford University Press.
Ryan, M. (1992) 'The Woolf Report: on the treadmill of prison reform?', *Political Quarterly*, 63(1), pp.50-56.
Ryan, M. and Ward, T. (1991) 'Restructuring, resistance and privatisation in the non-custodial sector', *Critical Social Policy*, pp.47-62.
Salter, A.C. (ed.) (1988) *Treating Child Sexual Offenders and Victims: A Practical Guide*. Newbury Park, London, and New Delhi: Sage.
Savage, M. and Witz, A. (eds.) (1992) *Gender and Bureaucracy*. Oxford: Blackwell.
Scheff, T.J. (1984) *Being Mentally Ill: A Sociological Theory*. Second edition. New York: Aldine Publishing.
Schuz, R. (1993) 'Divorce reform', *Family Law*, October, pp.580-81 and November, pp.630-32.
Scott, D. et al. (1985) *Going Local in Probation*. Norwich/Manchester: University of East Anglia and Department of Social Administration, University of Manchester.
Scott, J. (1993) 'Homelessness and mental illness', *British Journal of Psychiatry*, 162, pp.314-24.
Scull, A. (1983) 'Community corrections: panacea, progress or pretence?' in Garland, D. and Young, P. (eds.) *The Power to Punish*. London: Heinemann.
Senior, P. and Woodhill, D. (eds.) (1990) *Criminal Justice In The 1990s: What Future(s) For The Probation Service*. Sheffield: Sheffield City Polytechnic PAVIC Publications.
Shapland, J., Willmore, J. and Duff, P. (1985) *Victims in the Criminal Justice System*. Aldershot: Gower.
Shaw, S. (1993) 'Woolf warns against Howard's way with prisons', *Prison Report*, 25, Winter, p.12.
Shellice, A. and Gordon, P. (1990) *Black People, White Justice? Race and the Criminal Justice System*. London: Runnymede Trust.
Showalter, E. (1987) *The Female Malady: Women, Madness and English*

Culture 1830-1980. London: Virago Books.
Sim, J. (1991) ' 'We are not animals, we are human beings': prisons, protest and politics in England and Wales 1969-1990', *Social Justice*, 18(3), pp.107-29.
Sim, J. (1994) 'Reforming the penal wasteland? A critical review of the Woolf Report' in Player, E. and Jenkins, M. (eds.) *Prisons after Woolf: Reform Through Riot*. London: Routledge.
Simpkin, M. (1979) *Trapped Within Welfare: Surviving Social Work*. London: Macmillan.
Singh, G. (1992) *Race and Social Work: From Black Pathology to Black Perspective*. Bradford: Race Relations Research Unit, Bradford University and Ilkley Community College.
Sivanandan, A. (1991) 'Black struggles against racism' in Central Council for Education and Training in Social Work Northern Curriculum Development Project *Setting the Context for Change: Anti-Racist Social Work Education*. London: CCETSW.
Smart, C. (1976) *Women, Crime and Criminology: A Feminist Critique*. London: Routledge and Kegan Paul.
Smart, C. (1990) 'Feminist approaches to criminology or postmodern woman meets atavistic man' in Gelsthorpe, L. and Morris, A. (eds.) *Feminist Perspectives in Criminology*. Milton Keynes: Open University Press.
Smith, C. (1992) *Lesbians Talk: Queer Notions*. Newbury Park, London, and New Delhi: Sage.
Smith, D. (1993) 'Social circumstances of younger offenders under supervision', Speech given to Howard League 11th Annual Conference 8-10 September, *Criminal Justice*, II(4), 4 October, pp.7-8.
Smith, D., Paylor, I. and Mitchell, P. (1993) 'Partnerships between the independent sector and the probation service', *Howard Journal*, 32(1), pp.25-39.
Smith, K. (1988) 'Wormwood' in Astley, N. (ed.) *Poetry with an Edge*. Newcastle Upon Tyne: Bloodaxe Books.
Snaith, N. (1952) *Distinctive Ideas of the Old Testament*. Epworth Press.
Spencer, J. (1994) *The Loss of a Profession: The De Professionalisation of Social Work Services for Offenders and Its Effects on Criminal Justice in the UK*. Paper presented to the American Society of Criminology 46th Annual Conference, Miami, 9-12 November.
Statham, R. and Whitehead, P. (eds.) (1992) *Managing the Probation Service: Issues for the 1990s*. Harlow: Basingstoke.
Stern, V. (1994) 'The future of the voluntary sector and the pressure groups' in Player, E. and Jenkins, M. (eds.) *Prisons after Woolf: Reform Through Riot*. London: Routledge.
Stern, V. and Weston, B. (1990) 'Partnership between the statutory and voluntary sectors in criminal justice', *Justice of the Peace*, 2 September, pp.607-609.
Stewart, J. (1993) *The Rebuilding of Public Accountability*. London: European Policy Forum.
Stewart and Stewart (1993) *Social Backgrounds of Young Offenders*. London:

Association of Chief Probation Officers.

Stockdale, E. and Casale, S. (eds.) (1992) *Criminal Justice Under Stress*. London: Blackstone Press.

Stockley, D., Canter, D. and Bishop, D. (1992) *Young People on the Move*. Guildford: Department of Psychology, University of Surrey.

Stockley, D., Canter, D. and Bishop, D. (1993) *Homelessness: Young People on the Move*. Guildford: University of Surrey, Department of Psychology.

Stonewall (1992) *Briefing on the Equalisation of the Age of Consent*. London: Stonewall.

Sumner, C. (ed.) (1990) *Censure, Politics and Criminal Justice*. Milton Keynes: Open University Press.

Sutton, M. (1993) 'From receiving to thieving: the market for stolen goods and the incidence of theft', *Home Office Research Bulletin*, 34, Summer. London: HMSO.

Tarling, R. (1979) *Sentencing Practice in Magistrates' Courts*. Home Office Research Study No. 56. London: HMSO.

Tarzi, A. and Hedges, J. (1990) *A Prison Within a Prison: A Study of Foreign Prisoners*. London: Inner London Probation Service.

Tatchell, P. (1991) Speech presented to fringe meeting at Napo Annual Conference, October 1991.

Taylor, I. (1993) 'Driving the vermin off the street', *New Statesman and Society*, October, pp.16-18.

Thatcher, M. Rt. Hon. (1987) *Speech to Conservative Party Central Council*, Buxton, 19 March. London: Conservative Party News Service.

Thomas, D.A (1979) *Principles of Sentencing* . Second Edition. London: Heinemann.

Thomas, P. (1990) 'HIV/AIDS in prisons', *Howard Journal of Criminal Justice*, 29(1), pp.1-13.

Thornes, B. and Collard, J. (1976) *Who Divorces*. London: Routledge and Kegan Paul.

Thorpe, A. (1993) *Ulverton*. London: Minerva.

Thorpe, D.H., Smith, D., Green, C.J. and Paley, J. (1980) *Out of Care*. London: Allen and Unwin.

Tilling, R. (1982) 'Unemployment and crime', *Home Office Research Bulletin*, 14. London: HMSO.

Towry, M. (1987) *Sentencing Reform Impacts*. Washington DC: National Institute of Justice.

Travis, A. (1993) 'Inmates win right to see dossiers', *The Guardian*, 4 December.

Truax, C.B. and Carkhuff, R.A. (1967) *Towards Effective Counselling and Psychotherapy*. Chicago: Aldine.

United Nations (1948) *Declaration of Human Rights*. Geneva: UN.

United Nations (1985) *Declaration of Basic Principles of Justice for Victims of Crime and Abuse of Power*. New York: UN Department of Public Information.

Upshall, D. (1989) 'A criminal lack of justice', *New Statesman And Society*, 3 March, p.35.

Urmson, J.O. (1968) *The Emotive Theory of Ethics.* London: Hutchinson.
Van Dijk, J. et al. (eds.) (1986) *Criminal Law in Action.* Arnhem: Gouda Quint.
Vanstone, M. (1993) 'A 'missed opportunity' reassessed: the influence of the Day Training Centre experiment on the criminal justice system and probation practice', *British Journal of Social Work,* 23(3), pp.213-29.
Victim Support (1990) *Families of Murder Victims Project; Final Report.* London: Victim Support.
Victim Support (1991) *Royal Commission on Criminal Justice: Response by Victim Support.* London: Victim Support.
Victim Support Magazine (1993a) 'Commission recognises victims' place in court', *Victim Support Magazine,* 51, pp.2-3.
Victim Support Magazine (1993b) 'Home Secretary promises to implement some Royal Commission recommendations', *Victim Support Magazine,* 52, p.4.
Von Hirsch, A. (1976) *Doing Justice.* New York: Hill and Wang.
Von Hirsch, A. and Ashworth A. (eds.) (1992) *Principled Sentencing.* Edinburgh: Edinburgh University Press.
Walker, N. (1972) *Sentencing in a Rational Society.* Harmondsworth: Penguin.
Walker, N. (1981) 'Feminists' extravaganzas', *The Criminal Law Review,* pp.379-86.
Walker, N. (1983) 'Childhood and madness: history and theory' in Morris, A. and Giller, H. (eds.) (1983) *Providing Criminal Justice for Children.* London: Edward Arnold.
Walker, N. (1985) *Sentencing: Theory, Law and Practice.* London: Butterworths.
Walker, N. (1991) *Why Punish?* Oxford: Oxford University Press.
Warner, S. (1992) *Making Amends: Justice for Victims and Offenders.* Aldershot: Avebury.
Warner, S. (1993) 'Standing in the shadows with our backs against the sun' in Roberts, C. (ed.) *Changing Information Needs and the 1991 Criminal Justice Act.* Birmingham: Probation Research and Information Exchange.
Wasik, M. and von Hirsch, A. (1988) 'Non-custodial penalties and the principles of desert', *Criminal Law Review,* Sept, pp.555-72.
Webb, S.A. and McBeath, G.B. (1989) 'Political critique of Kantian ethics', *British Journal of Social Work,* 19(6), pp.491-506.
Weber, M. (1947) *The Theory of Social and Economic Organisations.* New York: Free Press.
Weißer Ring (1992) *Kriminalitätsopfer im Spannungsfeld der Interessen: 2. Mainzer Opferforum.* [Crime Victims' Interests in Tension, Second Mainz Forum on Victims]. Mainz: Weißer Ring.
Weistub, D. (ed.) (1984) *Law and Mental Health: International Perspectives.* Volume I. New York: Pergammon Press.
Wheeler Robinson, H. (1949) *Religious Ideas of the Old Testament.* Duckworth.
Whitehead, P., Turver, N. and Wheatley, J. (1991) *Probation, Temporary*

Release Schemes and Reconviction. Aldershot: Avebury.
Whiting, B.J. (1992) 'Hispanics at work in the 1990s: dealing with diversity and language Issues in the new American workforce', *21st Century Policy Review: An American, Caribbean and African Forum,* 1(1), inaugural edition, winter, pp.65-84.
Williams, B. (1991) *Work with Prisoners*. Birmingham: Venture.
Williams, B. (1992) 'Caring professionals or street-level bureaucrats? The case of probation officers' work with prisoners', *Howard Journal of Criminal Justice*, pp.263-75.
Wilson, P. and Shine, J. (1990) 'Characteristics and potential treatment needs of sexual offenders: young offenders', *Issues in Criminology and Legal Psychology*, 15, pp.50-58.
Witz, A. and Savage, M. (1992) 'The gender of organisations' in Savage, M. and Witz, A. (eds.) *Gender and Bureaucracy*. Oxford: Blackwell.
Woolf, Lord Justice and Tumim, Judge Stephen (1991) *Prison Disturbances April 1990*. Cmd 1456. London: HMSO.
Worrall, A. (1990) *Offending Women*. London: Routledge.
Wright, M. (1982) *Making Good: Prisons, Punishment and Beyond*. London: Burnett Books.
Wright, M. (1991) *Justice for Victims and Offenders*. Buckingham: Open University Press.
Wright, M. (1994) 'Volunteers or professionals?', *Victim Support Magazine,* 54, p.4.
Wright, M. and Galaway, B. (1989) *Mediation and Criminal Justice: Victims, Offenders and Community*. London: Sage.
Zimring, F.E. and Hawkins, G. (1994) 'The growth of imprisonment in California', *British Journal of Criminology*, 34, pp.83-96. Special Issue on *Prisons in Context*.

Notes on Contributors

Roy Bailey was with the Probation Service as Chief Probation Officer in Devon and as Secretary to the Central Probation Council. He then worked for Save the Children Fund in Northern Ireland for two years before beginning research at Nottingham University into attitudes to formalised helping in probation.

Rob Canton is a Senior Probation Officer with Nottinghamshire Probation Service and Special Lecturer in Criminology at the University of Nottingham. John Pendleton was one of his first and most influential teachers in probation practice.

Malcolm Cowburn is currently Lecturer in Probation and Social Policy at the University of Sheffield. Prior to this he worked at a NCH Sexual Abuse Unit. He was a Probation Officer for 12 years. He has written extensively on work with sex offenders and has developed training programmes on this subject. He is currently involved in a 3 year research programme with Derbyshire Probation and the NSPCC into the partnership treatment project.

Malcolm Cox joined the Probation Service in 1966, following training at Bristol University, and subsequently worked in a wide range of field posts and later as a Senior Probation Officer. After taking higher degrees at Surrey University, he started work as Research and Information Officer at the Dorset Probation Service in 1984. Since then he has worked extensively with Professor Pritchard on research projects with the Probation Service and is currently an Honorary Research Fellow with the University of Southampton.

David Faulkner served in the Home Office from 1959 until 1992, becoming Deputy Secretary in charge of the Criminal Research and Statistics Department in 1982 and Principal Establishment Officer in 1990. He is now a Fellow of St John's College Oxford and

Senior Research Associate at the Oxford University Centre for Criminological Research.

Norman Flynn is a Research Fellow at the London School of Economics and Political Science where he specialises in management in the public sector and directs the Public Services Management Programme. He has written *Public Sector Management* (Harvester-Wheatsheaf, 1993).

Steve Goode has been an Assistant Chief Probation Officer in Derbyshire for four and a half years. His chapter updates previous research and publications in this field. He was an appreciative student of John Pendleton whilst at Nottingham University in the late 1970s and has tried to emulate John's interest in scholarship and probation service management. He wrote this article just before his daughter Graihagh was born.

Basil W. Hylton is currently Assistant Chief Probation Officer with the West Midlands Probation Service responsible for Coventry. A Jamaican by birth, he has been a member of the Probation Service for 25 years, and was the first black Assistant Chief Probation Officer in this country. He was a co-founder member and first Chair of the Association of Black Probation Officers and has sat on a number of commissions including UKIAS and Catholic Commission for Racial Justice.

Malcolm Lacey joined the Probation Service in 1963. He was Regional Staff Development Officer for the Midlands from 1971 to 1976 and then went to Coventry Polytechnic as Head of Social Work. He became Chief Probation Officer for Dorset in 1982. Currently he represents the Probation Service on the Council of CCETSW.

Panna Modi is a Project Manager (Child Care) with the NSPCC. She qualified as a social worker in 1982 and after five years experience with local authorities, moved to the Leicester Family Service Unit as a Family Therapist. She has been Coordinator for a project involved in work with adult and adolescent sex offenders. Since 1992 she has lectured on the Diploma/MA Course in Child Protection Studies at Leicester University.

Mike Nellis is Lecturer in Probation Studies at the University of Birmingham. He worked as a social worker with young offenders, and was involved in the Intermediate Treatment Evaluation

Programme at the University of Cambridge, where he received his PhD. He is currently involved in research on probation and partnership with the voluntary sector.

Colin Pritchard has held the Foundation Chair in Social Work Studies at the University of Southampton since 1980. Previously he held posts at the Universities of Leeds and Bath. He trained at the Universities of Manchester and Bradford, and is a former Principal Psychiatric Social Worker, still maintaining a small NHS type practice. His researched work has ranged along international comparative studies of suicide, child abuse and, with Malcolm Cox, a range of consumer studies, including homeless people, truants and probationers, as well as analysis of statutory services caseload and drug experimentation in ordinary adolescents.

Peter Raynor is Reader in Applied Social Studies at the University of Wales, Swansea with a particular responsibility for probation training. He has published extensively on probation issues, including the books *Social Work, Justice and Control* (1985 and 1993), *Probation as an Alternative to Custody* (1988) and *Effective Probation Practice* (1994, with David Smith and Maurice Vanstone).

Helen Reeves has been Director of Victim Support since the organisation was established in 1980 (as the National Association of Victim Support Schemes). Previously she was a Medical Social Worker and then Probation Officer and Senior Probation Officer with the Inner London Service. She is a member of the National Board for Crime Prevention and the Home Office Victim's Steering Committee. She is Secretary of the European Forum for Victim Services and on the Executive Committee of the World Society of Victimology.

Marcia Francis-Spence is a Lecturer in the Centre for Applied Social Studies, University of Durham. Previously, she was a Probation Officer with Nottinghamshire Probation Service. She chaired the Black Staff Support Group, and was a member of the Association of Black Probation Officers. She is currently undertaking research examining whether probation is or should be social work.

David Ward is Professor and Head of the Department of Social and Community Studies, De Montfort University, and Co-Director of the Centre for Social Action there. Formerly, he was Head of the Social Work Programme at the University of Nottingham. His practice background is in the Probation Service, and he has wide experience of training, research and development in social work, probation and voluntary settings.

Brian Williams lectures in the Department of Applied Social Studies, University of Keele, having previously worked at Sheffield and Teesside Universities and as a Probation Officer. He has researched and written about probation work, victims of crime, bail and related topics.

Anne Worrall has been Lecturer in Criminology at Keele University since 1993. Prior to that, she was Director of the MA/Diploma in Social Work Programme at Keele and had responsibility for the Probation Option. She has been a Social Work Lecturer at Manchester University and Probation Officer in Staffordshire. She has researched and published in the area of women and crime. She is the author of *Offending Women* (Routledge, 1990) and Co-Editor with Pat Carlen of *Gender, Crime and Justice* (Open University Press, 1987). She has also researched the changing role of prison Boards of Visitors and is author of *Have Your Got a Minute?* (Prison Reform Trust, 1994).

Martin Wright is Visiting Scholar, Centre for Criminological and Legal Studies, University of Sheffield. He was formerly Librarian at the Cambridge Institute of Criminology, Director of the Howard League for Penal Reform and Policy Officer of Victim Support. He is a founder member of Mediation UK and a volunteer mediator with Lambeth Mediation Service. He is author of *Justice for Victims and Offenders: A Restorative Response to Crime* (Open University Press, 1991) and numerous articles. He was joint editor with Burt Galaway of *Mediation and Criminal Justice. Victims, Offenders and Community* (Sage, 1989).

Index

SUBJECT INDEX

AUTHOR INDEX